Heinemann ECONOMICS AS for AQA

Heinemann ECONOMICS AS for AQA

BY

Sue Grant *and* Chris Vidler

with Charles Smith

Heinemann Educational Publishers
Halley Court, Jordan Hill, Oxford OX2 8EJ
Part of Harcourt Education

Heinemann is the registered trademark of Harcourt Education Limited

First published 2003

07 06 05
10 9 8 7 6 5 4 3

British Library Cataloguing in Publication Data is available from the British Library on request.

10-digit ISBN 0 435330 80 2
13-digit ISBN 978 0 435330 80 4

Designed by Artistix

Typeset by Hardlines Ltd, Charlbury, Oxford

Original illustrations © Harcourt Education Limited 2003
Illustrated by Hardlines Ltd, Charlbury, Oxford

Cover design by Matt Buckley

Printed in the UK by The Bath Press Ltd

Picture research by Sally Cole

Acknowledgements
The authors and publishers would like to thank Dr. Charles Smith of Swansea Business School, AQA Principal Examiner.

P144 diagram from *Environmental Economics* by Turner, Pearce and Bateman (1993), reprinted by permission of Pearson Education Limited.

The publishers would like to thank the following for permission to reproduce photographs: p.34 (top) EPA/Press Association; p.34 (middle) Bennett Dean/Eye Ubiquitous; p.46 Mary Evans; pp.55, 147 Glyn Kirk/Action Plus; p.79 Peter Brooker/Rex Features; p.85 Bob Watkins/Photofusion; p.103 Robert Brook/Photofusion; p.106 John Stillwell/Press Association; p.135 Alamy; p.145 Press Association; p.153 James Davis World Wide.

Tel: 01865 888058 www.heinemann.co.uk

Websites

There are links to relevant websites in this book. In order to ensure that the links are up-to-date, that the links work, and that the sites are not inadvertently linked to sites that could be considered offensive, we have made the links available on the Heinemann website at www.heinemann.co.uk/hotlinks. When you access the Heinemann website, enter the express code **0802P**, and this will take you to the links you want.

Contents

General introduction

Welcome to *Heinemann Economics AS for AQA*. This book has been specially written for students taking the AQA course. This means that it:

- follows the AQA specification very closely
- has been written to ensure that all concepts are clearly explained in terms understandable by students taking this subject for the first time
- includes lots of advice written by examiners to help you get the best possible grade.

The introduction is divided into three parts. Firstly you will be reminded that you probably already know something about a subject which is not usually taught before AS level. This is followed by a more formal description of how your course is organised and finally you will be introduced to the features of this book, which have been designed to take as much of the pain out of learning as possible!

You might already be an expert

For many of you this will be the first time that you have studied economics for a formal qualification. This does not mean to say that you don't know anything about the subject. All of us have a basic understanding of many of the concepts that when put together, make up economics. Thus, you will know that prices go up if there is a shortage of something that people wish to buy and if the reverse were to happen, prices are likely to fall. Similarly if there is only one supplier of a particular good, customers may be forced to pay more than if lots of different companies are competing for custom. You did know that didn't you?

You will also realise that governments play a big part in influencing the provision of many services like health, education and housing, and that these are financed by the taxes we pay. It follows that the government will have to increase its spending in order to build more hospitals or increase the number of nurses and doctors. This could mean cutting spending elsewhere, on defence for example, raising more in taxation or, perhaps less obviously, borrowing more money. The point being that someone somewhere will have to pay for such improvements.

These examples should show that we probably all know something about economics but one of the things that makes the subject special is that it has a technical vocabulary all of its own. As will be repeated often in this book and by your teachers, economists are very precise in the way they use particular terms. This can be quite a challenge to students new to the subject; one of the main things that is tested in your AS examination is your knowledge and understanding of basic economic terms.

Getting to grips with economics

We all learn things in different ways, so it is hard to be too prescriptive about the best ways of getting to grips with economics. The special technical vocabulary mentioned in the last section can be a big barrier to some people. Sometimes economics can appear to be really confusing, especially when different meanings are given to words that we commonly use. Others can be put off by the diagrams and simple maths which can be involved in understanding some economics concepts. Finally, nothing in economics is black and white and some students may find it difficult to deal with these different shades of grey.

On the plus side, economics is about issues that confront all of us. It will help you understand the world as we know it and studying economics can involve lots of argument and debate.

Starting off with economics is usually the hardest stage. Once you get over the initial 'differentness' of the subject, it can be fun and really useful. Economics should help you think and argue more logically, and these skills are really valued in the employment market-place. So hang in there even when it seems tough – it will be worth it in the end. Incidentally economics has one of the highest progression rates from AS to A2 – in other words a large majority of students who take AS go on to take the full A level. That must say something for the subject.

Course structure

To get your AS you have to take three examination papers known as units. Although these can be taught in different ways, most students will start on module one which is called 'Markets and market failure'. As the title implies, this will require you to develop an understanding of how markets work and why they might fail. Central to understanding this module is learning about demand and supply. This involves the use of diagrams and building up logical arguments, which are often about controversial topics such as whether or not the government should charge motorists or whether or not large firms force us to pay more for goods than we should.

The second module is called 'The national economy', and involves learning more about inflation, the standard of living and the causes of unemployment. Again, diagrams are used to help you analyse the possible economic effects of events such as September 11, or changes in taxation. As with the first module, there should be lots of chances for debate and discussion and you should end up with a much better understanding of things in the news.

Definitions

Units = examination papers.

Modules = what you have to learn.

Finally, in the third unit, you are given a choice of topics in which you have to apply what you have learned in the first two modules:

- housing
- the environment
- sport and leisure.

There is not a great deal more to learn for this module but you will need to take an active interest in one of these topics and have some practise in answering the kind of questions you are likely to be asked in the examination.

Finding your way

This book is divided into three parts to reflect the structure of the specification outlined above. Part 1 is devoted to markets and market failure. Part 2 is about the national economy and part 3 is called 'Markets at work' which consists of the three options, housing, the environment and sport and leisure.

Each part is divided into neat sections devoted to the key material you have to learn. At the end of each part there are sections devoted to exam preparation. This consists of advice from examiners who work for AQA on good exam practice. They can give you a feel for what examiners actually look for when it comes to marking your work. Finally, there are sample questions and answers and further examination-style questions with which you can develop the skills which will be tested at the end of your course.

Sample section

The typical layout of each section is illustrated below.

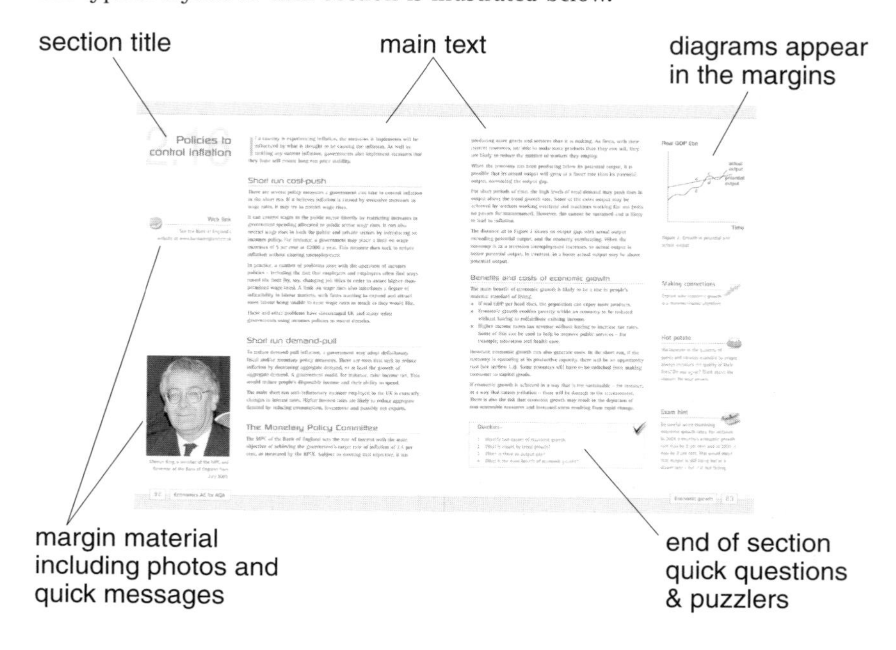

The central body of text is designed to explain the key concept(s) featured in each section. Quick questions to test your understanding can be found at the end of sections. The margins of each section will contain a different selection of quick messages designed to help your learning. These can relate to further research, web links, and controversial issues. Each is associated with a symbol and these are explained in more detail below:

Quickies – Quick questions designed to test your understanding of what you have just read.

Key concepts – Ideas that are essential to understanding the section.

Hot potatoes – Controversial issues you might want to argue about.

Definitions – You must know these and get into the habit of defining the main terms you use in all your exam answers.

Research tasks – Suggestions for more in-depth exploration.

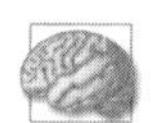

Thinking like an economist – Challenges you to consider an issue in a way an economist would analyse it.

Making connections - Encourages you to see the links between the topic and the world around you.

Exam hints – Little ideas that might make all the difference when it comes to the exam.

Puzzler – Tricky stuff to get your head round.

Web links – Hopefully they are still there when you need them.

You will also find that key words are emboldened and their definitions can be found in a glossary at the back of this book.

We hope that this book will develop your understanding and interest in economics. Our aims are to help you gain a high AS grade and to promote your enjoyment of the subject. Good luck!

PART I

MARKETS AND MARKET FAILURE

Markets and market failure

1.1

Part 1 of this book is concerned with microeconomics and in order to do well you need to understand how individual markets work, the strengths and weaknesses of freely operating markets, and how and why governments might intervene to either improve markets or to produce other desirable outcomes.

Although there are different ways of organising this module, it might be helpful to see it as consisting of five inter-related parts:

- Useful concepts
- Demand
- Supply
- Markets and the price mechanism
- Market failure.

These are illustrated by the diagram on page 17.

You will start with what are loosely called useful concepts and these are a mixture of concepts like opportunity cost which you will use again and again, and those that are necessary for you to understand what microeconomics is all about.

Demand, supply and markets

You will soon get into the nitty gritty of what economics is about i.e. demand and supply. These relate directly to the behaviour of consumers – that's us when we buy goods or services - and producers, which can also be us when we make something or provide a service. However, it is necessary to make a rigid distinction between these two sets of actions. Although there are books and books of theory to underpin the theories of demand and supply, at the end of the day all you need to know is that it is possible to model the behaviour of consumers and producers using demand and supply curves. Once you have understood this it will be possible to put these two concepts together to show how markets work to set the price of particular goods or services and also to determine how much is actually sold. This may sound very abstract but you only have to think of what happens to prices and sales of goods in the run up to Christmas and in the January sales.

Individual markets link to each other and chain reactions are set in motion, which theoretically allocate resources to those whose demand is strongest. This is known as the price mechanism and theoretically it should ensure allocative and productive efficiency. In other words consumers determine what is produced and this is produced at the lowest possible cost.

Market failure

There is always a gap between theory and practice, and markets don't necessarily work to produce outcomes which are economically and socially desirable. Pollution, deforestation and global warming can all be argued to be examples of failing markets. Left to their own devices markets might ignore a host of needs which we may consider important. This provides a reason for governments to intervene in the working of markets. Sometimes the government takes over providing services such as education and health which could be provided by the market system. Examples of such market failure and government intervention are dealt with in sections 1.19 – 1.24. For those of you who prefer to think visually the spider diagram on page 17 is designed to give you an overview of what is involved.

In a very short time you will find that news items in the papers and on TV will make more sense to you. Try to get into the habit of reading the financial sections of newspapers and take advantage of other magazines and periodicals. You should also build up an electronic file of resources and articles.

Web link

To access some good sites for economics students and information from your awarding body, AQA, go to www.heinemann.co.uk/hotlinks and click on this section.

The examination

The examination, known as Unit 1, lasts for one hour. You will have to answer 15 compulsory multiple-choice questions, and one data response question (from a choice of two questions).

The markets and market failure paper contributes 35 per cent of your final AS mark, and if you carry on for a second year, 17.5 per cent of your total A level grade. In reality it is even more important because in your first two modules you will be introduced to concepts which provide the foundation for further study of economics.

Definitions

The material you study for AS is divided up into three modules; micro, macro and contexts. When it comes to examinations, each paper is called a unit. In other words, modules = material you learn and units = examinations.

Exam timing

Most schools and colleges start their teaching programmes with Module 1 and it is possible for most students to be ready to take their first AS unit in January of the first year of their course. But, beware; some schools and colleges don't give that option to their students. They argue that too many examinations disrupt normal teaching too much. However, if you have the opportunity - take it. It will get you used to the new demands of AS rather than GCSEs and if you get a good grade you will become more confident. Even if you don't get a good grade you can try again in June.

Exam hint

It might seem a long way off but make a preliminary decision as to which context you are most interested in for Unit 3 and start building up a file of clippings about the topic. If your teacher sets you essays or other research tasks, use your chosen context for examples. If you do this you will cut down the amount of preparation you need do for Unit 3, and will probably get a better mark.

Exam hint

Irrespective of how good you are at economics you can boost your multiple-choice scores by lots of practise. Get hold of all the questions you can and keep going over them. Keep a record of your scores (as percentages) – over time you will get better and better (that's a promise).

Revision tactics

If you just study for this module, a typical student will take around 12 weeks to reach the required standard. It will take that long to really get used to demand and supply analysis, and confident about the various arguments about the strengths and weaknesses of the market system and government intervention. Although you should practise developing your examination techniques from the start you need a solid grounding in the underpinning theory and concepts before you are fully ready to prepare for the examination. Multiple-choice questions will be drawn from the whole of the module, and the data response questions will assume that you understand the whole of the module. So don't rush into exam preparation. Work through the three revision sections (1.25-1.27) after you have been through all the sections making up module 1 – *Markets and market failure.*

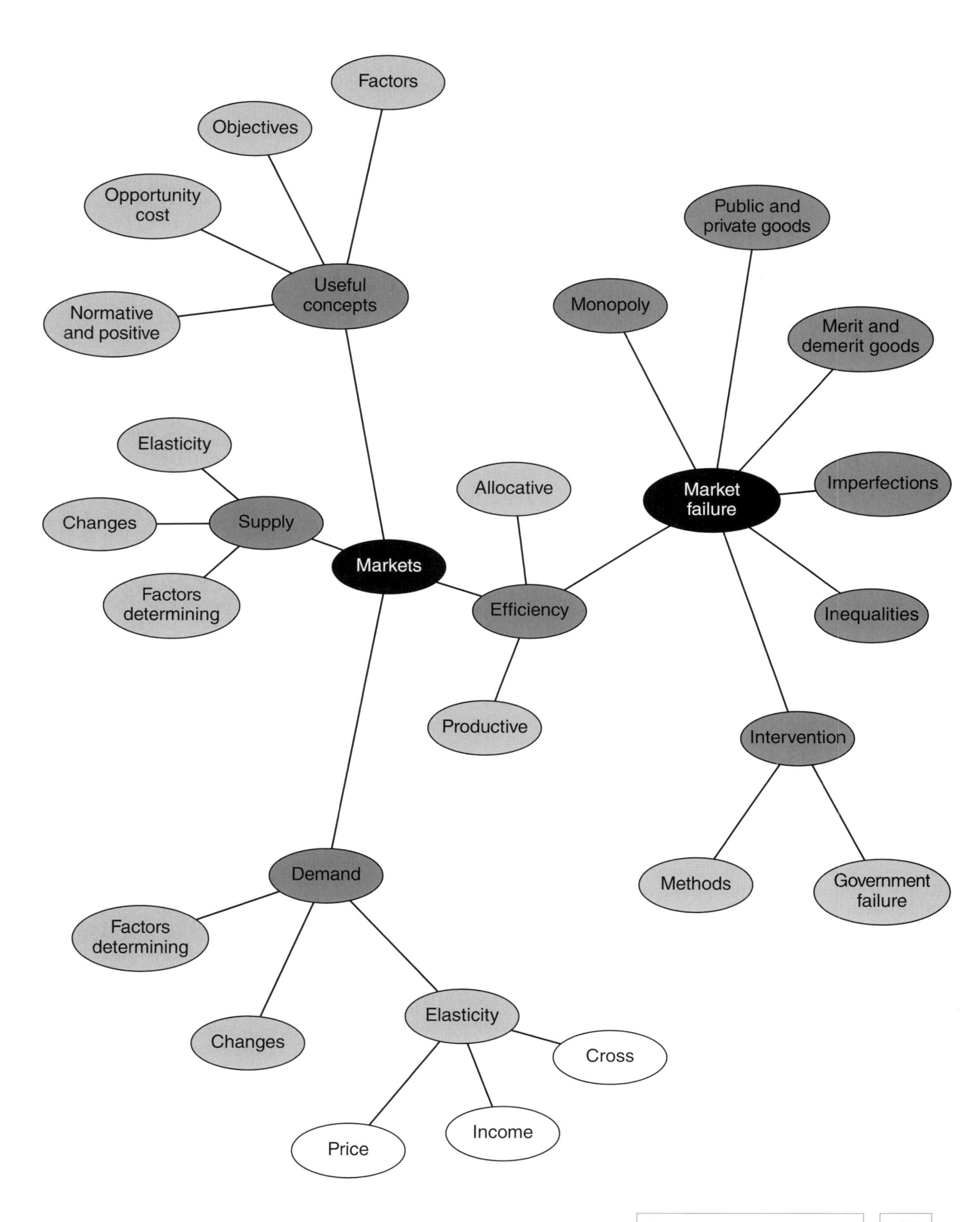

Markets
Useful concepts
Factors
Objectives
Opportunity cost
Normative and positive
Supply
Elasticity
Changes
Factors determining
Demand
Factors determining
Changes
Elasticity
Cross
Income
Price
Efficiency
Allocative
Productive
Market failure
Monopoly
Public and private goods
Merit and demerit goods
Imperfections
Inequalities
Intervention
Methods
Government failure

1.2 What is 'economics'?

Economics exists because we live in a world in which resources are finite. We don't have endless supplies of energy, minerals, foodstuffs and so on. Yet even though these resources are finite, many people aspire to improving their lifestyles by having more and better and newer and nicer things. In short, people have unlimited wants.

Our needs outstrip the means of satisfying them. There is not enough to go round. Some people starve while others enjoy fantastic luxury. This is not a morality tale. Rather, it is a description of the world in which we live. Economists use this image to explain why the discipline exists.

Making choices

People have virtually unlimited wants, yet resources are finite. Economics is about understanding that if one choice is made others have to be forgone. For example, it can be argued that if we want cleaner air, then we need to use cars less often. This sacrifice is called an **opportunity cost**.

Definition

Opportunity cost: the best possible alternative that has to be given up as the result of a particular choice.

An economic system

As we can't always get all we want, all societies need an economic system to decide:

- what gets produced
- how it is produced, and
- (crucially) who gets what.

Unravelling and understanding these types of issues is what economics is all about, and learning about the subject gives a better understanding of the forces that have shaped and will continue to shape our lives.

Starting to think like an economist

We all know about economics. We are all consumers and producers. All of us argue, knowingly and unknowingly, about economic issues. People have views about (for example) immigration, the destruction of rain forests or restrictions on tobacco advertising. But economics is about more than having views on a range of controversial issues. As it is a social science, economics involves:

- using evidence
- key economic theories and concepts
- a specialist technical vocabulary
- choice and politics.

Evidence

Economics is classed as a social science, which means that it has much in common with subjects like sociology and psychology. You can't subject people to strict laboratory conditions, although theories and concepts should be based on the careful collection of evidence. This means that numerical data is very important, as is the development of a logical and ordered argument.

Theories and concepts

Economics, as we know it today, has developed over the last 400 years. Some would argue that its origins are much older, but recent developments in economics are linked with industrialisation and the development of capitalism. Adam Smith, who wrote *The Wealth of Nations* in 1776, described how specialisation in particular tasks could lead to greater production (see sections 1.16 and 1.17).

As with other disciplines, the subject has constantly evolved and successive generations of economists have argued and debated each other's work. In this way, a body of knowledge and understanding associated with economics has developed. There is broad agreement about parts of this and dispute about others.

Key concept

Economics exists because, in the world we live in, we have to make choices. Wants are said to be infinite, whereas resources are finite.

Technical vocabulary

Economics is different to familiar subjects like history and english, because only a minority of students study economics before they are 16 years old. As with all disciplines, economics has its own technical vocabulary. Economists are also very precise in their use of particular terms. This precise use of particular terms takes some getting used to, but it is important – especially as you will need to clearly communicate your understanding of the subject and develop economic analysis and argument.

Hot potato

Brainstorm and agree the 10 biggest problems facing the world today. How many are economic?

Choice and politics

Finally, economics is about choices. It is often about controversial issues. Economic arguments are often used by politicians to support particular ideas. In fact, economics and argument go hand in hand. Often there are no right or wrong answers, and no clear-cut solutions to economic issues. Governments and political parties often disagree about economic issues. This means that economics often appeals to those who enjoy argument and debate, and also take an interest in current affairs and politics.

Quickies

1. What appeals to you about economics?
2. What puts you off?

Factors of production

Economists use the same or similar concepts again and again. You will need to practise applying them to a range of different contexts.

One way of looking at economics is that it is concerned with a study of how wealth is created. The creation of wealth involves taking resources and transforming them into products or services that can then be consumed or used in some other way. This process, illustrated in Figure 1, captures a wide range of issues and concepts important to economists. Let's break down the figure and look at each part.

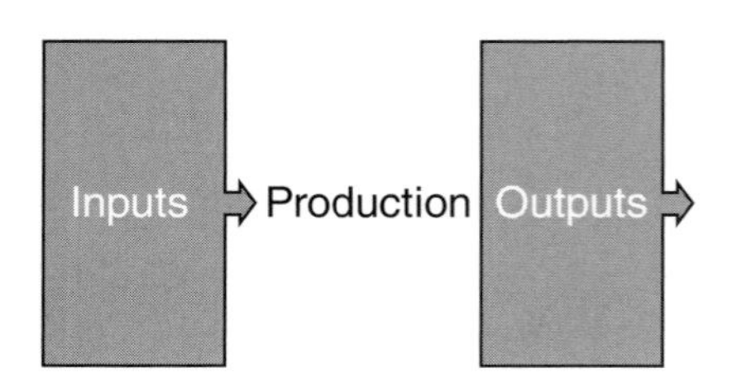

Figure 1: Simple input/output model

- 'Inputs' encompass environmental economics as it deals with the relationship between economic activity and the world's resources (both renewable and finite).
- 'Production' is concerned with how resources are transformed. Business studies students call this process 'adding value', and it can include complex processes involving the use of highly sophisticated technology or the more straightforward harvesting and packaging of an agricultural crop.
- 'Outputs' are concerned with the consumption of that which has been produced.

Types of resources

The simple input/output model shown in Figure 1 can be expanded to identify and classify different types of resources (see Figure 2). Economists call these '**factors of production**', and they are broken down into:

- land
- labour
- capital
- enterprise.

Each of these factors is explained more fully in the text that follows.

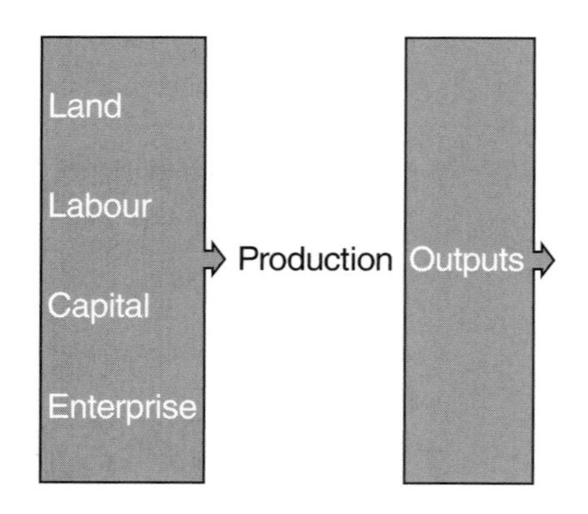

Figure 2: The four factors of production

Land

Land includes everything that is locked up in the earth's surface – not just land in the sense of farmland, building and factory sites, but also what we call 'natural resources' such as minerals, fossil fuels and timber, and what can be grown and harvested. Land includes:

- the products of the seas
- the content of our atmosphere, and
- (by implication) what has yet to be discovered in space.

Labour

Labour is a similar 'catchall' concept to land, and includes what we as people bring to the production process, such as:

- personal attributes (for example, strength or manual dexterity)
- individual aptitudes
- skills and capabilities that we can learn.

Capital

Economists refer to capital as those assets used to produce goods or services – including the factories, machinery and equipment used to transform 'land' into some particular form of output. The term 'capital' is used in everyday conversation to describe:

- money that is used to set up a business and keep it going
- savings in shares and so on.

All these uses are linked directly or indirectly to the actual production process, but economists use the term 'capital' in a more restricted sense. You might say they are not interested in money as such, but in the uses to which it can be put (especially uses that result in economic activity).

Key concept

The four factors of production (known as inputs) are land, labour, capital and enterprise. All outputs consist of varying combinations of each of these inputs. They are used by the public, private and voluntary sectors.

Enterprise

This is often described as the fourth factor of production. Economic activity involves the combination of particular quantities of land, labour and capital to produce something. Enterprise is the process of managing and deciding how factors should be confined and to what end. Being enterprising may also involve taking risks and guessing what goods or services are likely to be in demand. Economists consider enterprise as a separate factor of production as it emphasises the importance of decision making within the economy.

Hot potato

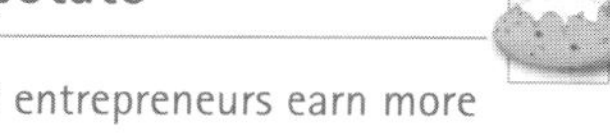

Should entrepreneurs earn more than workers?

Production

So who decides what is actually produced? This question has no simple answer. All societies are, to varying degrees, **mixed economies**. They consist of:

- privately owned organisations – known as the private sector
- national and local governments – known as the public sector
- a range of not-for-profit organisations (mainly including charities) – known as the voluntary sector.

Put simply, private sector organisations are primarily concerned with making a financial profit, the public sector provides services, and economic activity in the voluntary sector is not undertaken for financial gain. Although these definitions are simplifications (as your further study of economics will show), they do provide a starting point for your study.

Web link

Visit a virtual factory and learn about factors of production by visiting the Biz/ed homepage. Go to www.heinemann.co.uk/hotlinks and click on this section.

Quickie

Use the input/output model in Figure 1 to show what happens when beer and crisps are produced.

1.4 Trade and welfare

Two more key economic concepts useful in helping to develop an understanding of economics are trade and welfare. Trade refers to the exchange of goods and services. Welfare is used to indicate how well off a particular society might be.

The growth of economies can be seen to involve four important developments:

- **subsistence**
- **surpluses** and trade
- **specialisation**
- **division of labour.**

Subsistence

The development of western and other civilisations is closely linked to the development of trade. In the past, much economic activity could be described as subsistence – in other words, groups within societies attempted, through their own labour, to produce enough food and basic products to survive. But this was difficult. Poor harvests could result in too little food to go round, and natural disasters such as floods or earthquakes could wipe out shelter and possessions. Many people still live in conditions like these.

Surpluses and trade

Subsistence economies that became more successful were able to produce more food and other goods than needed for immediate survival. They were able to store unused produce to provide insurance against unforeseen disasters. These surpluses could also be traded with other groups producing surpluses. This trade enabled greater prosperity and higher standards of living.

Methods of payment

Early trade was probably by **barter**, with shells and other small precious items being used as early forms of money. Coins were first used about 3000 years ago.

Markets

The combination of surpluses, money and growing trade provided the foundation for the development of markets – places at which trade could take place. This provided stimulus for further economic growth and development.

Specialisation

Trade meant that an individual group no longer needed to produce all its own requirements. This allowed groups to concentrate on the commodities (products) they were best or most efficient at producing (perhaps because of different **natural conditions**). Concentration on producing particular goods could also increase overall production leading to even more trade, the development of larger surpluses and high standards of living.

Definitions

Barter: where one group of people with a surplus of something, say, fish, swaps with another group able to produce, say, more grain. As you can imagine, this isn't the most convenient or best way to trade.

Natural conditions: some countries have very warm weather; others may have a particular type of landscape; some land may have good soil drainage. These different natural conditions result in commodities that can be traded in areas not able to produce these things.

Division of labour

Similarly, within tribes and societies different tasks were increasingly delegated to particular individuals and groups. Through this division of labour, people were able to improve their skills and increase productivity. In this way, past empires and dynasties grew and developed. The most successful were able to use their surpluses to finance, for example, buildings, public works and religious celebrations. Those things that make a society better off without making others worse off are described by economists as 'contributing to the economic welfare of a society'.

Research task

Find the most ancient reference you can to economic activity. Where does this reference come from?

Production possibilities

Increases in economic welfare can also be illustrated using another key concept – **production possibility curves** (also known as production possibility frontiers). As with other models, these are simplifications of how the real world is thought to work. In Figure 1, it is assumed that an economy is capable of producing just two goods: corn and beer.

- If the economy were to use all its available factors of production to produce corn, it would produce **C**.
- Alternatively, if all resources were devoted to making beer, **B** would be made.
- The line between **C** and **B** is called a production possibility curve, because it shows all the different combinations of beer and corn that could be produced. It also illustrates opportunity cost – that is, what has to be given up as the result of a particular decision.
- The movement from ***a*** to ***b*** on the production possibility curve would indicate an increase in the production of corn. If all resources are being used, this can only be achieved by cutting the production of beer from x to z, which is the opportunity cost of increasing the output of corn.

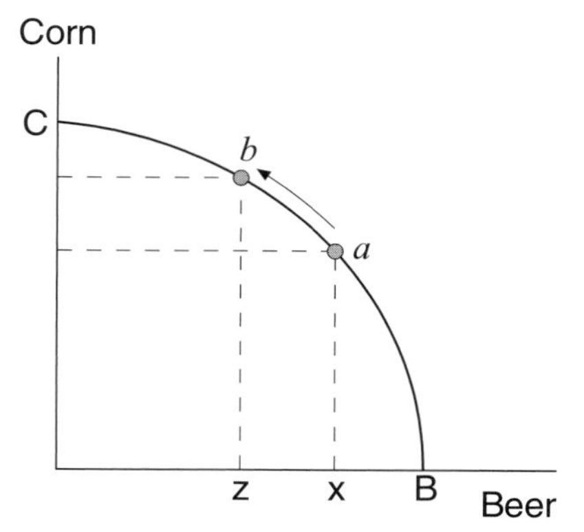

Figure 1: A production possibility curve

A variety of changes can be illustrated on a production possibility curve. For example, if a new technique were discovered that meant more beer could be produced with the same amount of resources, there would be a movement in the curve from **CB** to **CB1** (see Figure 2). This new production possibility curve indicates a higher possible standard of living and an increase in welfare. This society could now produce both more beer and corn, using the same amount of resources. Point *x* on Figure 2 illustrates an economy that is not making full use of all its resources. Both more beer and more corn could be produced. This failure to use all resources can be described as unemployment of resources.

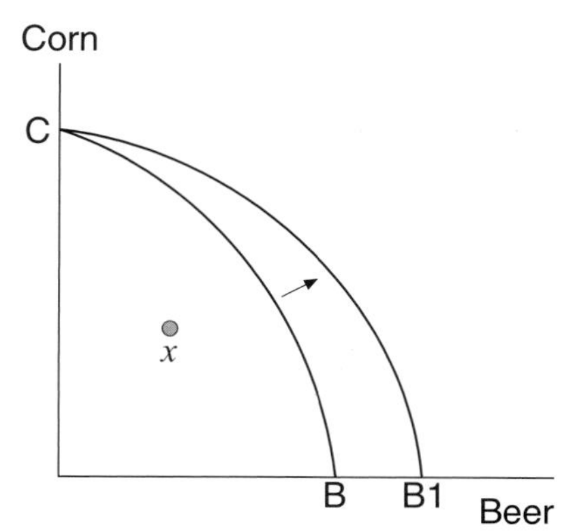

Figure 2: Changes to a production possibility curve

Quickie

Use production possibility curves to model the impact of spending more of a nation's resources on fighting aids rather than more arms.

1.5 Demand

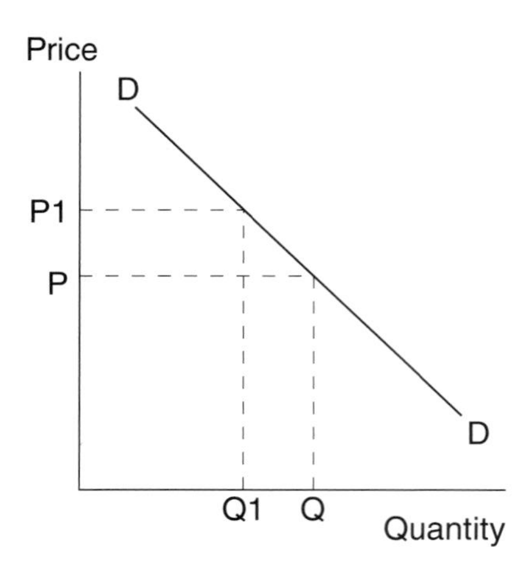

Figure 1: Demand 'curve'

Key concept

Demand curves show the likely relationship between the price of a good or service and the quantity sold. These curves usually slope downwards from left to right, showing either that as price falls demand is likely to rise, or that as price rises demand is likely to fall. (See Figures 1 and 2.)

Definition

Disposable income: income after direct taxation has been deducted and state benefits have been added.

Demand has a very precise meaning in economics – that is, how much of a product or service we are prepared to buy. Demand theory is based on a simple generalisation about customer behaviour: if the price of something rises, consumers are less likely to buy it, whereas falling prices lead to higher demand. This is illustrated in Figure 1.

The quantity demanded of a product or service is measured along the horizontal axis and its price on the vertical. The curve **D** slopes downwards from left to right. So, if the price is set at **P**, the demand will be at **Q**. If the price is increased to **P1**, the demand will fall to **Q1**.

Changes in demand

Many factors can potentially influence the demand for a product or service. Economists group these key variables under the following three headings:

- the price of other goods and services
- consumers' incomes
- consumers' tastes.

The price of other goods and services

Clearly, the decision to buy or not to buy something is not made simply on the basis of its price. Our choice to buy one product is often made by reference to prices of similar products.

- Products that can be seen as alternatives for each other – for example, a Ford Fiesta car and a Renault Clio car – are called **substitutes**.
- Products or services that can be brought together – for example, like shampoo and conditioner – are called **complements**.

Consumers' incomes

Obviously, the level of our income will have a powerful effect on our demand – the more money we earn, the more we can buy. Economists use the term **'disposable income'** to describe the amount of money available for spending, after the deduction of income tax and National Insurance contributions and addition of state benefits.

Demand for **normal goods** rises as income rises. Those products, for example, travel on luxury liners, where demand rises proportionally more than income are known as **superior goods** or luxury goods.

Other products are classified as **inferior goods** in the sense that as consumer income rises, demand for such products falls. Think of the example of terraced houses in some areas of northern cities: as owners of such houses become better off, they are more likely to purchase more expensive substitutes.

Consumers' tastes

This term is used by economists to capture a whole range of other influences on demand. At one level, we all like and dislike different things and these personal preferences are likely to affect what we wish to buy. These individual differences are hard for economists to model but it is easier to identify broad trends and changes in tastes. Advertisers in particular try to change our tastes in order to increase the demand for particular products or services.

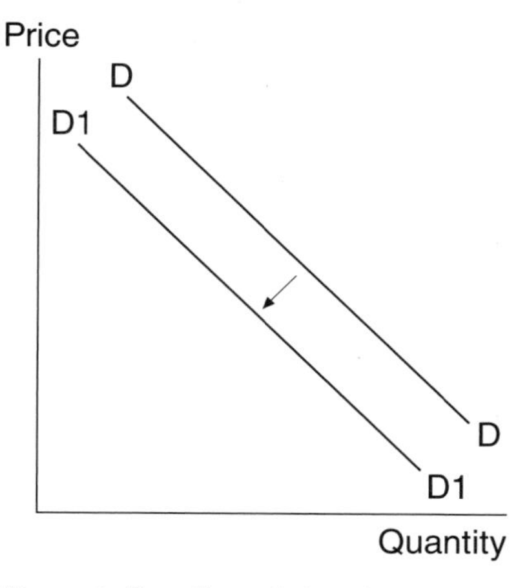

Figure 2: The effect of changing key variables

What if key variables change?

Figure 2 can be used to show the effects of changes in the three key variables mentioned above.

- If the price of a Renault Clio was to fall and the prices of other similar cars were to stay the same, the demand for Fiestas would fall. This is shown in Figure 2 by a shift in demand to the left. If the opposite were to happen, the curve should shift to the right. If goods are complements, a rise in the price of one good will lead to a fall in demand for the other.
- Rising incomes might lead to an increase in demand for, say, foreign holidays and this is shown by a shift in the demand curve to the right. If the good is considered inferior, then demand will fall as shown by the shift to the left.
- Changes in tastes can be treated in a similar way. The demand for goods that become more fashionable will shift to the right, whereas a leftward shift would show that something is no longer fashionable.

Thinking like an economist

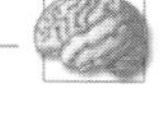

Model building is an essential part of the economist's toolkit. Demand and supply analysis is one of the most simple and powerful models used by economists. The value of any model is determined by how useful it is in predicting what might happen if changes occur.

Quickie

Which way will the demand curve for Mars Bars move if:

(a) the price of Twix is reduced
(b) child benefit is raised
(c) eating chocolate is proved to reduce your intelligence
(d) Tesco launches a two-for-the-price-of-one Mars Bar offer?

Puzzler

What do you think economists mean when they talk about the differences between a shift and a movement along a demand curve?

Price elasticity of demand

1.6

Definition

$^{P}\varepsilon_D$: price elasticity of demand

$$^{P}\varepsilon_D = \frac{\%\ \text{change in quantity demanded}}{\%\ \text{change in price}}$$

Elasticity – a measure of responsiveness – is a key concept in economics, that occurs many times in different contexts. This may be the first time you have come across it, so do spend some time making sure your understanding is secure.

As you will remember from section 1.5, basic economics indicates that if the price of a good or service changes, so the demand will also change. An increase in price is likely to result in a fall in demand, whereas a cut in price is likely to lead to an increase in demand. Understanding **price elasticity of demand** (often expressed as $^{P}\varepsilon_D$) is a way of measuring how much demand changes in response to a change in price. Price elasticity can be analysed in three ways:

- by diagram
- in words
- by using the formula.

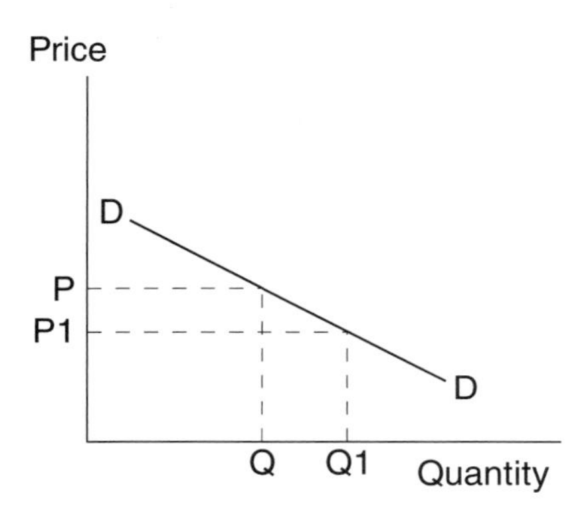

Figure 1: A response to a reduction in house prices

Diagrams

Figures 1 and 2 show two very different responses in demand to identical reductions in price.

- In Figure 1, a cut of around 20 per cent in house prices leads to a rise in demand of about 50 per cent. In Figure 2, the same price cut causes a much smaller rise in demand – about 10 per cent.
- Figure 1 shows demand to be very responsive to changes in price. In Figure 2, demand is much less responsive. Given the use of the same axis, the slope of the demand curve will indicate the degree of responsiveness to changes in price i.e. the price elasticity of demand.
- Another aspect shown by Figures 1 and 2 is to compare the revenue spent before and after the change. Revenue is simply: price × quantity. In Figure 1, revenue rises and in Figure 2 it falls. This has massive implications for businesses selecting an appropriate pricing policy.

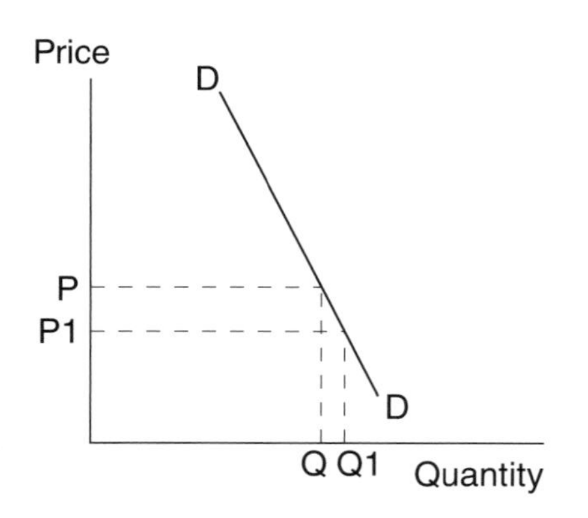

Figure 2: A different response to a reduction in house prices

Words

Using words to describe the differences between Figures 1 and 2 involves some specialist terminology.

- If the demand for a good or service is very responsive to changes in price, then the demand is said to be 'relatively **elastic**'.
- If the demand for a good or service is not very responsive to changes in price, then the demand is described as 'relatively **inelastic**'.

The formula

This representation of price elasticity of demand is a much more precise and mathematical way of dealing with the relationship between changes in price and changes in demand. Figures 1 and 2 show slope or gradient of the demand curve, which indicates its elasticity. This can be represented by the following equation:

$$^{P}\varepsilon_{D} = \frac{\text{\% change in quantity demanded}}{\text{\% change in price}}$$

So a price fall by 20 per cent, accompanied by a demand increase of 50 per cent, can be inserted into the equation above giving: $^{P}\varepsilon_{D} = \frac{+50}{-20} = -2.5$

Alternatively, if the price cut of 20 per cent prompted an increase in demand of 10 per cent, solving the same equation would give: $^{P}\varepsilon_{D} = \frac{+10}{-20} = -0.5$

These answers or values are called coefficients, and they give an instant insight into the responsiveness of demand for a product to a change in price. Any value (ignoring the + or – sign) that is less than 1 – for example, 0.6 or 0.2 – indicates that demand for the product is not very responsive to changes in price. To be more precise, any percentage change in the price of the product will result in a smaller proportional change in quantity demanded.

One the other hand, a value that is larger than 1 – for example, 2.5 or 6 – represents a demand that is very responsive to a change in price. The percentage change in quantity demanded for such a product will exceed the percentage change in price. Economists would describe this kind of demand response to be elastic.

Exam hint

- Elastic = stretches out = very responsive.
- Inelastic = doesn't stretch = not very responsive.

Why elasticities differ

Economists list the following four factors as having the greatest impact in determining the price elasticity of demand for a good or service:

- substitutes (for example, the demand for one brand of crisps will be more elastic if there are lots of similar brands on the market)
- absolute price (for example, the cheaper a good, the less sensitive it will make most buyers to price changes)
- consumer knowledge (if customers don't know what substitutes are available or what they cost, demand is likely to be more inelastic)
- time (it may take customers some time to adjust to changes in price; this would make price elasticity of demand more inelastic in the short run).

Making connections

What is the link between substitutes and competition?

Quickies

1. When will cutting the price of a good or service raise revenue?
2. When can the same objective be achieved by raising prices?
3. Why do UK governments often raise taxes on tobacco?

Puzzler

Why is the coefficient for price elasticity of demand almost always a minus figure? What if it were a positive value?

1.7 Other demand elasticities

In section 1.6, you looked at price elasticity of demand. Here, you will learn two more ways in which the concept of elasticity is used to help analyse different aspects of markets. They are:

- **income elasticity of demand**
- **cross elasticity of demand.**

Income elasticity of demand

Income elasticity of demand measures the responsiveness of the demand for a product to changes in incomes. It is also represented by a formula, or equation – in this case:

$$\text{Income elasticity of demand} = \frac{\text{\% change in quantity demanded}}{\text{\% change in income}}$$

Note: only the bottom of the equation is different to the equation given for price elasticity of demand in section 1.6.

If the government were to decide to cut income tax then all those people in work would have higher disposable incomes (see section 1.5). Having more money to spend might change people's spending patterns, especially if becoming better off makes it possible for them to afford what might previously have been considered a luxury item. For example, increasing incomes over the last 30 years have led to an even bigger proportionate increase in the demand for foreign holidays.

This could mean that a 10 per cent rise in incomes could lead to a 30 per cent increase in the demand for foreign holidays. In other words, income elasticity of demand for foreign holidays would be +30/+10 = +3.

On the other hand, rising incomes have also been associated with a fall in demand for traditional British seaside holidays. So the same increase in income of 10 per cent might be associated with a 40 per cent fall in demand for some British seaside towns.

The income elasticity in this case would be –40/+10 = –4 and, in this case, the coefficient for income elasticity of demand would be negative. Economists call goods such as these inferior goods, whereas the more attractive foreign holidays are called superior goods (refer back to section 1.5 for a further explanation).

Research task

You are going to investigate cross elasticity of demand.

(a) Select two clothing brands that you believe are close substitutes.

(b) Devise a suitable questionnaire to collect data to test whether or not you have made a good choice.

(c) Collect your data.

(d) Collate your findings. What do they tell you?

Cross elasticity of demand

As indicated in sections 1.5 and 1.6, it is often helpful to categorise goods as being either substitutes or complements. These can be analysed using the concept of cross elasticity of demand, which is used to measure the responsiveness of demand for one good in relation to a change in the price of another.

Substitutes

Many people might regard, for example, peaches and nectarines as being close substitutes for each other. In this case, an increase in the price of peaches may lead to an increase in the demand for nectarines. The formula that is used to work out the coefficient of cross elasticity of demand is similar to that used on page 27:

cross elasticity of demand of good x in relation to a change in the price of good y

$$= \frac{\text{\% change in quantity demanded of good } x}{\text{\% change in the price of good } y}$$

So a 50 per cent increase in the price of peaches might result in a 40 per cent rise in demand for nectarines. The cross elasticity would be:

$$= +40/+50$$
$$= +0.8$$

The value of the coefficient will always be positive if you are considering two goods that are substitutes for each other.

The size of the coefficient indicates how substitutable the two products are for one another. If there were little **brand loyalty** and a high degree of customer knowledge, the value of the co-efficient would be much larger.

Complements

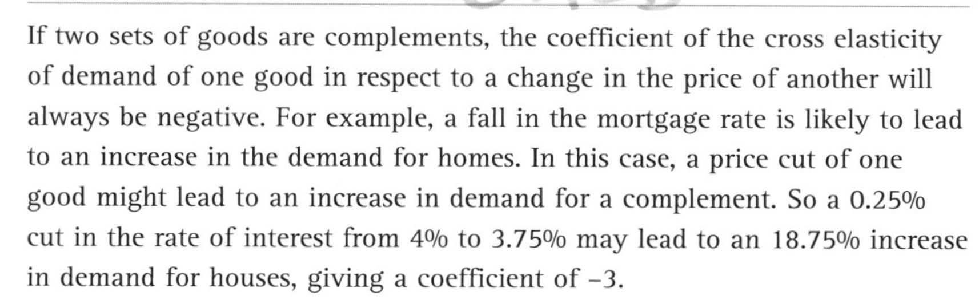

If two sets of goods are complements, the coefficient of the cross elasticity of demand of one good in respect to a change in the price of another will always be negative. For example, a fall in the mortgage rate is likely to lead to an increase in the demand for homes. In this case, a price cut of one good might lead to an increase in demand for a complement. So a 0.25% cut in the rate of interest from 4% to 3.75% may lead to an 18.75% increase in demand for houses, giving a coefficient of –3.

This relatively large negative figure would indicate that the demand for houses is very sensitive to changes in the mortgage interest rates. If two goods are complements, their coefficient for their cross elasticities will always be negative and, as with all the other uses of the concept of elasticity, the smaller the value the less responsive the relationship (and vice versa).

Hot potato

Why is branding so important in marketing?

Definition

Brand loyalty: a term often used in business to explain why customers stick to the same brand. This can apply to a whole range of products from cornflakes to cars (e.g. Kelloggs and VW).

Exam hints

1 Don't worry if you initially get a bit confused about different elasticities. You need only remember two things:
(a) always define the concept you are using
(b) the change in demand always goes on the top half of any equation.

2 Try to remember the following:
(a) small value to elasticity coefficient = weak relationship
(b) large value = strong relationship
(c) negative value = inverse relationship.

1.8 What is 'supply'?

Key concept

Supply curves show the likely relationship between the price of a good or service and the quantity supplied. These curves usually slope upwards from left to right showing that as price rises supply is also likely to rise, whereas if price falls supply is likely to fall.

Thinking like an economist

It would be difficult to assess what would happen to coffee supply if there was a frost in Brazil, revolution in Columbia, collapse in tea prices and so on. To make these situations more manageable, economists freeze all but the variables they want to analyse. To ensure everyone knows what's happening, they use the phrase '*ceteris paribus*' (which means 'other things being equal').

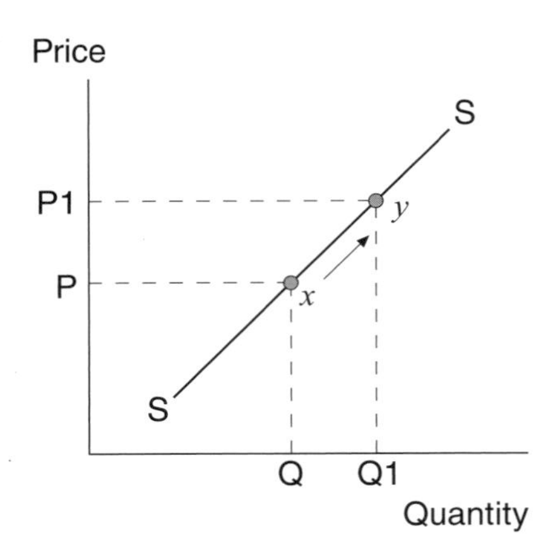

Figure 1: A typical supply curve

Supply refers to the willingness of a producer to supply a good or service. A typical **supply curve** is illustrated in Figure 1. It slopes upwards from left to right showing that as the price of a good or service rises, suppliers are likely to want to produce and supply more of that good or service. Economists consider price to be the most important variable affecting supply, but they also recognise that supply will be affected by changes in four other factors:

- costs
- technology
- relative profitability
- business objectives.

Price and supply

Supply refers to the willingness and ability to supply goods to a market and, as with demand, price is considered to be the most important variable. ***Ceteris paribus***, if the price of a good or service rises it will become more profitable to sell that good or service. If there are greater potential profits, it is reasonable to expect that producers will wish to produce more. Therefore it is argued that a rise in price will lead to an increase in supply. This is illustrated in Figure 1 by the movement along the curve from x to y. The converse (or opposite) of this is true. If prices fall, supply should also fall.

Costs of production

Costs refer to all payments that have to be made in order to produce a good. *Ceteris paribus*, a rise in costs will lead to a fall in profits and the incentive to make a particular product or service will drop. This will lead to a shift in supply to the left, showing that, at all possible prices, less will be supplied, as illustrated in Figure 2. The reverse argument applies – if costs fall, potential profits rise and supply will rise, shown by a shift in the supply curve to the right, as illustrated in Figure 3.

Changes in technology

The use of technology in the production of goods or provision of services is changing all the time. Improvements in the way in which things are made or how services are provided can have a major impact on supply. Car producers, for example, have reduced both production and running costs by using plastic components rather than those made of metal.

Improvements in technology are often associated with reductions in the cost of production and they can be illustrated in a similar way. The adoption of better and cheaper ways of making something will shift the supply curve downwards to the right (Figure 3). On the other hand, the use of more complex or difficult technologies will shift a supply curve to the left (Figure 2).

Relative profitability

The importance of profits has previously been considered, but a further issue – especially for those firms who have an easy choice between producing different products or providing different services – is the relative profitability of producing different goods or services. For example, if Tesco can negotiate a better deal with the suppliers of Whiskas cat food rather than Felix, it may be inclined to supply more of the former and less of the latter.

Not all businesses have such easy choices, because changing what is produced or sold may take time. However, the general rule is that if supplying an alternative product becomes more profitable, the supply of the good in question will fall, as shown in Figure 2. On the other hand, if the supply of an alternative becomes less profitable, there could be shift to the right, showing an increase in supply, as illustrated in Figure 3.

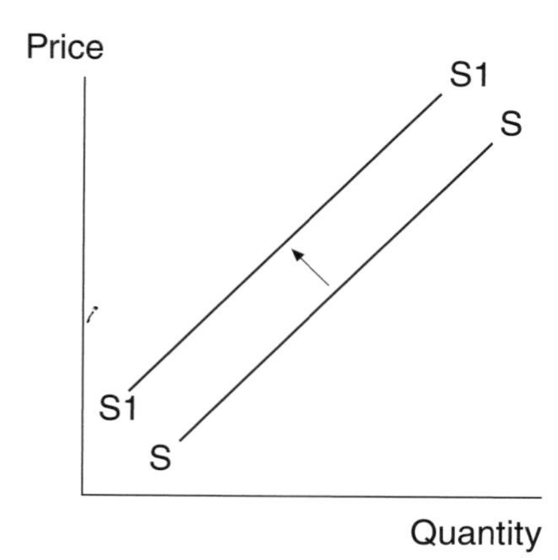

Figure 2: The result of a rise in costs

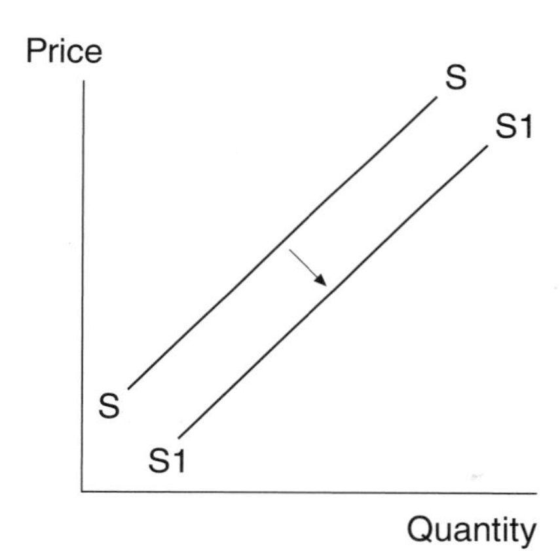

Figure 3: The result of a fall in costs

Business objectives

So far, we have assumed that businesses will respond in similar ways to changes in factors affecting their supply of a good or service. Obviously no two businesses are the same.

- Some businesses are interested in quick profits at all costs.
- Others might place greater emphasis on, for example, ethical considerations.

Business decision makers don't necessarily respond immediately to small changes in price. In this case, rising prices might not lead to increased output, or improvements in technology might allow the same level of profit in return for working less hard. How individual businesses work and make decisions will affect supply, and this makes it harder for economists to make simple generalisations about supply.

Quickie

Which way will the supply curve for Mars Bars move if:

(a) there is a severe frost in Ghana

(b) producing chocolate truffles becomes more profitable

(c) an ethical chocolate-producing company (for example, Fairtrade) mounts a successful advertising campaign

(d) Mars Bars are shown to improve energy levels?

Puzzler

What do you think economists mean when they talk about the difference between a shift and a movement along a supply curve?

1.9 Elasticity of supply

The responsiveness of supply to changes in price is measured using the concept of **price elasticity of supply formulae.** As with other applications of this concept, written, graphical and formulaic treatments are used by economists.

Words

- If it is easy and quick for a producer to change the output of a good or service in response to changes in price then the supply of that good is described as relatively elastic.
- Alternatively, if it is difficult and time consuming to change output in response to price changes then supply is relatively inelastic.

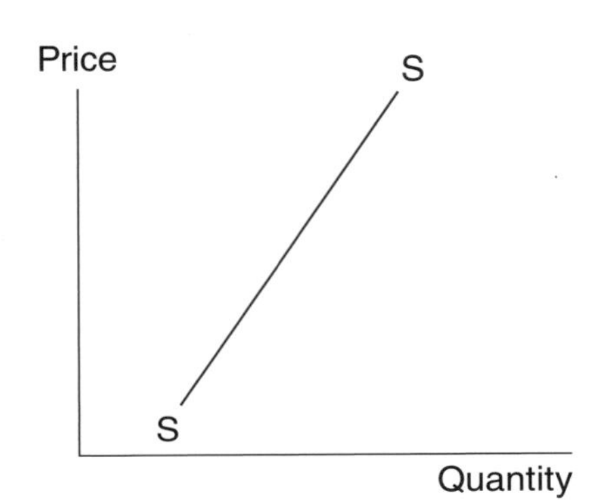

Figure 1: Inelastic supply

Graphs

Graphical analysis can be quickly used to illustrate supply elasticity. Figure 1 illustrates inelastic supply and Figure 2 illustrates elastic supply.

The formula

The formula for working out the coefficient is very similar to that relating to price elasticity of demand (see section 1.6). It is:

$$\text{Elasticity of supply} = \frac{\text{\% change in quantity supplied}}{\text{\% change in price}}$$

- So if the price of cars rises by 10 per cent and car producers struggle to raise output, increasing supply by 2 per cent, the coefficient would be + 0.2.
- On the other hand, if car manufacturers have large stocks of unsold cars and can change output quickly in response to a price rise, the coefficient is likely to be larger than 1.

It is very unlikely for a negative coefficient to occur, as this would mean that producers expand production in response to a fall in price or cut output in response to a rise in price.

The opposite analysis also applies. Falling prices are associated with a decrease in willingness to produce and supply. Some producers are able to adjust quickly to falling prices, while others will find it harder to do.

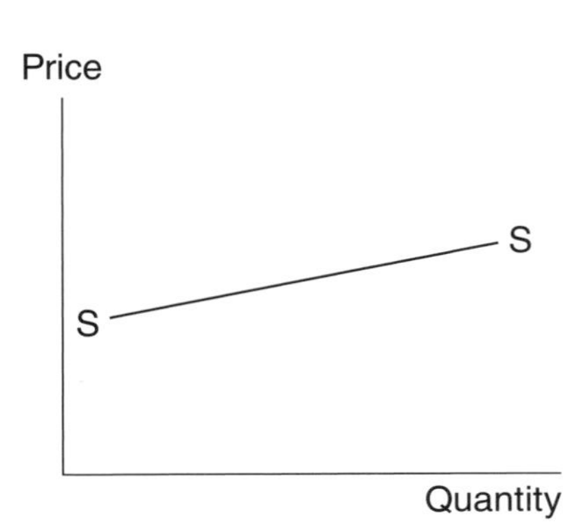

Figure 2: Elastic supply

Factors affecting the elasticity of supply

If prices rise, producers are likely to want to respond by increasing production, and this could be achieved by undertaking a number of measures. The elasticity of supply of any product or service is likely to depend on the following factors.

- Availability of stocks, and raw materials. (If there are stocks of finished goods, components and other materials, it will be relatively easy to expand production and sales. Conversely, expansion could be checked by the unavailability of one small component.)

- Unused productive capacity. (If existing factories and production lines are not being used all the time, supply is likely to be more elastic.)
- Availability of imports. (Many industries are global and companies can switch supplies from contracting markets to those that are growing.)
- Availability of suitably trained labour. (The difficulty and extra costs of attracting skilled workers may limit the responsiveness of producers in meeting increases in demand.)

The significance of these factors can be viewed in a different way by using the concept of 'time' – the supply of most products and services is likely to become more elastic over a longer time scale. Changes in elasticity of supply over time are shown in Figure 3, where:

- S represents the elasticity of supply in a very short timescale as unused stocks of materials and under-utilised labour is used
- S1 represents the elasticity of supply for a longer period in which existing productive capacity can be brought into production, and
- S2 represents the elasticity of supply over an even longer period to allow for the acquisition of a new plant and machinery along with the training of new workers.

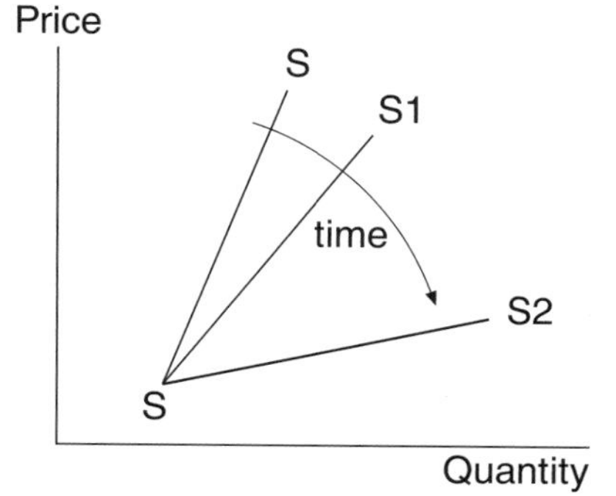

Figure 3: Changes in elasticity of supply over time

The significance of technological change

Technological change refers to changes in the way in which goods and services are actually produced. Over the last two decades tremendous advances have been made in communications technology. We all know about the importance of IT in our lives, but there have been similar, if less spectacular, advances in air and sea transport. These developments have been paralleled by the growth of transnational corporations – many of whom have more economic power than most nations. Nissan and Shell are examples of such transnational corporations.

The cumulative effect of these changes is often referred to as **globalisation.** It is now possible for production and sales to be organised on a global scale, which means that the supply of many products and services has become more and more elastic. As will be shown in sections 1.18 and 3.8, globalisation is having a major effect on how economies and economists work.

Thinking like an economist

You already know that demand analysis focuses on behaviour of customers or consumers. But don't forget to think also of producers making goods and providing services.

Quickies

1 What factors are likely to affect the elasticity of supply in the following markets?
   (a) Wheat production.
   (b) Electrical generation.
   (c) T-shirt manufacture.
2 Which supply is likely to be most responsive to changes in:
   (a) demand
   (b) price?

1.10 Markets at work

Stock exchange

A flea market

Markets exist wherever those who demand products or services meet those who supply goods or services. Many different kinds of markets exist.

The earliest markets moved around the country. They were often celebrated as fairs and special events at which all kinds of resources were traded. Some were devoted to selling surplus production at harvest time. Others involved selling labour to the highest bidders.

Cattle markets retain some of the features of these earlier trading events. Towns and city centres now take on several functions of traditional markets, and the sellers of products and services use a wide variety of strategies to appeal to consumers. There are many other forms of market:

- classified advertisements
- the stock market
- wholesale markets
- futures markets
- auctions
- flea markets
- grey markets
- the Internet.

This list could easily be extended, but regardless of the form and frequency of such markets they all involve:

- buyers
- sellers
- a means to reach a deal.

Putting demand and supply together

As demand curves and supply curves are drawn against the same axes, it is possible to superimpose one on top of another – as illustrated in Figure 1.

- The demand for new houses slopes downwards to the right. It is relatively inelastic, as there are not many close substitutes. This factor is likely to outweigh the significance of housing taking up a very large portion of most customers' budgets.
- Supply slopes upwards to the right. For the new houses, this is also relatively inelastic as it is not always easy for producers to quickly change output in response to changes in demand and price.
- The point *a*, where the supply and demand curves cross, shows the price at which demand and supply are equal.

In the example given in Figure 1, the average price of a new house coming onto the market will be £85,000, and 100 houses would be sold each month. This is called the **equilibrium** price, and in a free market this will be established automatically.

If, for some reason, the price were to be £95,000, demand would equal 90 whereas supply would be 120. The producers of new houses would be attempting to sell more than could be sold. This excess supply of 30 homes would mean that some houses were being made, but not sold. Stocks of unwanted houses would build up and sellers would be tempted to cut prices.

Falling prices would make new houses more attractive to some consumers – for example, those on lower incomes, who might now be able to borrow enough money. However, some builders may find house building less attractive and seek alternative building contracts. Demand would rise as supply would fall.

According to price theory, this process would stop when the equilibrium price had been reached. This pincer movement towards an equilibrium is shown by ***b*** and **c** along the demand and supply curves. The process by which markets are brought into equilibrium is called '**market clearing**'.

The same logical analysis can be applied to a situation in which new houses are being sold for less than £85,000 each. Excess demand would apply and some prospective house buyers would be forced to go without. New houses coming onto the market would be snapped up quickly, and enterprising estate agents might well attempt to take advantage of the shortage of new houses by raising their prices.

This process would set a similar pincer movement in operation to that described earlier. Rising prices would put off some potential house buyers but would also make house production more attractive. Demand would fall and supply would rise until equilibrium is reached.

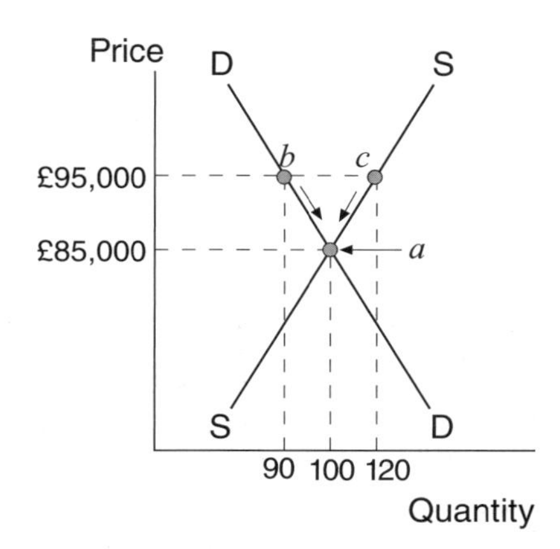

Figure 1: The market for new houses

Summary

The key point to remember is that as long as demand curves slope downwards to the right and supply curves slope upwards to the right, and as long as they both cross, there will be one equilibrium – and that is the price where demand is equal to supply. In other words, both buyers and sellers can make a deal.

Quickie

Draw a diagram to explain why a price set below the market equilibrium will not persist.

Thinking like an economist

The concepts on these pages are simple but central to microeconomics. Markets in different forms are key to how all economics operate. Diagrams are used to model market behaviour. Analysis should be accurate, precise and to the point. This is what economics is all about.

Hot potato

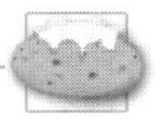

Are markets a good idea?

1.11 Markets and changes in demand

If one of the key variables that determine the demand or supply for any product or service changes, the equilibrium will change, leading to a change in price and sales.

Now may be a good time to look back to section 1.5 to remind yourself of key variables. However, in summary, demand curves shift if any of the following change:

- the prices of substitutes
- the prices of complements
- consumers' incomes
- consumers' tastes.

Decrease in the price of a substitute

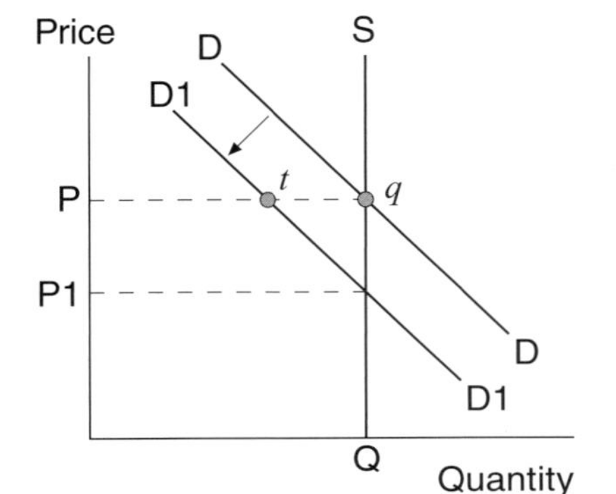

Figure 1: Market for seats at Wimbledon

Consider the market for seats at the Centre Court for the Wimbledon All-England Open Tennis Championship (see Figure 1).

- The supply is fixed, and this would appear as a vertical line as shown by **S**.
- Demand is represented by **D** giving an equilibrium price of **P** and ticket sales of **Q**.

Those thinking of buying a ticket will consider not only the price of the ticket, but also the price of alternatives. This would include prices of tickets for other courts or a whole range of other leisure products. If, for example, a Test cricket match were being staged in London at the same time and seat prices for that were reduced, some people might be attracted to cricket rather than tennis and this would cause the demand for Wimbledon tickets to fall – as shown by the shift from **D** to **D1**.

If the price were to remain at **P** there would be disequilibrium between demand and supply. Supply would exceed demand by ***tq***. **Excess supply** would exist – that is, some tickets would be unsold. The managers of Wimbledon might consider cutting prices to **P1** in order to make sure all seats were sold. This change in price would be described by economists as being the outcome of 'market forces' at work.

Making connections

What pair of goods are the closest substitutes for one another?

Decrease in the price of a complement

A number of other products or services are likely to be jointly consumed by visitors to Wimbledon. Travel to the courts, the famous strawberries and cream, and perhaps having something new to wear could be considered to be complements. So, reduced public transport prices to Wimbledon could result in an increase in demand for Wimbledon tickets, as shown in Figure 2.

In this case, demand increases, as indicated by the shift to the right from D to D1. If the price remained at P, excess demand of *xy* would occur. This would give Wimbledon's managers the opportunity to raise seat prices and a new equilibrium could be established with a higher price at P1. If they didn't, opportunities would arise for ticket touts to exploit the situation by selling tickets at inflated prices.

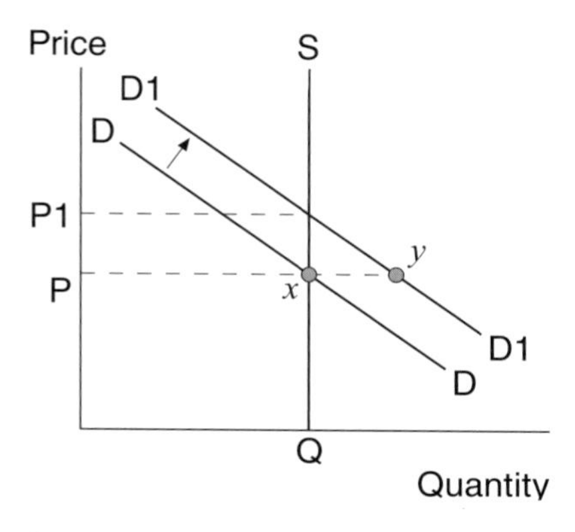

Figure 2: Effects of a decrease in the price of a complement

Changes in incomes

If the country as a whole becomes better off, potential ticket sales at Wimbledon are likely to rise. Studies show that the income elasticity of demand for 'products' such as this is highly positive. If incomes in general rise, it is likely that demand for tickets will rise, and the effects of this would be similar to those illustrated in Figure 2.

If the product or service under consideration were an inferior good then an increase in income would be associated with a fall in demand; the demand curve shifts to the left, leading to a fall in prices and sales.

Changes in tastes

The effects of changes in tastes can be modelled in the same way. If a good or service becomes more fashionable, demand shifts to the right resulting in higher prices and sales. On the other hand, going out of fashion would be represented by a shift in demand to the left, leading to falling prices and sales.

Thinking like an economist

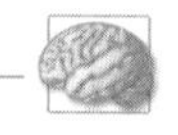

Make sure you understand the distinction between shifts and movements in demand curves.

Quickie

What will happen to the price and sales of tennis rackets if:

(a) there is a rise in membership fees for tennis clubs
(b) footballers get even higher incomes
(c) there is a reduction in income tax
(d) cat gut (once used for stringing tennis rackets) is shown to be carcinogenic?

Puzzler

Why might an understanding of cross elasticity of demand be helpful in forecasting the effects of changes in the price of other goods?

1.12 Markets and changes in supply

Changes in supply are considered in this section in the context of the market for organically grown carrots. In this case, supply will change if any of the following happen:

- changes in costs of production
- technological changes
- changes in the objectives of producers.

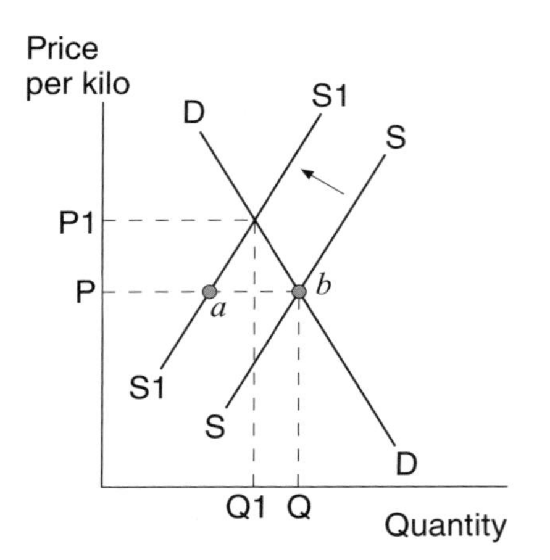

Figure 1: Effects of increased costs faced by organic carrot producers

The market for organic carrots

In this market there will be a considerable number of producers, both in this country and abroad. Individually, they will have much less influence over the price charged for their product. However, you could reasonably assume that the supply of organic carrots will slope upwards from left to right – as with **S** in Figure 1 – which shows a greater willingness to produce if prices are high and vice versa.

The demand curve for organic carrots is likely to be relatively inelastic, and this is shown in Figure 1 by the steep gradient of **D**. In this market, demand and supply are equal at price **P**, leading to sales of **Q**.

Increasing costs of production

Organic producers face additional costs in order to assure buyers that their produce is really organic. So the Soil Association, which promotes organic production methods, operates a certification scheme to guarantee the organic origins of products. If it were to increase its registration fees, organic carrot producers would face an increase in costs. This is shown in Figure 1 by the leftward and upward shift in supply to **S1**.

If the price were to remain at **P** per kilo, demand would now exceed supply by ***ab***. Excess demand means that some potential buyers might have to go without. Enterprising greengrocers might raise their prices. The price would be likely to rise until a new equilibrium is reached. In this case, demand would be equal to the reduced supply at **P1** per kilo, and sales would fall to **Q1**.

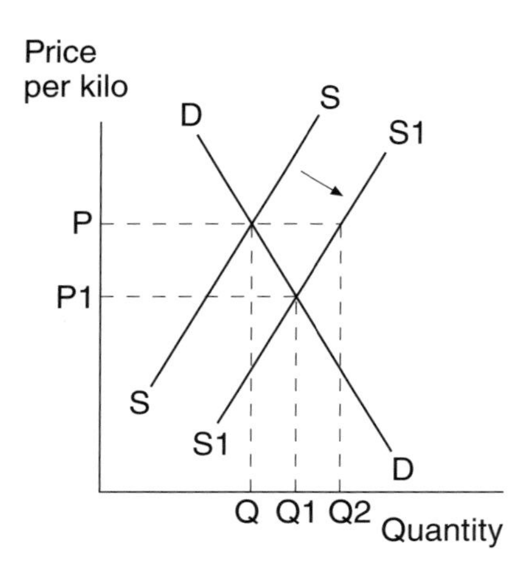

Figure 2: Effects of technological improvements on the organic carrot market

Improvements in technology

Alternatively, an improvement could be made in the production process that reduced costs of supply. Potential profits would be higher, production would be more attractive and the supply curve would shift downwards to the right. If the old price were maintained, disequilibrium would arise in which supply would be greater than demand. Prices would fall until a new equilibrium had been established, showing both a lower price and higher sales. This is illustrated in Figure 2.

Objectives of producers

An increasing number of farmers are turning away from inorganic fertilisers, herbicides and pesticides, and may prefer to adopt organic techniques for ethical reasons. This trend is likely to lead to an increase in the supply of organic products (as shown in Figure 2). The long-term effect of these trends is that the supply and sales of organic carrots (and other products) should increase and prices should fall.

The importance of elasticity

The significance of elasticity of demand is illustrated in Figures 3 and 4.

- In Figure 3, the demand is highly inelastic.
- Figure 4 shows a highly elastic demand.

The same change in supply in both markets will have very different effects.

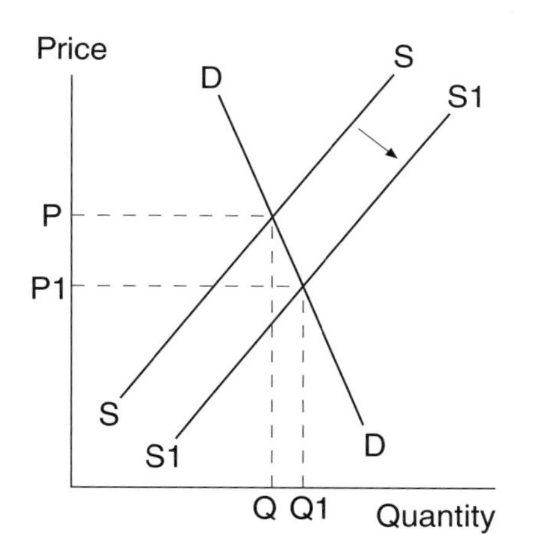

Figure 3: A highly inelastic demand

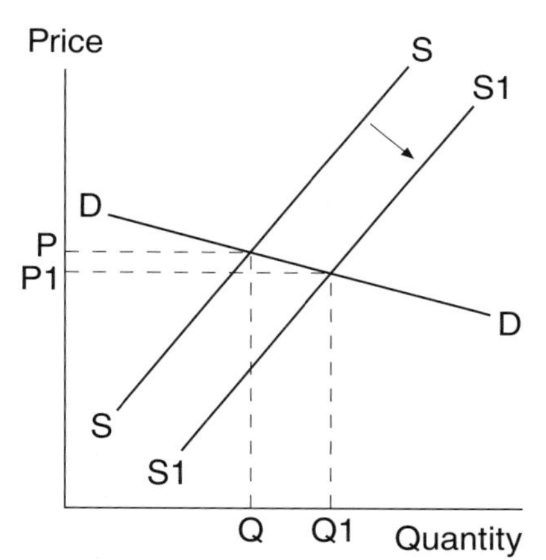

Figure 4: A highly elastic demand

Quickie

How might the price and sales of hot chocolate in the UK be affected by:

(a) easier access for African producers to European markets
(b) a new outbreak of foot and mouth disease in the UK
(c) hurricanes in the West Indies
(d) lower tea prices?

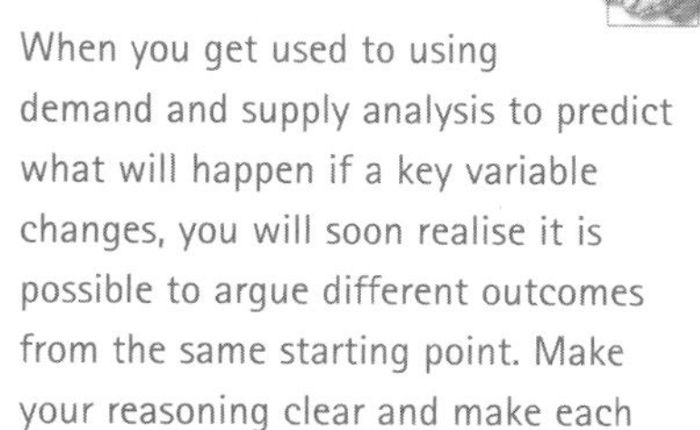

Thinking like an economist

When you get used to using demand and supply analysis to predict what will happen if a key variable changes, you will soon realise it is possible to argue different outcomes from the same starting point. Make your reasoning clear and make each step in your analysis logical.

Hot potato

'The case for organic food production in the UK is overwhelming.' Do you agree?

1.13 More market analysis

In this section on market analysis, we will use the example of personal computers (PCs). In analysing this market, an economist would look first at demand, then at supply.

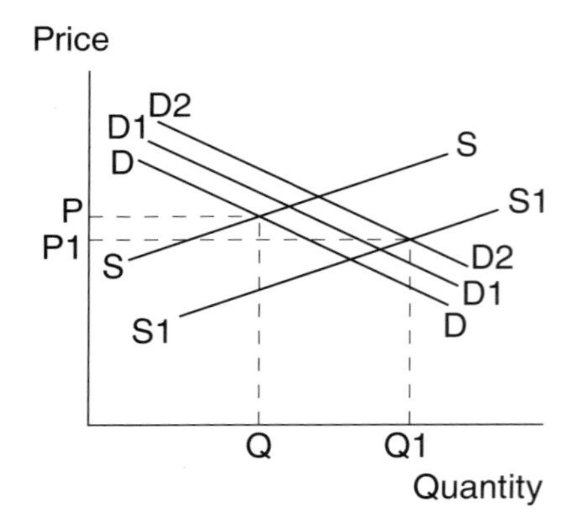

Figure 1: Market for Dell PCs

Analysing the PC market in terms of demand

There is nothing special about the demand for PCs that would challenge the generalisation that, *ceteris paribus* (see section 1.8), lower prices will lead to higher sales (and vice versa). So the demand curve for a given PC is likely to be downward sloping from left to right. Moreover, PCs from different manufacturers can often look and perform in the same way, which should mean the market is very competitive. So the demand for Dell PCs, for example, is likely to be relatively elastic because there are other close substitutes. If these assumptions and observations are accurate, the demand curve for an entry-level Dell PC is likely to look something like that shown by D on Figure 1.

Analysing the PC market in terms of supply

Although individual components are very sophisticated, most PCs are relatively simple to make – essentially, they are sets of standard components, simply linked together and put in a box. Another key supply factor is the rapid changes in technology, with faster equipment and increasingly bigger memories continually being developed. In short, PCs can be made relatively easily and in a short period of time, but their technical specifications change very quickly.

As this is a fast-moving market, stocks are likely to be small. The supply curve for an entry level Dell PC is probably fairly elastic, as shown by S in Figure 1.

Exam hint

Year after year examiners complain about the poor quality of diagrams. This may be boring, but:

- get into the habit of labelling diagrams
- make sure they are a reasonable size
- use them to help you write your analysis and to check the outcomes are logical.

How the analysis helps

Demand and supply analysis can help us to understand why the price of this kind of PC fell dramatically during 2002.

It is likely that the business demand for these PCs has slowed, reflecting the weaker performance of the US economy and possible saturation of the market for home users. However, income elasticities of demand tend to be high and positive, expenditure on advertising is high, and the price of complementary products and services (for example, access to the Internet) continue to fall. It is possible that demand will continue to grow, but at a slower rate. This is shown in Figure 1 as a series of shifts to the right from D to D2.

Such developments would normally lead to rising prices, but this ignores changes in supply. Competition between the suppliers of components is intense, and the cost of many PC components has fallen significantly. Some have been over supplied, and those imported from countries in the Far East have become cheaper with the fall in value of those countries' currencies. The effect of this is that there has been an increase in supply, illustrated in Figure 1 by the shift from **S** to **S1**.

This analysis of a particular market shows that prices have fallen but their sales have increased.

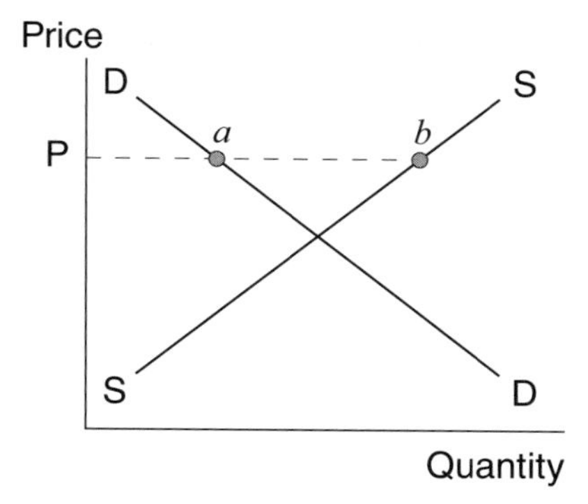

Figure 2: Disequilibrium resulting in excess supply

Price fixing

Market analysis can also be used to examine what happens if attempts are made to fix prices.

Manufacturers might try to set prices above the equilibrium level. Governments might want to reduce the prices consumers have to pay for essential items. The possible outcomes of these two kinds of intervention are illustrated in Figures 2 and 3. In both cases, disequilibrium is likely. Attempts to set a price above equilibrium result in excess supply of ***ab*** (Figure 2), whereas setting a price below equilibrium will lead to excess demand of ***xy*** (Figure 3).

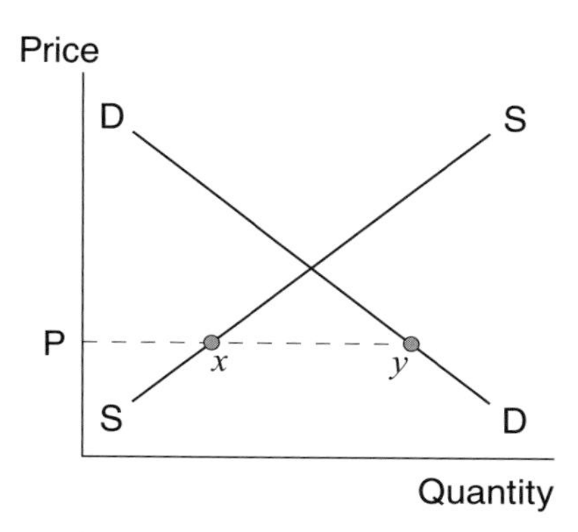

Figure 3: Disequilibrium resulting in excess demand

Summary

Markets bring demand and supply together to determine price and sales. Changes in demand or supply will lead to changes in price and sales. Demand and supply conditions always differ between different markets, and it is advisable always to consider what might make one set of demand and supply conditions differ from another set.

Quickies

Use demand and supply diagrams to offer a possible explanation for each of the following scenarios.

1. Adopt the role of a promoter of musical events. You have hired a venue with a capacity of 2000 people. Show the effects of:
   (a) overpricing tickets
   (b) underpricing tickets.
2. The market for grapes shows widespread fluctuations at different times of the year. Prices can vary from £1.39 a kilo to £5.98 a kilo. Why might this be so?

Research task

Use the tools of economic analysis developed in this section to analyse market forces at work in a market of your choice. Use demand and supply analysis to explain trends in prices in this market over the last five years. Present your findings as a report to your class.

1.14 The market system

Knowing how individual markets work is a key step to understanding how whole market economy works. No market works in isolation. Changes in one will lead to changes in others, which will have further effects. These chain reactions have a big impact on our lives (for example, they can cause us to become richer or poorer). They can also have an impact upon the environment. This section examines what happened in the housing market in London and south-east England in 2002/3 to show how markets for a series of products or services are interlinked.

Local market inter-relationships

The housing boom of 2001/2 was caused by a major imbalance between the supply and demand for housing. Greater London is home to many different businesses, corporate headquarters, government departments and so on. Although people do exist on low incomes in London, the city contains a disproportionate number of people earning high incomes. House buying has a high positive income elasticity of demand, and the demand for houses in London and the south-east has always been stronger than in other parts of the country.

Supply

The supply of houses in the short run is relatively inelastic, resulting in relatively high house prices. At the end of 2002, the cheapest starter home in London was about £130,000. People moving away from London could make large profits selling in London and buying relatively cheaper property elsewhere. Land prices continued to rise in the early part of 2003.

Demand

The demand for workers with building skills was subsequently high, boosting the earnings of bricklayers and other skilled trades. Estate agents found both sales and high profits easy to achieve. The demand for all kinds of building materials rose. Earnings of workers and the profits of the owners of such businesses also climbed.

Rising house prices in London forced some potential buyers to look further afield, increasing the demand for housing in areas around London and causing a similar chain reaction as increases in demand in one market rippled over into closely related markets.

Consequences and reactions

All of the above only describes part of the picture. There are great pressures to turn farmland into new estates, road congestion is getting worse and so on. It is easy to see how such ripples and waves would set off further reactions. It is also possible to anticipate how the rise in property prices in the south-east might reach out and affect the whole local economy.

Messages and signals

Any local economy consists of thousands of interconnected markets, each with its own demand and supply curves, shifting and adjusting to change after change. The key links between these individual markets are price changes.

- Thus, the rise in the price of houses is a signal to those who supply associated products, like paint, nails, furnishings and washing machines, that they should consider increasing their supplies and raising their prices.
- Rising incomes in the building trade are a signal that attracts more workers to move to the region and more young people to undertake training.
- Rising profits lead to increases in the share prices of leading building firms.
- The demand for water, electricity and other utilities also rises.

Thinking like an economist

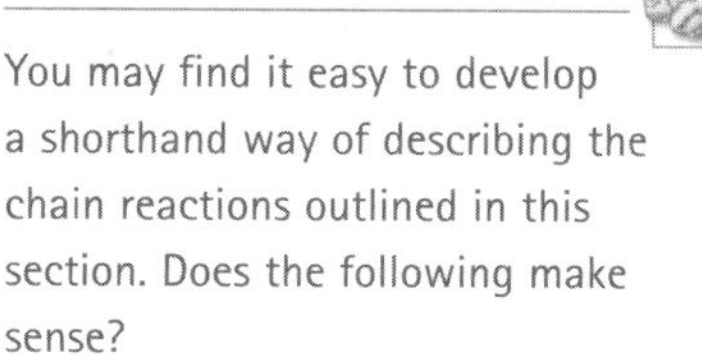

You may find it easy to develop a shorthand way of describing the chain reactions outlined in this section. Does the following make sense?

↑ price cocoa →↑ price chocolate
↓ Q sold

National inter-relationships

The impact of the property boom discussed in this section was not confined to the south-east. Brickmakers in Bedford, timber suppliers in Scotland and screwmakers in Birmingham, for example, are all likely to have experienced growing order books. Demand for their products would have risen, as would the demand for labour and other resources. A whole series of demand curves shifted to the right, and prices and outputs rose.

Ever-growing congestion and rising land prices in the south-east might encourage some employers to re-locate to other parts of the country. Spreading business activity from London also affects motorways and rail links.

Global effects

The effects of the property boom spread beyond the UK. Foreign suppliers of building materials, furnishings and white goods (refrigerators, washing machines, etc.) enjoyed increased demand for their products. Workers from other parts of Europe have been attracted to the UK because of labour shortages. The property boom has spread to northern France and southern Ireland, as those with increasing incomes looked for holiday and weekend homes.

Web link

For many resources on Markets go to www. heinemann.co.uk/hotlinks and click on this section.

Quickie

Use the style of analysis described in this section to show what impact war with Iraq might have had on the UK economy.

1.15 Factor markets

The market system includes a whole series of markets for land, labour, capital and enterprise. Collectively, these are called **factor markets.** They play a crucial role in ensuring that customers get the goods and services they wish to purchase. Although economists consider that there are special features of these markets, demand and supply analysis is used to model the behaviour of those working in factor markets.

Key concepts

- The demand for factors is a derived demand from the demand for a final product or services.
- The supply of factors in some cases may be fixed or immobile.

Demand for factors

In many ways, factors of production are like any other product that is traded in the marketplace. They have a price. For example, the price of labour is the wage or salary that has to paid. Rent is the return earned by the owners of land. Profit is a reward for enterprise. Interest or dividends can be seen as the price paid to the owners of money or capital. If a factor of production *ceteris paribus* is expensive, then demand is likely to be low. If, on the other hand, it is cheap, demand will be high. Thus the demand for building land will be lower as it becomes more expensive. In other words, the demand for factors is likely to slope downwards from left to right, as shown in Figure 1.

Supply of factors

Similar analysis can be applied to the supply of factors. If you assume that the owners of factors of production want a good financial return then the supply of land, labour, capital or enterprise can be treated in a similar way to any other commodity. The supply of workers to higher-paying jobs is likely to be higher than that to similar jobs paying lower wages. Alternatively, if wages are low then the supply is likely to be low. This means that a supply curve for any factor will slope upwards to the right – see Figure 1.

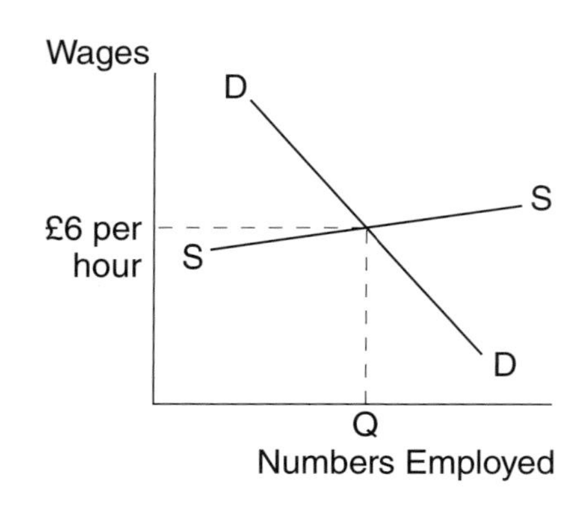

Figure 1: Factor market equilibrium

Factor market equilibrium

Factor market equilibrium is illustrated in Figure 1. Although this looks like other demand and supply diagrams, the axes measure different variables. Thus, if the market for shop workers in Cheltenham is being modelled, wages are represented on the vertical axis and numbers employed on the horizontal. The equilibrium wage rate is given as £6 per hour, at which the demand for shop workers is matched by the supply. Any change in demand and supply will lead to the establishment of a new equilibrium.

Derived demand

Final goods like cars or houses are demanded for what they are. Factors are demanded because they are required to produce something else. The nature of demand for that final product will have a direct impact on demand for the factors required to produce that product. For example, the demand for pesticide-free land will increase as a result of the increase in demand for organic foodstuffs. On the other hand, the demand for meat-processing equipment will fall if the demand for meat products falls. Premier division footballers command enormous salaries because they contribute to the success and earnings of top clubs.

Thus, although the demand curve for a factor of production looks like any other demand curve, its gradient and position will be heavily influenced by the demand for the final product. If the demand for that final product is highly price elastic, it is likely that demand for factors to make that product will also tend to be relatively elastic. Similarly, if the demand for the final product is relatively inelastic, factor use is likely to be more stable.

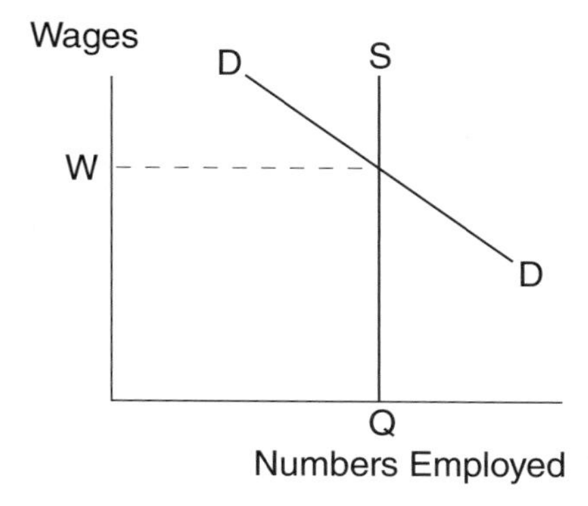

Figure 2: An extreme supply curve indicating the 'fixed supply' of a footballer like David Beckham

Factor immobility

The supply of factors is also special in some ways. In the case of labour markets we are considering people, and it may not be appropriate to treat them as commodities. Moreover, people may not work solely for monetary reward. Some jobs are more attractive than others, regardless of wages or salary levels. Some people are loath to leave some parts of the country for others, even though wages and salaries might be higher.

The use of others factors of production may be even less flexible because some may be fixed in supply. Thus, in the UK, the amount of land for new housing developments tends to be fixed for a mixture of reasons. Land itself is finite – it can't be moved from one part of the country to another.

The mobility of labour, or any other factor of production, can be illustrated by the gradient of the supply curve. In the most extreme case (there is only one David Beckham – see Figure 2) the supply curve will be vertical, indicating a fixed supply, regardless of the wage or return offered. On the other hand, the supply of Division 3 football players is much more elastic – see Figure 3.

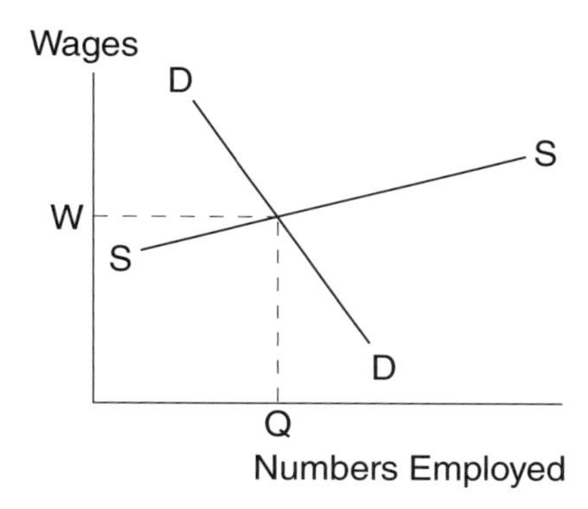

Figure 3: An elastic supply indicating the market for Division 3 footballers

Quickie

How far can the concepts of demand and supply be used to explain the differences in earning between successful pop bands and those struggling to make ends meet?

Hot potato

Why do women often get paid less money than men?

1.16 Adam Smith's hidden hand (1)

This section builds on earlier treatments of how individual markets work and interact with each other. It features the work of Adam Smith (1723–90), one of the most famous economists to have lived.

The Wealth of Nations

In his book *The Wealth of Nations* (published in 1776), Smith argued that if all members of society pursued what they perceived to be their selfish interest then society would improve if its individual members were left to their own devices. They would be driven, as if by instinct, to make profits from their activities. Those who were most successful would make the greatest profit. Those who were less successful would fail. Smith argued that an '**invisible hand**' linked producers to consumers and society as a whole. That invisible hand would help to ensure that what is actually produced is what people want.

A free market economy

For this invisible or hidden hand to work, Smith argued that all resources should be owned privately and that all members of society would be free to engage in any kind of business activity. Thus, the owners of factors of production should be free to sell their resources, but self-interest should ensure that factors are sold to the highest bidder.

- Some people will choose to be entrepreneurs and take risks in combining particular factors of production in order to produce goods or services that earn them the maximum return possible.
- People will also act in this system as customers or consumers whose motive is to consume as many chosen products as possible for the minimum outlay.

Interaction

The interaction of the independent actions of these economic agents will determine the resources used to produce various goods and services and who will consume them. Smith's invisible hand will, it is argued, ensure that this web of independent yet inter-dependent actions produces outcomes that benefit all of society.

In the following analysis, it is important to understand that markets are assumed to be highly competitive – that is, there are many firms producing similar products. If these conditions are satisfied, it can be argued that allocative and productive efficiency will be maximised. The rest of this section examines **allocative efficiency**, while section 1.17 looks at productive efficiency.

Making connections

The uniform, constant and uninterrupted effort of every man to better his condition, the principle from which public and national as well as private opulence is originally derived, is frequently powerful enough to maintain the natural progress of things toward improvement, in spite both of the extravagance of government, and of the greatest errors of administration.

Adam Smith, writing in *The Wealth of Nations*

Adam Smith, a Scottish political economist and philosopher who became famous for his influential book *The Wealth of Nations*

Definition

Allocative efficiency: refers to who gets what. An economy would be allocatively efficient if everybody received exactly those goods and services for which they were prepared to pay the market price.

Allocative efficiency

This relates to the central questions that a study of economics is meant to answer.

- What gets produced?
- How is it produced?
- Who gets what is produced?

In a free market it is argued that the consumer (rather than the producer or anyone else) is 'king'. In other words, customer preference will determine what is produced. **Consumer sovereignty**, as this concept is known, means that the free market will adapt and change to ensure that what is produced is what customers want. This outcome will be achieved by means of a price mechanism that should work as follows.

Exam hint

Make sure you understand each step in the mechanism outlined in this section by working out the effects of everyone demanding to have red hair.

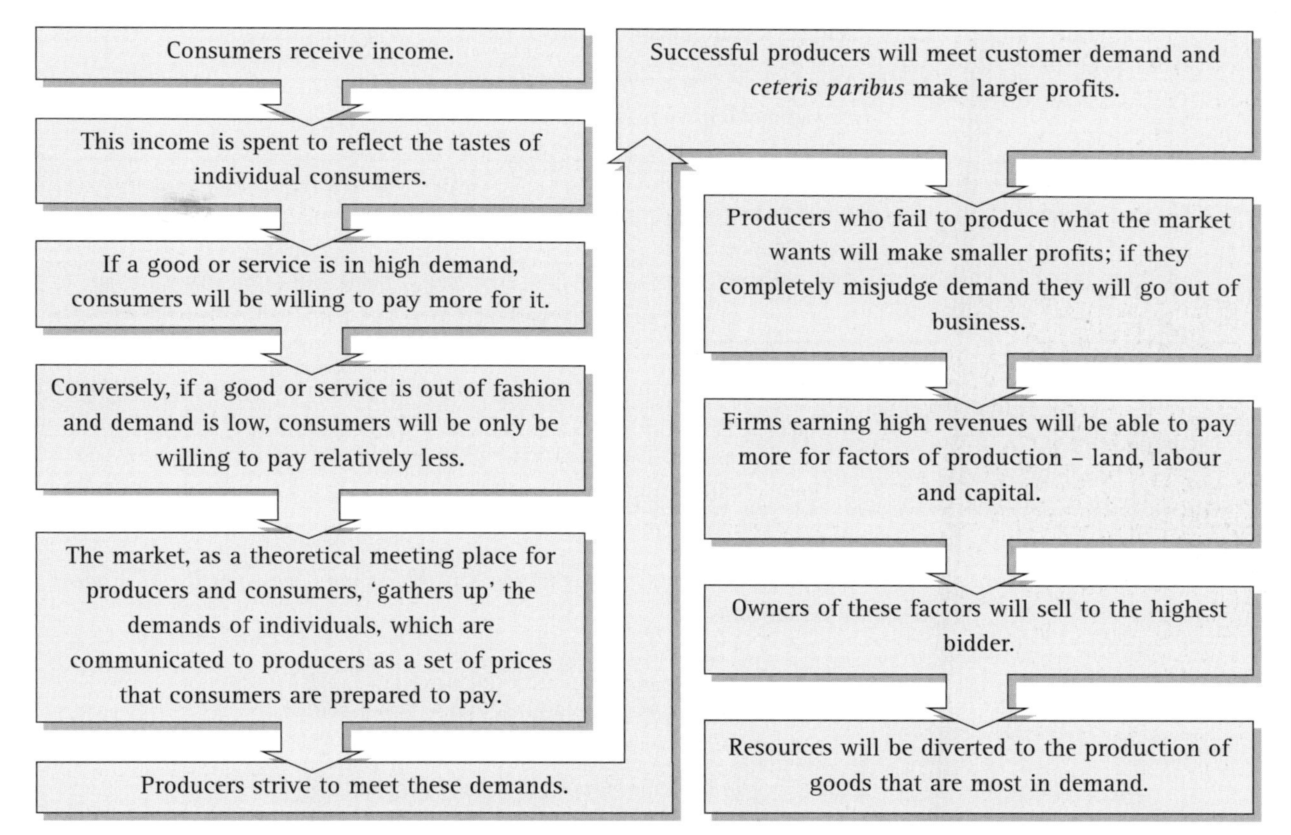

Hot potato

Divide into two groups.

- One group should develop arguments to support the notion that all health care should be provided privately.
- The other group should develop counter-arguments.

Discuss the rival viewpoints.

Quickies

1. How do consumers decide (in a free market economy) which resources get used to produce which goods and services?
2. Why is competition so important in a free market economy?
3. What happens to ineffective firms?

1.17 Adam Smith's hidden hand (2)

Definition

Productive efficiency: producing goods and services at the lowest possible average cost.

In section 1.16, Adam Smith's hidden hand was used to discuss how a free market economy might work and lead to allocative efficiency. This section deals with **productive efficiency** and the implications of Smith's analysis.

Productive efficiency

If markets are truly competitive, individual producers will be forced by market pressures to produce outputs at which costs of production are minimised. This concept relates to the basic question 'How are goods and services produced?', and it follows that if markets are competitive and if there is relative freedom of entry and exit, that costs of production for an individual firm will be squeezed to a minimum.

The reasons for this were given in section 1.16. However freely operating markets should enable the price mechanism to work as follows.

Assume one firm operating in one industry discovers a new, more efficient way of making what it produces.

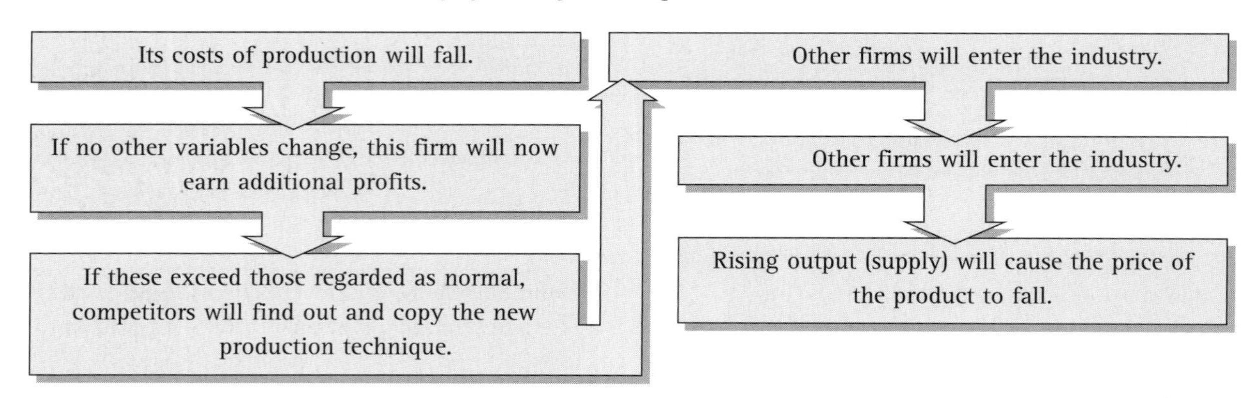

Alternatively, consider what happens if the demand for a particular product or service falls.

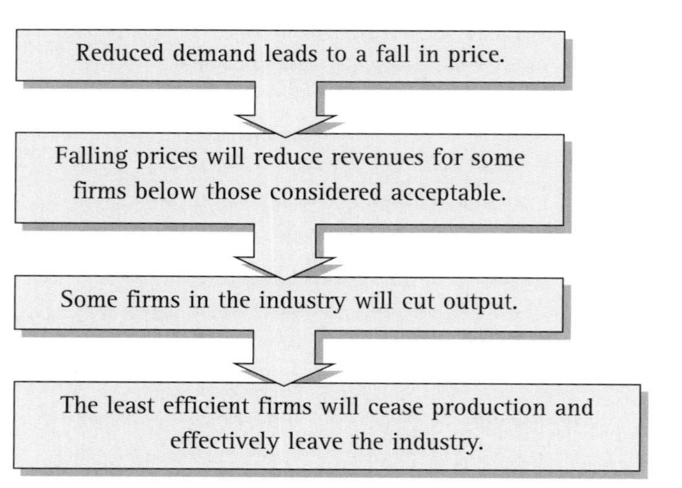

In short, the forces of competition are such that:

- any tendency by one firm to be more efficient and cut costs will be copied by competitors
- any decrease in demand will be accompanied by the disappearance of the least efficient producers.

This is a continuing process that should result in ever-growing efficiencies in those markets that are truly competitive.

Implications

Back to Smith ... He argued that two things would get in the way of this perfectly operating invisible hand, ensuring not only that we get what we want but also that we get it at the least possible cost:

- government interference, and
- monopoly.

Discussing the role of the government, Smith said:

> *Little else is requisite to carry a state to the highest degree of opulence from the lowest barbarism but peace, easy taxes, and a tolerable administration of justice: all the rest being brought about by the natural course of things.*

As to the dangers of monopoly, he said:

> *A monopoly granted either to an individual or to a trading company has the same effect as a secret in trade or manufactures. The monopolists, by keeping the market constantly under-stocked, by never fully supplying the effectual demand, sell their commodities much above the natural price, and raise their emoluments* [salary or fee], *whether they consist in wages or profit, greatly above their natural rate.*

Similar analysis is used by some economists to argue that governments should play a much smaller role in the economy.

Summary

A competitive economy, in which the role of the government is minimised and in which there are no monopolies, should ensure that customers determine what is produced and that competitive pressures compel firms to be as efficient as possible.

Quickie

Adam Smith considered that monopoly and government interference were both threats to the efficient and effective working of the economy. Why?

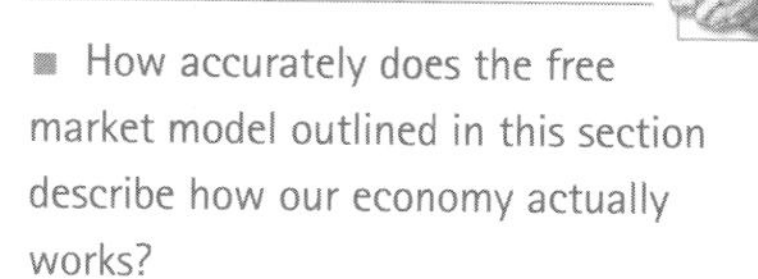

Thinking like an economist

- How accurately does the free market model outlined in this section describe how our economy actually works?
- Are consumers sovereign?
- Are firms compelled to be as efficient as possible?

Make a note of your conclusions. Think about the evidence you would need to collect to check whether or not the economy works in the ways described.

Hot potato

'Bus services would be much better if local transport officials stepped out of the way and allowed private bus operators to manage things freely,' says Professor John Hibbs, from the Adam Smith Insititute – a right-wing think-tank and pressure group. Do you agree?

Web link

What other right-wing economic perspectives can you find? Start by going to www.heinemann.co.uk/hotlinks and click on this section, to find a web site on The Adam Smith Institute.

1.18 Monopoly power

In the purest sense, a **monopoly** exists when one organisation is the sole producer or provider of a good or service. Adam Smith argued that monopolies:

- charge higher prices
- restrict customer choice.

Thinking like an economist

When you analyse a market, ask yourself where would you place it on the following continuum:

Pure monopoly ⟵⟶ Pure competition

Most markets will fall somewhere in the middle between these two extremes.

Higher prices

If a company has monopoly power, it will have much greater freedom to set its own prices – for example:

- a petrol station that has no local competitors is likely to charge more for its petrol
- we are likely to pay more for branded goods than we do for non-branded goods.

But if there is a lot of competition, individual companies will be strongly influenced by the prices charged by other businesses.

Economists describe companies who have market power as **price makers**. If they know that demand for their product is relatively inelastic, they can boost revenue by putting up prices. In other words, a monopolist provides goods or services for which there are few close substitutes (see section 1.5). Moreover, a monopolist will have less incentive to keep costs low because if they are a price maker, they can pass on additional costs to their customers.

Another aspect of market power is that a monopolist can also charge different sets of customers different prices for the same product. For example, a Mazda 323 car is nearly £5000 more expensive in the UK than in the rest of Europe. This particular form of monopoly power is called **price discrimination**. Companies have used this technique to boost profits by charging higher prices to those with more inelastic demands and lower prices to those whose demand is relatively more elastic. This is becoming an increasingly common practice.

Restricted choice

Web link

For information on consumer competition policy visit the Department of Trade and Industry website by going to www.heinemann.co.uk/hotlinks and clicking on this section.

Monopolies can exploit the dependence of their customers on their products by restricting choice. Henry Ford was famous for saying that customers could buy a Model T Ford in any colour, as long as it was black. More modern forms of this kind of behaviour include limiting the number of retailers allowed to sell particular products. Some electrical goods manufacturers do this, arguing that particular expertise is required to sell their products. Such practice makes it easier for manufacturers to ensure that retailers do not cut prices.

Companies also create market power, and what might be described as illusionary choice, by marketing very similar products under a range of brand names. The two major soap powder manufacturers Unilever and Proctor and Gamble are experts at this strategy.

Monopolies are good for you

Like most controversial topics in economics there are also strong arguments in favour of monopolies. These include the benefits of:

- economies of scale
- innovation
- national security.

Economies of scale

Monopolies will tend to be large companies. If firms produce high volumes of particular products, they may be able to cut costs of production because they enjoy **economies of scale**. The largest supermarkets have been able to invest millions in using IT to record sales, make orders, change stocks and control expenses that could not be afforded by smaller competitors. Larger businesses can also force down the price of their suppliers and use specialisation to reduce costs.

Innovation

Large companies with monopoly power might be more able to afford research and development that leads to the creation of newer and better products. Major drug companies like GlaxoSmithKline use this argument to justify their monopoly position in the provision of some drugs.

National security

This is not really an economic argument, but over the years it has been said that having national monopolies might safeguard a country in times of war when supplies from other countries might be cut off. This argument has been used in favour of keeping British coal mines open, rather than depending on foreign imports.

Conclusion

Economic arguments can be developed to both support and defend monopolies. The important point is that monopoly power can be used to distort free markets upsetting both productive and allocative efficiency. Whether or not this happens in practice is a job for economists to solve.

Quickie

Survey prices of TVs in local stores. What evidence does this reveal of competition in this particular market?

Puzzler

Who provides the greatest choice on television – the BBC or ITV?

Definition

Economies of scale: reductions in costs associated with larger outputs; they can occur because it is possible to invest in more efficient technology.

Thinking like an economist

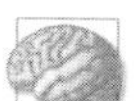

Birds Eye Wall's Ltd., a subsidiary of the Unilever group, supplies 70 per cent of wrapped ice-cream to the UK market. It distributes ice-cream through wholesalers with whom it has contracts, stopping them distributing products made by competitors. It also gives better deals to retailers who stock only its products. Is this in the public interest?

Making connections

Identify three local monopolies.

1.19 Market failure (1)

Market failure is a major concept that you are expected to understand for your AS examination. It is a blanket term used by economists who recognise that if markets are left to themselves, they may produce socially unacceptable outcomes. Markets might be said to fail if they fail to account for **externalities**. Other sources of market failure are considered in section 1.20.

Key concept

Externalities occur when there is a divergence between private and social costs and/or between private and social benefits.

Externalities

Externalities are defined by economists as third-party effects of any transaction between a consumer and a firm. Externalities can either be positive or negative. It can be argued that if markets are left to themselves:

- too many goods and services will be produced that have harmful third-party effects, and
- too few goods and services will be produced that have beneficial third-party effects.

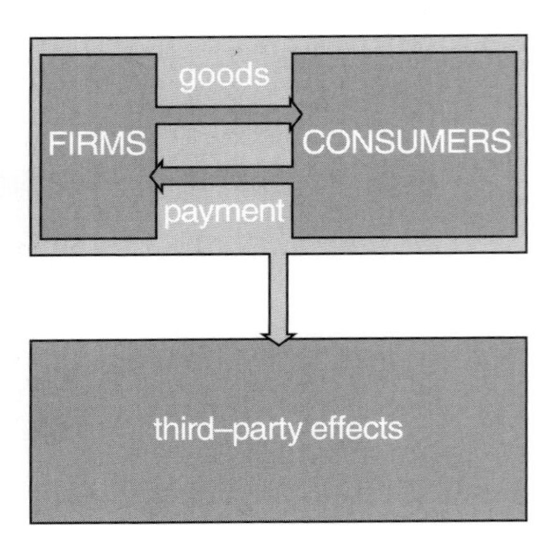

Figure 1: Third-party effects

The potential existence of externalities is illustrated in Figure 1. Figure 1 illustrates a transaction in which firms supply goods to consumers in return for payment. There may be unintended third-party effects whereby others are positively or negatively affected by the transaction. These are called externalities.

Negative externalities

A whole range of industrial and commercial activities can give rise to **negative externalities.** Pollution of various kinds is an obvious example. Some businesses may pay little regard to the effects of their activities on others. Pure water might be used to cool, clean and wash, only to be returned to rivers and watercourses as pollution. Forests are exploited for their timber, giving rise to erosion, floods, infertile soil and even global warming. Anti-social behaviour by consumers of alcohol and tobacco can affect the well-being and health of 'innocent' third parties.

Negative externalities and market failure

Negative externalities are significant to economists; they cause arguments about the strengths and weaknesses of the market system because their existence places additional costs on other members of society. For example, we all know there are links between smoking tobacco and a range of serious diseases. Treatment of patients with smoking-related diseases means that the National Health Service (NHS) and private health insurance companies are faced with additional expenditure.

If markets operate freely and effectively, the price that a customer pays for a product or service should represent the actual costs involved in the production of that product or service. If this production generates additional costs that are incurred by other members of society, the market system can be said to have failed.

In Figure 2, **S** represents the costs of production faced by the producer of a good. These are known as **private costs. S1** includes the additional external costs that the production of this product creates.

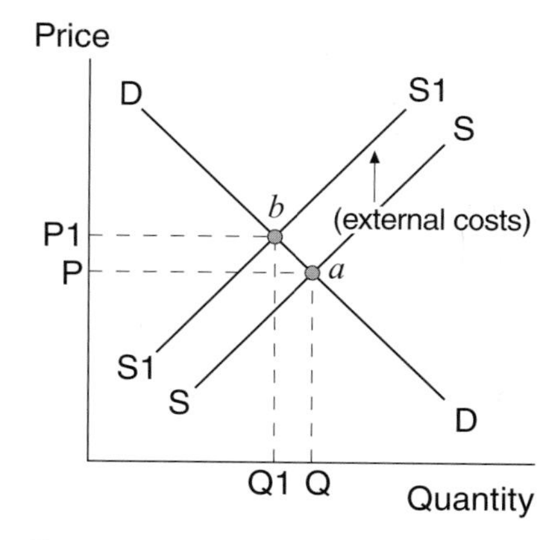

Figure 2: Negative externalities

Private costs + external costs = **social costs** (that is, the full costs to society of making the product).

- If there were no government or other intervention, equilibrium would be reached at **a**, **P** would be the price charged for the product and **Q** would represent the quantity sold.
- However, if it were possible to calculate the external costs, if these were to be added to the private costs and if consumers were required to pay the full social cost of production, a different equilibrium would prevail at ***b***, giving a higher price of **P1** and reduced sales of **Q1**.

In other words, a freely operating market would lead to lower prices and higher outputs of goods having harmful environmental and/or social consequences.

Positive externalities

Unintended external effects do not necessarily lead to greater costs for society as a whole. Some economic transactions generate more beneficial third-party effects. Thus, the provision of clean piped water will directly benefit those who are supplied but it may also contribute to better standards of health, less illness and disease, and greater productivity. Similarly, improvements to education and training may benefit society as a whole, as well as those individuals who are directly concerned with the improvements.

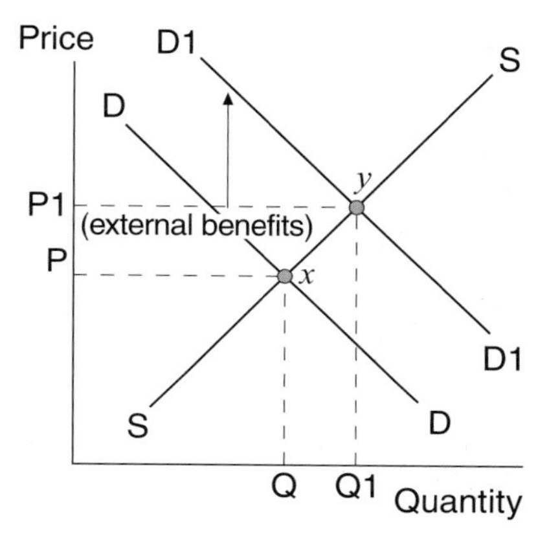

Figure 3: Positive externalities

- In Figure 3, **D** represents the demand from individuals – that is, the private benefits gained from purchasing a particular good or service – and **S** represents the costs of providing that good or service. The market equilibrium is given at **x**, with a price of **P** and sales of **Q**.
- If, however, it were possible to quantify the **positive externalities** associated with the provision of this good or service, these could be represented by **D1** showing the full **social benefits** that would benefit society as a whole. If these additional benefits were to be taken into account, output would be increased to **Q1**.

In this example of market failure, freely operating markets would be said to be failing because fewer socially useful goods would be produced.

Work in groups to brainstorm those economic activities that generate positive and negative externalities. Choose three that your group consider the most beneficial and then three that are the most harmful to third parties.

Thinking like an economist

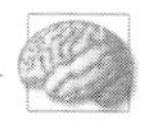

Discuss as a class, and note if a consensus is reached or whether differences persist.

1.20 Market failure (2)

Markets might also be said to fail if they result in the under- or overproduction of certain types of goods, or if they contribute to greater inequalities in society.

Underproduction

The free market system might lead to underproduction of:

- **merit goods**
- **public goods.**

This might be something society considers to be desirable.

Merit goods

Prior to 1947, health services in this country were provided by a free market. Those needing a doctor had to pay, and poor people often suffered ill-health because of this financial barrier. The Labour government elected in 1945 was committed to the notion of a health service which was free at the point of use. Economists call this type of provision of something that is socially desirable a 'merit good'.

Other merit goods include the provision of library services, job centres, state education, and health and recreational services. In each case, there may be significant positive externalities that could be used to justify tax-funded government provision to ensure that full social benefits are enjoyed.

Public goods

These are products or services for which it is difficult to identify who benefits most. In a free market, those who derive the greatest satisfaction from the consumption of a good or service are thought likely to be prepared to pay the most. In this way, resources are rationed to those who believe they will benefit most. This works well enough with consumer goods, but it is harder to apply to a range of services such as the police. It is impossible to predict who needs the police and when, and it would be hard to work out a means by which consumers of police services would actually pay for the resources used for their benefit.

Economists argue that public goods have two important features that differentiate them from other goods:

- non-rivalry (that is, if one person consumes a good or service, others are not prevented from doing the same)
- non-excludability (in other words, once a public good is provided to one person it is not possible to stop others from enjoying it).

Thinking like an economist

The unconstrained action of Adam Smith's hidden hand (see sections 1.16 and 1.17) can lead to socially unacceptable outcomes. Agreement about what is acceptable and what is unacceptable in terms of inequalities, the overproduction of socially harmful goods and services, and the undersupply of socially valued outputs is very difficult.

Overproduction

Left to its own devices a free market could lead to the overproduction of goods and services that a society might judge to be socially harmful. Consideration has already been given to circumstances in which companies will overproduce if private costs are far less than social costs.

A free market system might also produce goods and services that society believes to be harmful, and various measures are taken by governments to reduce the consumption of commodities such as alcohol and tobacco. The provision of other goods and services such as cannabis, prostitution and offensive weapons is banned.

Goods that are judged to be harmful to society are called **demerit goods.** It might be that their production involves the generation of significant negative externalities, and this could be used to justify intervention to limit production and therefore protect society.

The Government has passed a bill to ban tobacco advertising. Formula 1 racing will be given until 2006 to find alternative sponsors

Inequalities

A freely working market will create both losers and winners. For example, many British and other European farmers are currently losers because they are finding it increasingly difficult to compete with cheaper imported foods and cope with changes in customer tastes away from products such as meat. Similarly, the coal industry in the UK has almost disappeared because of the greater use of alternative energy sources and the availability to cheap imports.

Other members of our economy can also be described as losers. These include:

- some older people whose skills are no longer in demand
- young people who lack both skills and qualifications, and
- owners of businesses that have become uncompetitive.

On the other hand, the price mechanism rewards those owners of resources who are able to produce goods and services in anticipation of changes in demand. These free markets result in inequalities, one outcome of which might be the existence of poverty for losers and material benefits for the winners. This might not be socially acceptable.

Hot potato

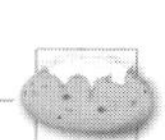

Should the government protect farmers' incomes?

The distribution of rewards

Not only do free markets create inequalities in income, but also they allocate resources to those members of society who are prepared to pay the most. Some economists have likened the price mechanism to a system of votes.

- Each pound of income is the equivalent of one vote.
- Those with the most votes will determine not just what is produced for society but who consumes such production.
- If there is a shortage of a good or service, competition between buyers will force up prices until equilibrium between buyers and sellers is reached.
- Those who cannot afford the market price of the good or service will go without.

Those members of society who have larger incomes will be able to consume more resources than those with relatively smaller incomes. Some people would regard such inequalities as unfair.

Research task

Find out what you can about the economic implications of leaving health care to market forces.

1.21 Market imperfections

Sections 1.14 to 1.17 outlined the theory of how free markets might work and lead to socially desirable outcomes – for example, efficient production and consumer sovereignty. The existence of monopoly and externalities can also prevent free markets from working to the advantage of society as a whole. Similarly, markets may help to create unacceptable levels of inequality. This section is devoted to other issues that might limit the effective working of markets.

Economists refer to market imperfections when considering those factors that might inhibit markets from working as efficiently and effectively as has been argued earlier. Three factors can contribute to market imperfections:

- **factor immobility**
- imperfect knowledge
- imperfect competition.

Thinking like an economist

There are times when you might despair at economists, because they tend to say things like 'On the one hand, we have ... Yet on the other ...' The answers to most controversial issues are not black and white. Always beware of those who claim otherwise.

Factor immobility

Free markets require factor mobility. Land, labour, capital and enterprise are all meant to be attracted by the prospect of better returns and repelled by the threat of worse returns. There are many reasons why this might not be so.

Land

Economists define land as including not just farms, factory sites and building lots but also those resources contained within the Earth's crust. Whereas natural resources such as timber, minerals and energy can be relatively easily transported and switched from use to use, particular sites with particular qualities are more likely to be locked in time and space.

Labour

Free market theory requires that workers work primarily for money and that changes in wage and salary levels not only signal to workers that they should consider changing employment but that they should also be geographically mobile. In spite of higher wages elsewhere, some workers are reluctant to leave areas of high unemployment such as Cornwall, Merseyside and Teeside. Family and community links are hard to break. It is not clear what primarily motivates workers. Some workers indicate that 'job satisfaction' is more important than financial return. Others value 'status'. Given the complexity of human behaviour, economists have to be very careful when making assumptions about motivations.

Capital

Finance capital has become a much more mobile factor of production compared to land and labour. Governments have historically tried to control international flows of finance capital but such intervention has become increasingly difficult and ineffective, especially as global capital markets have developed. If investments in a particular sector or country become more attractive relative to those in others, finance capital is likely to flow to that new use, away from uses where the returns are less.

Enterprise

By definition, enterprise should be the most mobile of all factors. If enterprise is about taking risks and identifying where greatest profits can be made, it follows that entrepreneurs will be mobile in pursuit of profit. However, as with labour, human factors are likely to influence decisions of entrepreneurs. Thus, owners of small businesses may be reluctant to sack workers when orders fall. Alternatively, there is evidence to suggest that some owners forgo greater sales and profits associated with growth because such expansion may threaten lifestyles and informal relationships with employees.

Research task

Conduct a survey into a product of your choice to find out how knowledgeable a group of consumers are.

Imperfect knowledge

If consumers are to make informed and effective choices of those products and services they may wish to purchase, they need knowledge and understanding of the prices and qualities of potential purchases. In theory, they need perfect knowledge, which is the term used by economists to describe a total and all-encompassing knowledge. However, numerous studies indicate that consumer knowledge is far from perfect.

- Customers perceive there to be differences between products when there are none, and keeping track of the prices of competing products is too demanding for all but the most expert buyers.
- Similarly, it is assumed that customers base purchases on rational decisions, that they are consistent and not swayed by irrational considerations. But customer choices are often unpredictable. Fashions and tastes change, as do perceptions as to what is good quality.

Imperfections in customer knowledge imply that markets may not respond quickly to changes in demand or supply conditions.

Making connections

How perfect is your knowledge about women's deodorant?

Imperfect competition

Firms spend considerable sums on advertising and promotion to encourage customer loyalty and repeat custom. Branding is used to create particular images for products. Psychological factors are exploited to promote sales. Some firms bewilder potential customers with choices of complicated tariffs or alternative prices. All these practices inhibit the working of a free market.

Summary

Anything that stops factors moving freely will result in sub-optimal outcomes, i.e. free markets will not guarantee productive and allocative efficiency.

Hot potato

Is there such a thing as a free market?

1.22 Government intervention and externalities

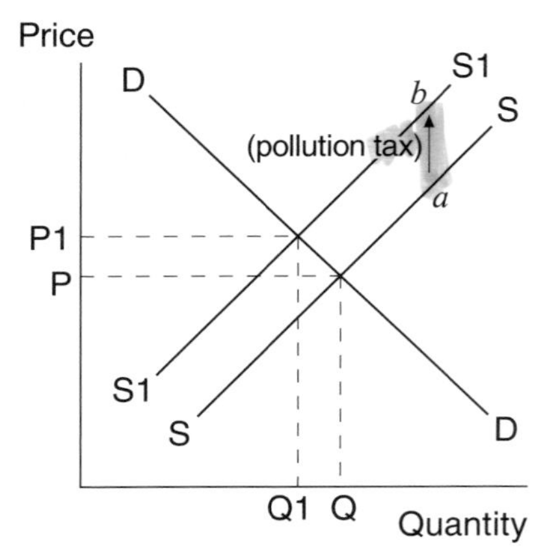

Figure 1: Taxing away negative externalities

Web links

For a government initiative providing health information to teachers and other useful websites go to www.heinemann.co.uk/hotlinks and click on this section.

The possible existence of market failure provides governments with a reason to intervene in the free working of markets. In reality, there are very few markets in which governments do not intervene.

Negative externalities

If governments wish to reduce, say, pollution – a negative externality – they can use:

- the **price mechanism**
- direct controls
- persuasion
- tradable permits.

Price mechanism

This approach is illustrated in Figure 1. If a government is able to calculate accurately the external costs attributed to a polluting company, it could introduce a tax equal to the vertical distance ***ab***. This would force consumers of this product to pay a price that represented the full cost to society of its production. Output would be reduced to **Q1** and the government would actually use the price mechanism to cure market failure.

Direct controls

Governments can choose to pass laws and use the existing legislative framework in an attempt to control and constrain the behaviour of firms and industries that generate negative externalities. For example, in the UK:

- emissions of potentially dangerous chemicals are subject to regulations
- advertising by the tobacco industry is limited, and
- car safety is promoted by annual car tests.

Persuasion

Some people consider that changing customer and producer behaviour to ensure greater account is taken of externalities is so complicated, it is more effective in the long term to change the attitudes of those who demand and supply products and services creating negative externalities. For example, the UK government part-funds the Health Education Council, whose role includes encouraging people to eat healthier diets. If these approaches are successful, the effects will be fed through the market system. It can be argued that demand for organic produce is a result of greater awareness of healthy eating.

Tradeable permits

Another market-based means of limiting some negative externalities involves the government giving or selling permits to polluters to emit a certain amount of waste. These permits can then be bought and sold. A company successful in cutting its pollution could sell its permit to one that was less successful. The company producing the lower emissions would gain and the heavier polluter would be forced to pay. By setting an overall limit to how much pollution would be allowed, governments could reduce this negative externality. However, it would be left to market forces to determine where emissions would be reduced.

Positive externalities

Governments could use similar techniques to deal with positive externalities.

Price mechanism

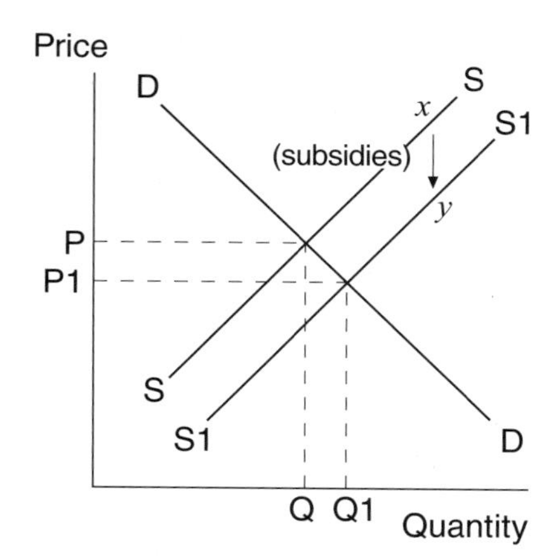

Figure 2: Using subsidies to account for positive externalities

Figure 2 illustrates a possible approach. If the government wished to work through the price mechanism to try to boost production of a product or service that a free market would overprice and underproduce, it could estimate the value of the positive externality and it would need to pay a subsidy to producers equal to this amount – shown by the vertical distance *xy*. The outcome would be production rising to Q1 and price falling to P1.

Direct controls

A government might decide that the production of a particular good or service has significant positive externalities that society would not benefit from if markets were left to operate freely. Thus, in many market-based economies, governments directly provide merit goods such as education and health services. Prices charged to the consumer are not used to allocate such products but decisions as to who gets what still have to be made.

Persuasion

It could be argued that much of any government's work is concerned with persuasion in the form of advertising, political campaigning and so on. Changing attitudes to education, healthy living, sustainability, preventive medicine and so on can all be seen as attempts to change free market outcomes.

Summary

This section has considered both positive and negative externalities. The existence of these third-pary effects can distort the price mechanism and lead to socially undesirable outcomes, providing a rationale for government intervention. Governments may seek to encourage greater production where positive externalities exist and limit production if negative externalities are identified.

Puzzler

How would you deal with the negative externalities of car use in London and other large cities?

Research task

Undertake an investigation of a market in which you consider there to be significant positive or negative externalities. How would you try to estimate the monetary value on such externalities? Suggest possible government intervention strategies to take account of the externalities you have identified.

1.23 Other forms of government intervention

The government can use techniques other than those discussed in section 1.22 to overcome market failure, for example:

- **price controls**
- **buffer stocks**
- **legal checks.**

Price controls

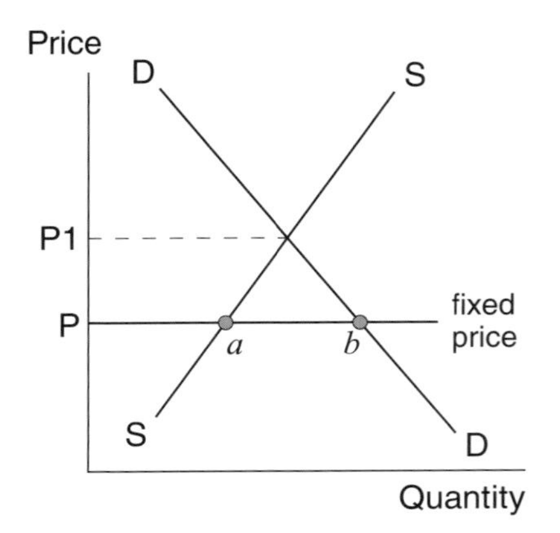

Figure 1: Maximum price set below equilibrium

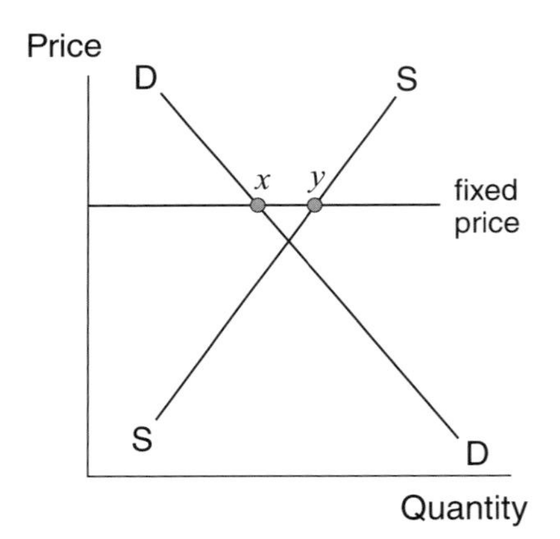

Figure 2: Minimum prices and excess supply

Price controls may be used to deal with inequalities generated by free markets, and also to deal with merit and demerit goods.

Governments can intervene by using price controls. These are usually maximum prices, which limit what can be charged for a good or service. They may be used to encourage the consumption of merit goods or to compensate for inequalities caused by free markets.

A number of governments in developing countries impose maximum prices for basic foodstuffs in order to ensure that poor people avoid going without. If prices are fixed below the equilibrium, then these low prices will create excess demand. This is shown in Figure 1, where the price has been capped at P, which is below the market-clearing price of P1.

The effect of government intervention will be to create a shortage at ***ab***, and a government might be prompted to introduce some form of rationing in order to ensure 'fair shares'. In this case, a market-based solution is linked to the introduction of direct controls.

Governments might also introduce minimum prices, especially if they wish to encourage production. If these are set above the equilibrium that would apply without government intervention, excess supply will occur. This is shown in Figure 2, where the oversupply is represented by ***xy***. The European Union's Common Agricultural Policy (CAP) sets a minimum price for a range of agricultural products. It does this to increase agricultural output and to protect farmers' incomes.

Buffer stocks

Buffer stocks can be used to reduce the undesirable effects of widespread fluctuations in prices that will occur if demand and/or supply changes frequently. It could be argued, for example, that fluctuations in farm prices might give farmers problems, as their incomes will also fluctuate widely.

This can be illustrated in Figure 3, which shows price on the vertical axis and time on the horizontal; ***tp*** is a target price and ***mp*** is the free market price.

- In 1999, overproduction would have resulted in additional supply, forcing the market price down to P. The government could intervene and purchase surplus supply, forcing the actual price up to the target price.
- These government purchases could be stockpiled; if in the following year shortages threaten to push the price up to P1, release of government stocks from the previous year will bring down prices to the target level. In this way, prices would be stabilised, not only protecting farmers' incomes but also benefiting consumers.

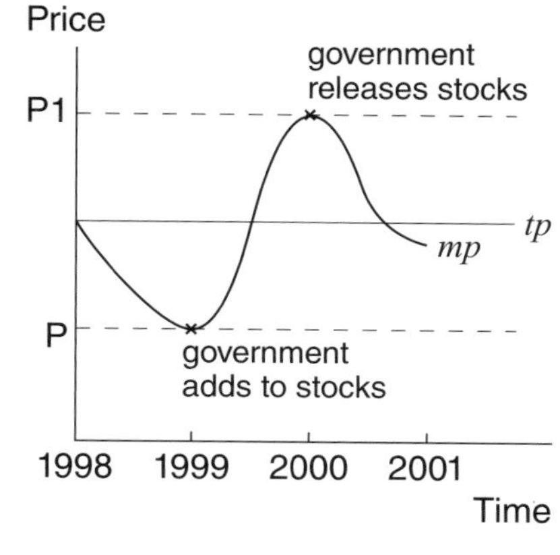

Figure 3: How buffer stocks are used

Legal checks

Company and other laws provide a framework to protect consumers, producers and factor suppliers from being exploited. This legal framework helps ensure that markets works and trusted. Such confidence is vital especially in matters relating to banking and company finance.

Summary

Governments can try to set prices below or above the market-derived equilibrium. This is likely to cause excess demand or excess supply. Where a government uses these excesses in conjunction with buffer stocks, it may be possible to stabilise fluctuating prices in particular markets.

Quickie

Use diagrams to illustrate what went wrong with the European Union's Common Agricultural Policy.

Puzzler

What happens if a government sets a maximum price above the equilibrium?

1.24 Government failure

Government intervention to correct market failure does not always work. Policies might fail because of:

- inadequate information
- administrative failings
- unintended effects
- political conflicts.

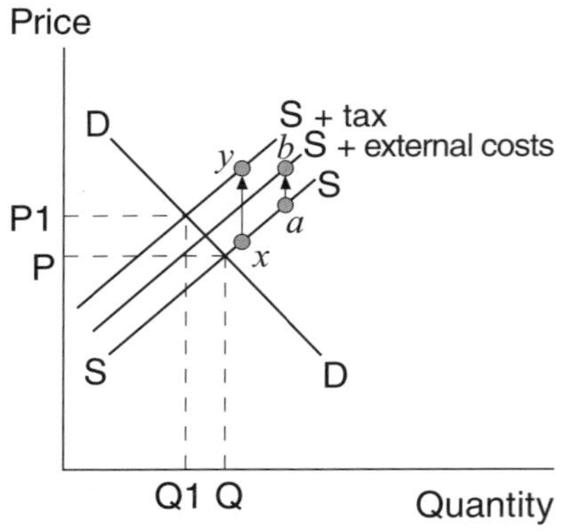

Figure 1: Overtaxing

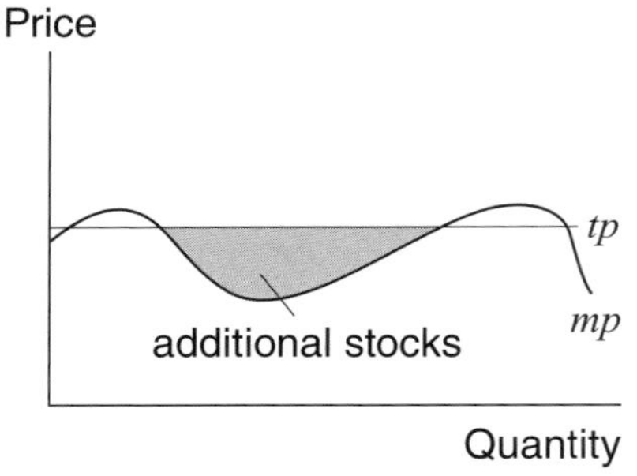

Figure 2: Incorrect price level leading to bigger stocks

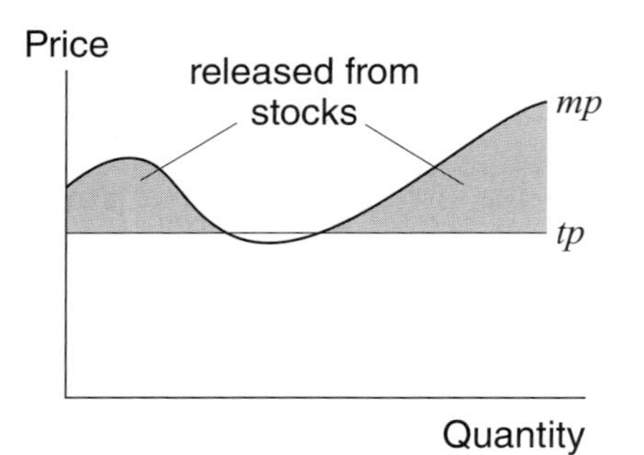

Figure 3: Incorrect price level leading to buffer stocks running out

Inadequate information

Many of the policy options outlined in sections 1.22 and 1.23 rely on the government having excellent data and information on the markets in which it wishes to intervene. For example, if a government is using some form of tax to correct a negative externality, it has to be able to estimate accurately the external costs. If its estimates are too high, then the market will be further distorted. This is shown in Figure 1, where the additional tax is set at ***xy*** rather than ***ab*** resulting in consumers paying more than the product is worth in terms of resources used.

Similarly, failure to set target prices at the right level will result in the failure of buffer stock policies, as shown in Figures 2 and 3. In Figure 2, the price is set too high resulting in ever bigger stocks. In Figure 3, buffer stocks would soon run out.

Administrative failings

Governments and civil servants make mistakes. The imposition of any control or regulation provides scope for evasion. Policing emission controls is very difficult and in many cases the penalties for non-compliance are not very strong deterrents.

Changing the behaviour of people involves affecting complex and deep-rooted attitudes. Public relations campaigns do not always work in the ways in which they were intended. Some are far more successful than anticipated. Many depend on the coincidence of other events. The problems faced by the British government in 1999–2003 when trying to gather evidence about the effectiveness of GM (genetically modified) foods is an example of a government attempt to change attitudes that many believe failed.

Unintended effects

The growth of unofficial markets are a good example of unintended effects, especially if the result of government policies is to create shortages of goods that are in demand. Unofficial markets arise when maximum prices are set so that shortages of products or services are created. Some customers are prepared to pay more than the set price, and this also creates a new or unofficial market for such products. If governments introduce maximum prices at times of war, they usually outlaw unofficial markets. As unofficial markets are illegal anyway, lawlessness is encouraged, and this may have further repercussions. Much of modern gangsterism in the USA is said to have developed in the 1920–30s when many states banned the consumption of alcohol.

The incentive for unofficial markets to develop is shown in Figure 4 in which the supply of a good is fixed at **Q**. Some customers are prepared to pay up to **P** for these limited supplies. This could provide an incentive to engage in illegal activity.

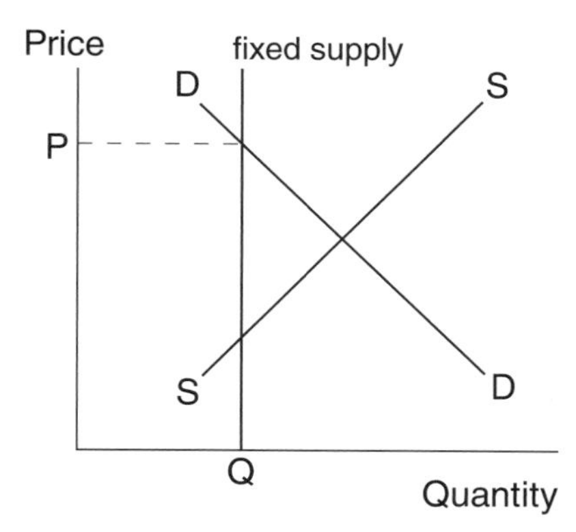

Figure 4: How unofficial markets develop

Hot potato

What are the economic arguments for and against controls on sales of alcopops?

Political conflicts

Politics can be seen as a means of reconciling conflicts. Politicians need the support of voters who may have different objectives. In 1999, the government announced that not all cigarette advertising was to be banned as quickly as originally intended. It has been argued that groups such as those promoting Formula 1 motor racing have been able to persuade the government to change its policies. In this case, there was a conflict between the Labour Party raising revenue and its desire to reduce smoking.

The jobs of politicians can be made harder as a result of the pressure applied to the government by the media, various pressure groups and lobbyists. Sometimes politicians just cannot win.

Reconciling political differences is even harder in an international or global context. This is particularly significant in dealing with negative externalities. Pollution and pollutants do not recognise national boundaries. Countries need to agree common approaches. The failure of the US government to cut greenhouse gas emissions is considered by some to be one of the biggest threats facing global society.

Research task

Find out about the implications on the agriculture industry of moving towards a much more market-based economy by ending government indirect taxes and the provision of subsidies.

Quickie

Do governments always fail?

1.2.5 Activities: markets and market failure

Activity 1

Answer the following objective test questions.

1 Which one of the following is a normative statement?
 (a) Petrol is more expensive than bottled water.
 (b) Bottled water costs more to produce than petrol.
 (c) Petrol is more useful than bottled water.
 (d) Bottled water has a bigger market than petrol.

2 The idea of opportunity cost suggests that all of the following are limited in supply except people's
 (a) time
 (b) wants
 (c) resources
 (d) incomes?

3 A mixed economy is said to exist when there is a combination of
 (a) different types of goods and services on sale
 (b) economic goods and free goods available
 (c) capital and labour used in production
 (d) government and markets allocating resources?

4 When a market is at equilibrium
 (a) all consumers can afford the product
 (b) there is no shortage or surplus at the equilibrium price
 (c) all producers are equally efficient
 (d) the equilibrium quantity is at its highest possible level?

5 The demand for season tickets at a railway station rose from 800 to 1000 a month following a 10 per cent increase in the price of bus travel. What will the cross elasticity of demand of train season tickets with respect to the price of bus travel be?
 (a) −2.5
 (b) −0.4
 (c) +0.4
 (d) +2.5

6 The fact that most airlines and train operators in the UK have banned smoking suggests that cigarettes are
 (a) demerit goods
 (b) merit goods
 (c) public goods
 (d) private goods?

7 Which one of the following would cause a shift of the supply curve for new cars?
 (a) An increase in advertising expenditure for new cars.
 (b) An increase in the price of new cars.
 (c) An increase in the level of incomes.
 (d) An increase in wages of car factory workers.

8 A new growing technique reduces the cost of producing cabbages. What is likely to happen to the quantity supplied and demanded?

	Quantity supplied	Quantity demanded
(a)	Increases	Increases
(b)	Increases	Decreases
(c)	Decreases	Decreases
(d)	Decreases	Increases

9 The consumption of Good X is widely regarded as creating positive externalities. The production of Good Y is known to create negative externalities. Which of the following would a government wishing to increase economic welfare be likely to do?
(a) Tax consumers of X and subsidise producers of Y.
(b) Subsidise consumers of X and tax producers of Y.
(c) Tax both consumers of X and producers of Y.
(d) Subsidise both consumers of X and producers of Y.

10 A product has a price elasticity of supply of 0.25, and a demand curve with zero elasticity. The government imposes a sales tax on this product. Which of the following can be predicted to happen?
(a) Producers pay a quarter of the tax.
(b) Producers pay all the tax.
(c) Consumers pay a quarter of the tax.
(d) Consumers pay all the tax.

Activity 2

Study Table 1 and answer the questions that follow.

Price (pence)	Quantity supplied (units)
3	100
5	50
8	40

Table 1: Demand schedule

1 Calculate the price elasticity of demand for a change in price from:
(a) 3p to 5p
(b) 5p to 3p
(c) 5p to 8p
(d) 8p to 5p
(e) 3p to 8p
(f) 8p to 3p

2 Explain carefully why elasticity changes depending on:
(a) the starting price
(b) whether price increases or decreases.

1.26 Exam practice

Figure 1: Four supply curves

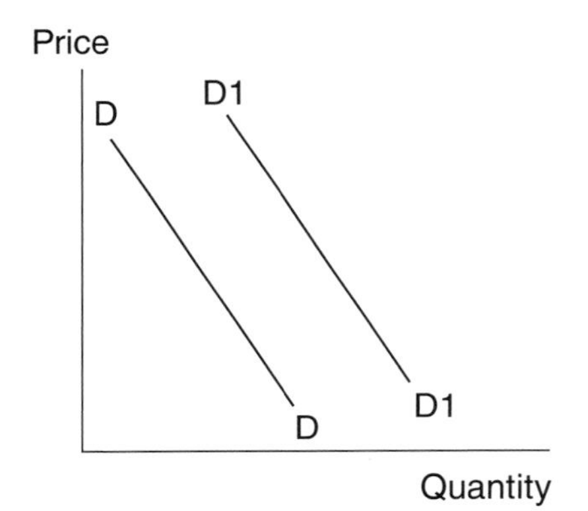

Figure 2: Demand curves for petrol

Figure 3: Production possibility curve

Objective test questions

1 Which one of the following is NOT a scarce economic resource?
(a) Land.
(b) Labour.
(c) Money.
(d) Enterprise.

2 Which of the following questions cannot be answered using positive economic analysis?
(a) Are doctors more efficient than nurses?
(b) Do doctors earn less than nurses?
(c) Why do the wages of doctors and nurses differ?
(d) Is it fair to pay doctors more than nurses?

3 Ambridge Parish Council needs to relay the village cricket pitch and extend the village hall. The Council receives £25,000 from National Lottery funds and spends it on extending the village hall. As a result, the hall is used more frequently by villagers, who were previously using the Scout Hall. What is the opportunity cost of this decision?
(a) Zero, since lottery funds are not public money.
(b) £25,000.
(c) Earnings lost by the Scout Hall.
(d) The improved cricket pitch.

4 Figure 1 shows four supply curves. Which of these lines has a price elasticity of supply of 1?
(a) S1
(b) S2
(c) S3
(d) S4

5 Figure 2 shows two demand curves for petrol. Which of the following would have caused the shift from D to D1?
(a) An increase in public transport fares.
(b) An increase in the price of oil.
(c) An increase in income tax.
(d) An increase in interest rates.

6 Figure 3 is a production possibility curve for a country. Which of these points has the least productive efficiency?
(a) Point w.
(b) Point x.
(c) Point y.
(d) Point z.

Data-response question

Study Extract 1 and Figure 4 and then answer all the questions that follow.

Extract 1: Health and efficiency

Many economists would argue that efficiency in the NHS cannot be measured in quite the same way as in the world of business, and would put forward several reasons why the idea of a 'market' cannot easily be applied to health.

A. Unpredictability. With most goods and services, consumers can plan their purchases ahead. The family car, for example, usually wears out gradually. An individual or family can plan ahead and budget for a replacement. It is much more difficult to predict and budget for a broken bone or a sudden serious illness.

B. Lack of knowledge. Market theory suggests that consumers have plenty of knowledge about what they are buying. In health care, the patient is in the hands of the specialised knowledge of the doctor.

C. Externalities. Health care often tends to benefit not only the user, but also the non-user. Some types of health care are clearly 'merit goods'.

D. Unusual elasticities. In countries where health is dominated by the private sector, people pay for health insurance. The insurance policy to some extent breaks the link between a spending decision and the cost of treatment. There is some evidence from the USA that there is a temptation for doctors to prescribe over-expensive medicines and even perform unnecessary operations, believing that insurance companies will pay the bill.

When treatment is a matter of life and death, from the patient's point of view, the price elasticity of demand for treatment might be very low or even zero. At the same time, health insurance becomes more affordable as incomes increase, and consumers will demand the latest 'hi-tech', most expensive treatments. High income elasticity coupled with low price elasticity makes medical provision more and more costly as time goes on.

(a) Give an example of a type of health care which is clearly a 'merit good' and describe its 'externalities'. (4 marks)

(b) Explain why the statistics shown in Figure 4 may or may not be good indicators of the efficiency of health spending (6 marks)

(c) Evaluate the case for and against government involvement in the provision of health care. (15 marks)

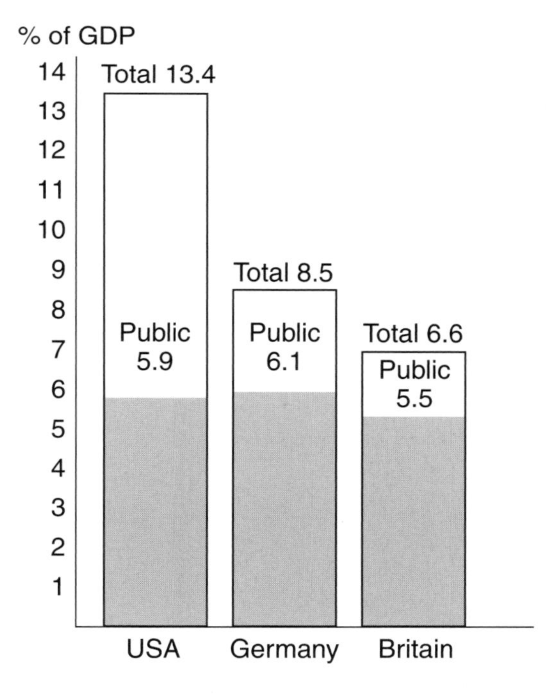

Figure 4: Health spending as a percentage of GDP in the 1990s

1.27 Exam guidance

Answers to objective test questions

1 Answer (c)
The idea of 'scarcity' is a basic principle of economics. Believe it or not, money is not scarce (a government could easily print more of it if it wished). What are scarce are the things that money can buy. These things are scarce because producing them uses up resources, and since resources are limited we have to make economic choices.

2 Answer (d)
Positive statements or questions refer to objective reality (the world around us), for example: 'Is this table made of wood?' They can be answered using tests whose validity can be agreed among the majority of people. Normative questions, on the other hand, refer not to objective reality, but to our views of the world around us (what is known as subjective reality), for example: 'Is this a beautiful table?' Normative issues often involve ideas of justice or fairness. Answers (a) (b) and (c) might be difficult questions to answer but they can be answered using positive economic analysis. Answer (d) is very much a matter of opinion, depending on the way in which we view the world, and so it is normative.

3 Answer (d)
There is a 'sacrifice' involved in the Council's choice, and so the answer is not (a). Opportunity cost is *not* the same thing as money cost, and this eliminates answer (b). Earnings lost by the Scout Hall are a money cost to the Scout Leaders, but this is not an *overall* loss to society since the earnings are transferred to the village hall. If the Council had chosen its next best alternative it would now have an improved cricket pitch; this is what has been sacrificed or foregone, and so this is the opportunity cost.

4 Answer (b)
If a supply curve is a straight line through the origin, it has a price elasticity of supply of 1.

5 Answer (a)
Answers (c) and (d) would reduce people's spending power, and so shift demand to the left. Answer (b) refers to a production cost, and would shift the supply curve, not demand. (Alternatively, we could argue that this would increase the price of petrol, causing movement along the demand curve, rather than a shift.) Answer (a) refers to an increase in the price of a substitute, which would lead people to use their cars more, and therefore increase the demand for petrol.

6 Answer (a)
Point w is the one that is nearest to the origin, showing the lowest productive efficiency (least output in return for resources used up). Note that points y and z have equal productive efficiency, as both are on the production possibility curve.

Exam hint

The 15 multiple-choice questions are often described as *items* rather than questions, because they do not always contain a question mark. You get 1 mark for each correct answer you choose. You do *not* lose marks for wrong answers so you should *always* attempt *all* of these items. Before you enter your choice on the answer sheet, consider each option carefully, to convince yourself that you know *why* your chosen option is correct, and *why* each of the other 'distractors' are incorrect.

Exam hint

Multiple-choice questions (and data response questions) often require you to work with *index numbers*. These numbers require you to compare quantities with a base year. This is the year in which the quantity being measured is converted to 100. For example, £2847 and £1423.50 are awkward numbers; but if we convert £2487 to 100, £1423.50 becomes 50, and it is easy to see that one is half of the other. Similarly, 200 would represent an amount of £5694 (twice £2847).

Answers to the data response question

(a) Although the distinction is not required by this question, generally speaking you should be careful to distinguish between a merit and a public good. A public good is one which is non-excludable and non-rival. Provision at all is provision for all. A mass vaccination programme eliminating a contagious disease (such as smallpox) would be a good example, as the whole of society, and not just individuals, would benefit, and no individual would be excluded. However, most health services are best regarded as 'merit goods'. A hospital bed is 'rival', as one person's occupancy deprives another, and 'excludable', because it can be rationed using price. So it is not a 'public' good; however, we choose not to treat hospital beds as private goods, since their benefits are not confined to the prime user (this is how a merit good is defined). It is in society's interests to cure people of illnesses as quickly and effectively as possible, so the benefits of hospital treatment are not confined to the patient. Having read the above detailed explanation you should note that part (a) is meant to be a relatively straightforward question, requiring a basic or descriptive answer. It carries just 4 marks, so keep your answer brief and to the point. Do not allocate too much time to part (a); you need to reserve the most time for part (c).

(b) This part of the question goes beyond description and requires some analysis. A high amount of spending on health (as in the USA) might be a good thing, showing that health has a high priority. On the other hand, it might indicate unnecessary spending. The extract suggests that the balance between public and private spending can affect efficiency, and also that private spending is not necessarily efficient.

(c) This part of the data response is marked using 5 levels of response mark bands. To enter the highest bands (4 and 5) you should identify several issues and discuss them critically. In other words, you must *evaluate*. You could do this by considering the advantages and disadvantages of public versus private provision, and come to a judgement about whether the advantages outweigh the disadvantages, justifying your conclusion. Another way to evaluate is to mention several points or issues, and then to say which of these are the most important or significant.

Exam hint

Data response questions are usually designed to have an 'incline of difficulty'. The first part of the question will be relatively easy, earning a few marks. The last part of the question will have more marks available, and the question will be more challenging, with higher order skills required to earn these marks.

1.28 Further reading

1.2

C. Bamford & S. Munday. *Markets*. Heinemann, 2002. Chapter 1.
S. Munday. *Markets and Market Failure*. Heinemann, 2000. Chapter 1.

1.3

C. Bamford & S. Munday. *Markets*. Heinemann, 2002. Chapter 1.
G. Hale. *Labour Markets*. Heinemann, 2001. Chapter 1.

1.4

C. Bamford & S. Munday. *Markets*. Heinemann, 2002. Chapter 1.

1.5

C. Bamford & S. Munday. *Markets*. Heinemann, 2002. Chapter 2.

1.6

C. Bamford & S. Munday. *Markets*. Heinemann, 2002. Chapter 3.
G. Hale. *Labour Markets*. Heinemann, 2001. Chapter 2.

1.7

C. Bamford & S. Munday. *Markets*. Heinemann, 2002. Chapter 3.

1.8

C. Bamford & S. Munday. *Markets*. Heinemann, 2002. Chapter 4.
G. Hale. *Labour Markets*. Heinemann, 2001. Chapter 4.

1.9

C. Bamford & S. Munday. *Markets*. Heinemann, 2002. Chapter 4.

1.10

C. Bamford & S. Munday. *Markets*. Heinemann, 2002. Chapter 5.

1.11

C. Bamford & S. Munday. *Markets*. Heinemann, 2002. Chapter 5.

1.12

C. Bamford & S. Munday. *Markets*. Heinemann, 2002. Chapter 5.
G. Hale. *Labour Markets*. Heinemann, 2001. Chapter 5.

1.13

C. Bamford & S. Munday. *Markets*. Heinemann, 2002. Chapter 5.

G. Hale. *Labour Markets*. Heinemann, 2001. Chapter 4.

1.14

C. Bamford & S. Munday. *Markets*. Heinemann, 2002. Chapter 6.
G. Hale. *Labour Markets*. Heinemann, 2001. Chapter 6.

1.15

C. Bamford & S. Munday. *Markets*. Heinemann, 2002. Chapter 7.

1.16

C. Bamford & S. Munday. *Markets*. Heinemann, 2002. Chapter 6.

1.17

S. Munday. *Markets and Market Failure*. Heinemann, 2000. Chapter 3.

1.18

S. Munday. *Markets and Market Failure*. Heinemann, 2000. Chapter 3.

1.19

C. Bamford & S. Munday. *Markets*. Heinemann, 2002. Chapter 7.
G. Hale. *Labour Markets*. Heinemann, 2001. Chapter 8.

1.20

C. Bamford. *Transport Economics*, 3rd edn. Heinemann, 2001. Chapter 6.
S. Munday. *Markets and Market Failure*. Heinemann, 2000. Chapters 2-3.

1.21

C. Bamford. *Transport Economics*, 3rd edn. Heinemann, 2001. Chapter 5.
S. Munday. *Markets and Market Failure*. Heinemann, 2000. Chapters 4-5.

1.22

S. Munday. *Markets and Market Failure*. Heinemann, 2000. Chapter 6.

1.23

S. Munday. *Markets and Market Failure*. Heinemann, 2000. Chapters 6-8.

1.24

S. Munday. *Markets and Market Failure*. Heinemann, 2000. Chapter 7.

PART 2

THE NATIONAL ECONOMY

2.1 The national economy

Part 2 of this book is concerned with macroeconomics – that is, the performance of the whole economy. How well the economy performs affects all our lives. It influences:

- the quantity and quality of goods and services we can enjoy
- our chances of gaining a job, and
- the prices we pay for the products we consume.

As you progress through this module, you will explore how economists and politicians measure macroeconomic performance and the key government macroeconomic objectives. You will consider the causes of economic growth, inflation, unemployment and a balance of payments disequilibrium.

Aggregate demand and aggregate supply analysis

You will use aggregate demand and aggregate supply analysis to examine how the level of economic activity is determined. You will also see some similarities with the demand and supply analysis you are familiar with from Part 1 including the widespread use of diagrams. However, it is important to realise that there are differences. In Part 2, you will be analysing *total* economic activity, whereas in Part 1 you studied the activity in single markets.

For instance, while price is measured on the vertical axis of a demand and supply diagram, it is *price level* on an aggregate demand and aggregate supply diagram. Also, on the horizontal axis on an aggregate demand and aggregate supply diagram it is *real GDP* (gross domestic product – in other words, output) that is measured, and the letter y is usually used to represent a particular level of output.

You will find aggregate demand and aggregate supply analysis useful as you consider the main types of economic policies the government implements in pursuit of its objectives. You will learn the differences between the main types of policies and explore which policy instruments can be used to achieve specific objectives.

Objectives

When you have completed this module, you should be able to:

- explain how the performance of an economy is measured
- compare the performance of the UK with other economies
- explain the causes and consequences of economic growth, inflation, unemployment and balance of payments deficit
- apply aggregate demand and aggregate supply analysis to explore current economic behaviour and issues
- assess fiscal, monetary and supply-side policies.

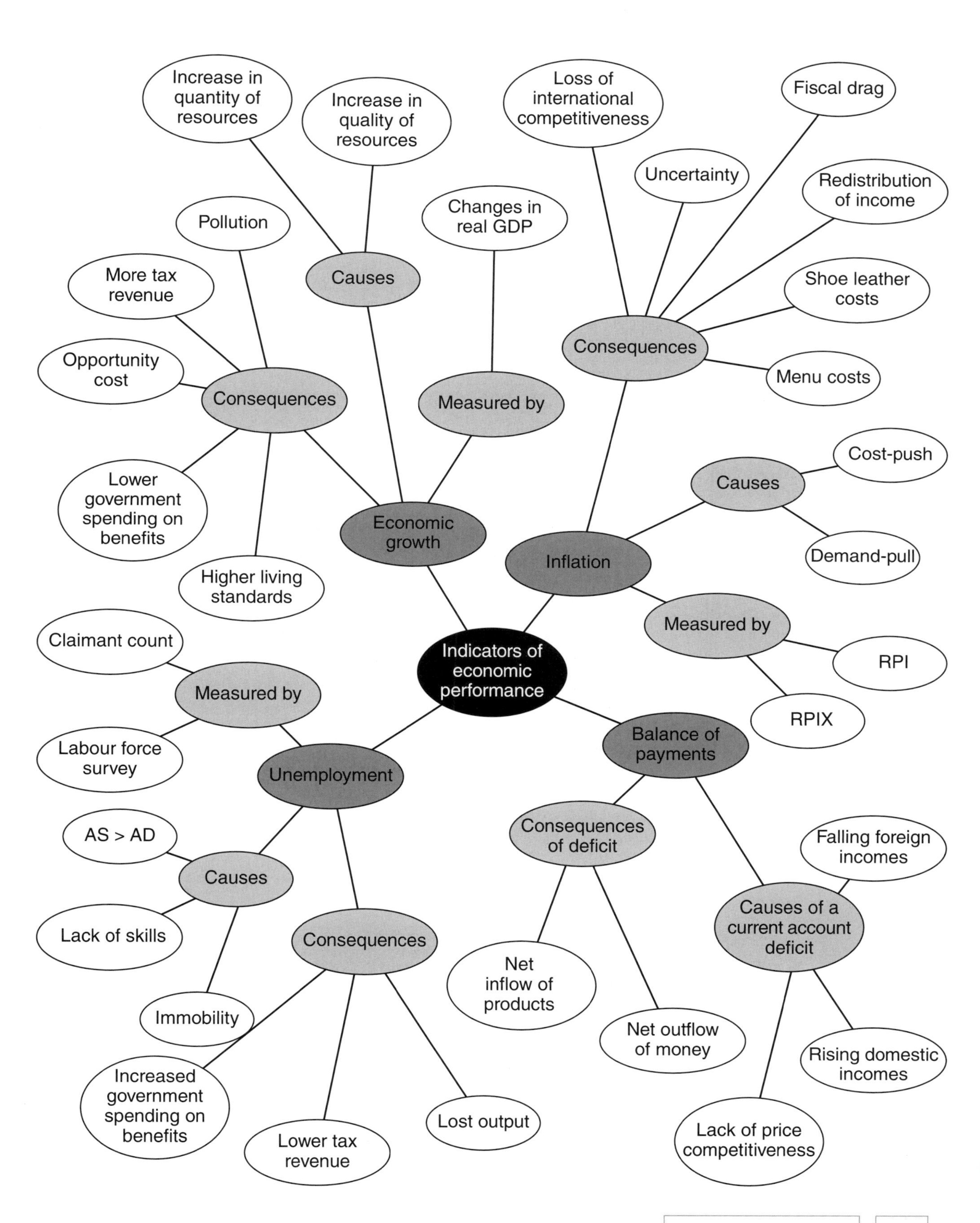
Indicators of economic performance
Economic growth
Causes
Increase in quantity of resources
Increase in quality of resources
Measured by
Changes in real GDP
Consequences
Pollution
More tax revenue
Opportunity cost
Lower government spending on benefits
Higher living standards
Inflation
Consequences
Loss of international competitiveness
Uncertainty
Fiscal drag
Redistribution of income
Shoe leather costs
Menu costs
Causes
Cost-push
Demand-pull
Measured by
RPI
RPIX
Balance of payments
Consequences of deficit
Net inflow of products
Net outflow of money
Causes of a current account deficit
Falling foreign incomes
Rising domestic incomes
Lack of price competitiveness
Unemployment
Measured by
Claimant count
Labour force survey
Causes
AS > AD
Lack of skills
Immobility
Consequences
Increased government spending on benefits
Lower tax revenue
Lost output

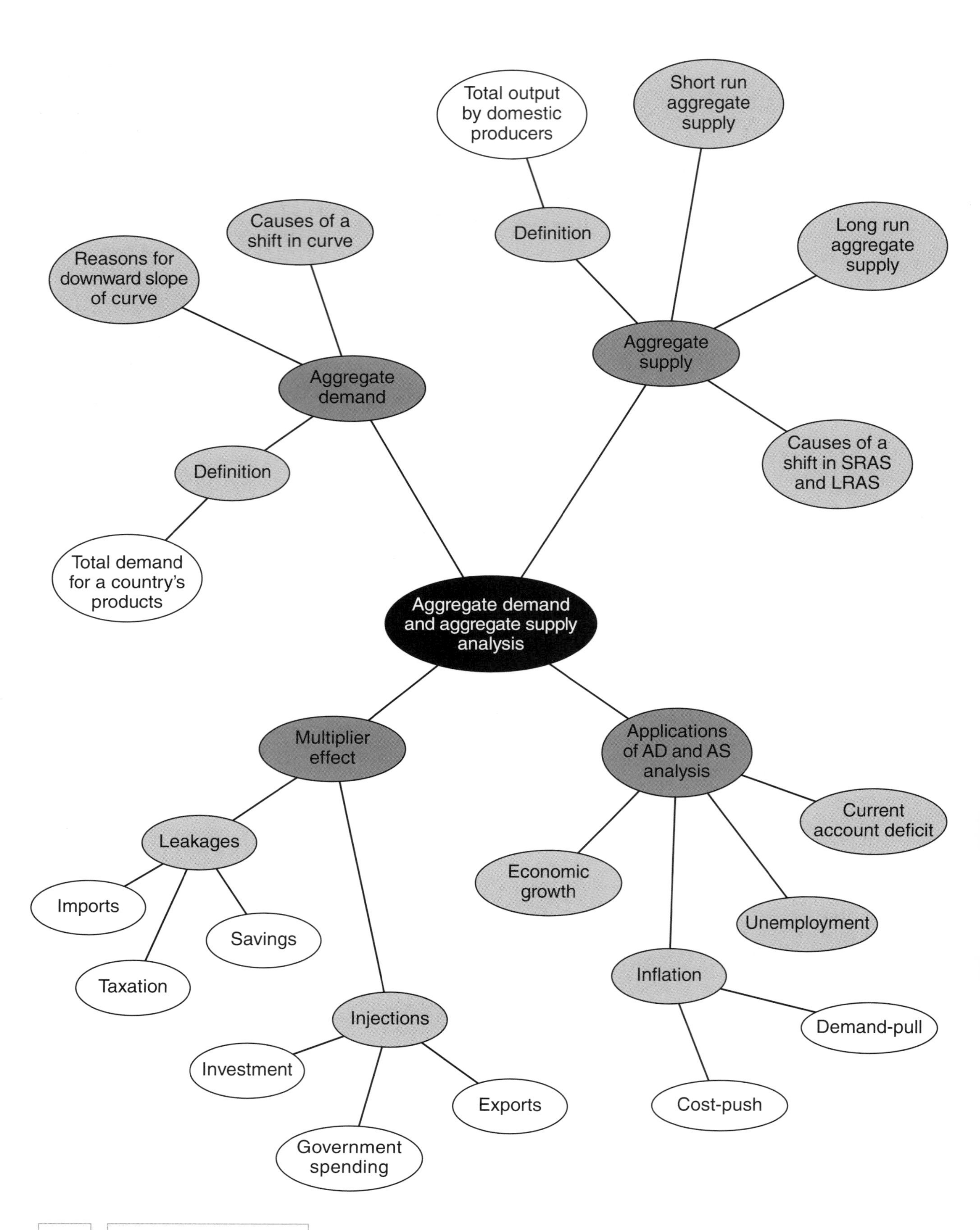

Aggregate demand and aggregate supply analysis
Aggregate demand
Reasons for downward slope of curve
Causes of a shift in curve
Definition
Total demand for a country's products
Aggregate supply
Definition
Total output by domestic producers
Short run aggregate supply
Long run aggregate supply
Causes of a shift in SRAS and LRAS
Multiplier effect
Leakages
Imports
Savings
Taxation
Injections
Investment
Government spending
Exports
Applications of AD and AS analysis
Current account deficit
Economic growth
Unemployment
Inflation
Demand-pull
Cost-push

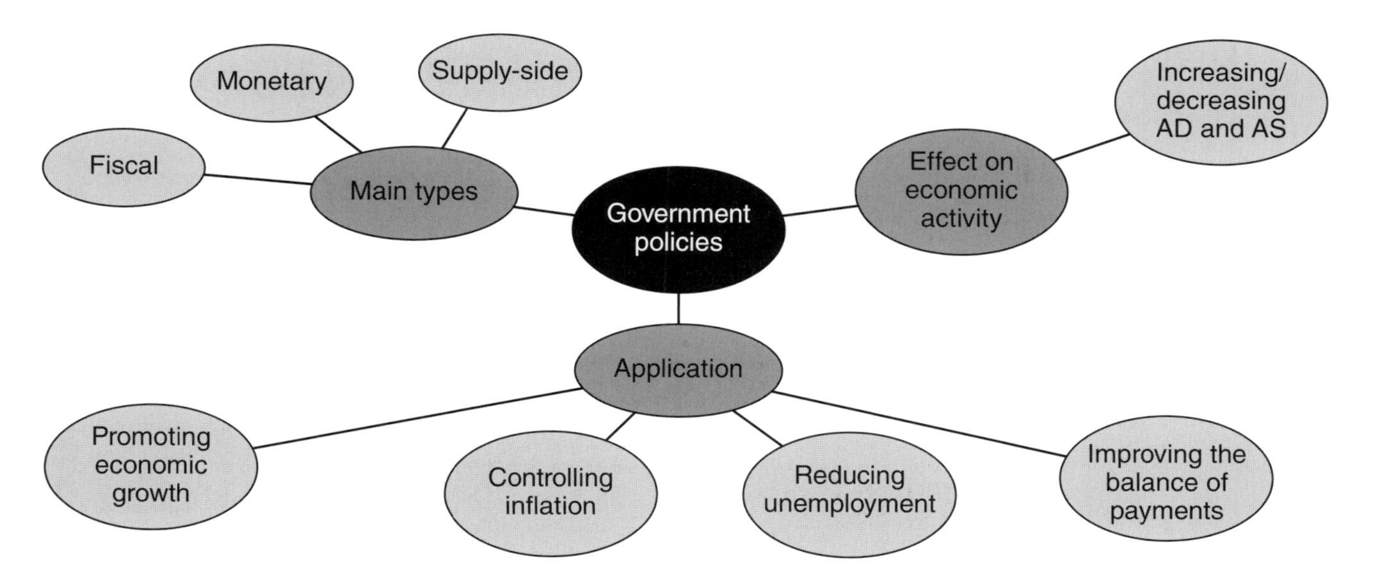

Spider diagrams

The three spider diagrams on pages 75–77 provide an overview of the three main areas covered in Part 2. It would be useful to review these again when you have completed the module.

The examination

The examination, known as Unit 2, lasts for one hour. You will have to answer a set of objective test questions (multiple-choice) and a data response question.

The national economy paper contributes 35 per cent of your marks for AS and 17.5 per cent of your final total for A Level.

Exam hint

Boost your objective test scores by getting lots of practice using past examination papers.

Revision tactics

A typical student will take around 12 weeks to reach the required standard when studying this module. It will take that long to get used to applying aggregate demand and aggregate supply analysis, and to understand, analyse and evaluate indicators of macroeconomic performance, policy objectives and policy measures. You will need a good grounding in the underpinning theory and concepts as well as a good grasp of examination techniques before you are fully prepared for the examination. Objective test questions will be drawn from the whole of the module and the data response questions will assume that you understand the whole of the module. Work through the five revision sections (2.19-2.23) after you have completed module 2 – The national economy.

Indicators of economic performance

Economists compare the performance of the UK with that of other national economies by examining a number of key indicators including:

- economic growth
- **inflation**
- unemployment
- the balance of payments position.

Definitions

Inflation: a sustained rise in the general price level.

GDP (Gross Domestic Product): total output of the economy.

Economic growth

Economic growth is measured as the change in real **GDP**. Real GDP can be measured by totalling the output, income or expenditure of the country.

- When using the output measure, it is important to avoid counting the same output twice – for example, including the output of raw materials, then including it again in the value of finished products.
- In the income measure, only incomes earned in return for producing products are included so, for example, pensions are not included.
- With the expenditure measure, it is important to remember to include exports (because they are produced by domestic firms) and to exclude imports (because they are produced by other countries' firms).

Real and money GDP

To assess economic growth, it is important to use real GDP. A real figure (one measured in constant prices) is one that has been adjusted for inflation. The GDP of a country, measured in the prices operating in the year in question (money GDP), may rise from, say, £500,000 million in 2003 to £550,000 million in 2004. This would appear to suggest that output has risen by:

$$\frac{£50,000m}{£500,000m} \times 100 = 10\%$$

However, at least part of this increase may be due to a rise in the price of the products produced. To assess the rise in volume, the effects of price rises are taken out by using the following formula:

$$\text{Current year GDP figure} \times \frac{\text{base year price index}}{\text{current year price index}}$$

So, if the price index in 2003 was 100 and 106 in 2004, real GDP would be:

$$£550,000m \times \frac{100}{106} = £518,867.92m$$

In real terms, GDP has risen by:

$$\frac{£18,867.92m}{£500,00m} \times 100 = 3.77\%$$

Thinking like an economist

When examining a country's performance in terms of inflation and other main indicators, economists use index numbers. These provide a measure of the relative change in a set of figures. They enable users of the data to assess quickly the percentage change on some previous year without having to undertake any difficult calculations. The year against which such comparisons are made is known as the base year. It is given a value of 100. To convert data into an index, the following formula is used:

$$\frac{\text{current year figure}}{\text{base year figure}} \times 100$$

Economic growth rate

The economic growth rate is the percentage change in real GDP. If a country's annual economic growth rate is 3.77 per cent, it means that the country has produced 3.77 per cent more this year than the year before.

Countries do not always experience steady economic growth. There can be booms, which are characterised by a high unsustainable economic growth rate, low levels of **unemployment** and accelerating inflation. There can also be **recessions**, during which aggregate demand (see section 2.8) is usually falling, unemployment is high and output is declining.

Inflation

The inflation rate is the percentage change in the general price level. In assessing a country's inflation performance, it is important to consider the rate over time and in comparison with other countries' rates – that is, relative inflation.

To measure the rate at which prices are changing, governments construct **price indexes** (or indices). In the UK the main price index is the **CPI**, which is a **weighted consumer price index**.

Unemployment

There are two main measures of unemployment in the UK.

- The claimant count. This includes as unemployed anyone who is receiving Jobseeker's Allowance. However, it misses some of those who are involuntarily unemployed because some unemployed people are not entitled to unemployment benefits.
- The labour force survey measure. This uses the International Labour Office (ILO) definition, which includes those without a job and who are actively seeking employment.

As well as the number of people unemployed, the government also publishes the unemployment and employment rates – the percentage of the labour force who are out of work and the corresponding percentage in work.

The balance of payments

The **balance of payments** is a record of a country's transactions with other countries over a 12-month period. The section that receives the most attention in the media is the current account (see section 2.7), which includes exports and imports.

Another main section is the financial account, which show the movement of direct investment (for example, the purchase of a factory), portfolio investment (for example, the purchase of shares) and other investments (for example, bank loans).

Quickies

1 What is the difference between real and money GDP?
2 What is meant by the unemployment rate?

Definitions

Unemployment: a situation of being willing and able to work, but not having a job.

Recession: a period of falling real GDP that lasts for at least six months.

CPI: Consumers Prices Index.

Weighted consumer price index: changes in the prices of goods and services that people spend more on are given more importance than those on which they only spend a small amount.

RPIX: the RPI minus mortgage interest payments.

Balance of payments: a record of transactions between a country's residents and the rest of the world.

Counting those claiming Jobseeker's Allowance is one way of measuring unemployment

Objectives of government policy

Government policy objectives and the emphasis placed on them can change as **government administrations** and economic theories change. However, the main objectives for the economy (macroeconomic objectives) pursued by most governments are:

- control of inflation
- minimising unemployment
- a steady rate of economic growth
- a satisfactory balance of payments.

Control of inflation

The UK government has charged the **Bank of England** with responsibility for achieving a 2.5 per cent target on the RPIX measure, with a 1 per cent margin either side. The government is aiming for low and stable inflation. A high and accelerating rate of inflation can be harmful to an economy. It may reduce the international price competitiveness of the country's products, lower the real value of some people's incomes and savings, and is likely to create uncertainty (making planning difficult).

However, zero inflation, with the general price level remaining unchanged, has always been regarded as difficult to achieve and not particularly desirable. A low level of inflation, rather than zero inflation, may bring benefits. It may enable firms to reduce their costs by not raising wages in line with inflation rather than making some workers redundant.

Minimising unemployment

Unemployment involves a waste of resources, a loss of potential output and gives rise to a number of social problems. In contrast, high employment confers several important advantages, including the possibility of high output and high living standards. The highest possible employment may be referred to as **full employment**. This still does not mean zero unemployment, as there will always be some people who are between jobs.

A steady rate of economic growth

A steady rate of economic growth may provide many advantages in an economy, including increasing material living standards. It also enables a government to reduce poverty without having to lower the living standards of the rich and middle-income groups. This is because higher output will mean higher total income, some of which can be used to increase the employment opportunities of the poor – for example, by providing training and increased benefits. If total income does not rise, the only way to increase government spending to reduce poverty is to increase taxes on the rich and middle-income groups.

As well as steady economic growth, governments also aim for **sustainable economic growth**.

Definitions

Government administrations: government regimes that run the length of a parliament e.g. the Labour Government 1997-2001.

The Bank of England: the UK's central bank. Founded in 1694 it issues notes and coins and implements the government's monetary policy including changing interest rates when it is thought appropriate.

Full employment: a situation where those wanting to work can gain employment at the going wage rate – often taken as an unemployment rate of three per cent.

Sustainable economic growth: economic growth that does not endanger future generations' ability to expand productive capacity.

A satisfactory balance of payments

In the long term, a government may seek to match revenue and expenditure on the current account of the balance of payments. However, in the short term, it may be content to see a deficit or a surplus. For example, a deficit may arise when an economy is expanding and buying more raw materials that will be converted into finished products – some of which will be exported. The deficit may also be offset by a surplus on another section of the balance of payments.

Web link

Go to www.heinemann.co.uk/hotlinks and click on this unit to link to the website for the Office for National Statistics.

Influencing factors

There are several factors that influence a government's ability to achieve its macroeconomic objectives. One is the level of economic activity. An economic boom, for instance, is usually associated with a significant rise in real GDP and falling unemployment. However, the high and increasing level of **aggregate demand** (see section 2.8) that exists during a boom may lead to inflation and a current account deficit.

The level of economic activity in the UK's main trading partners also influences the UK government's ability to achieve its objectives. If the US, Japanese, German and other EU (European Union) economies are performing well, they are likely to buy more products from the UK. This should help the UK's current account position, employment and economic growth rate.

Another influencing factor is the appropriateness of government policies. For instance, it would be inappropriate for a government to cut income tax when a country is experiencing high inflation because the reduction in income tax will increase total demand in the economy and may raise the general price level even further.

Definition

Aggregate demand: the total demand for a country's goods and services at a given price level.

Policy conflicts

In the short run, a government's objectives may conflict. There is a risk that reducing unemployment, for instance, may generate a higher rate of inflation. This is because as the number unemployed falls, there is increased competition for workers. This may push up wage rates and so raise firms' costs of production and prices.

A government seeking to reduce spending on imports may introduce measures to cut spending in general. Such measures may reduce employment and the economic growth rate.

Quickies

1. What is the government's inflation target?
2. Why is there always some unemployment?
3. Identify a benefit of economic growth.
4. What effect is a cut in income tax likely to have on total demand?

Hot potato

Between 1998 and 2001 the price level in Japan fell. This caused major problems. Consumers delayed their purchases, expecting prices to be lower in the future. Lower spending resulted in higher unemployment and falling output. The situation became so desperate that the Japanese government tried to generate inflation!

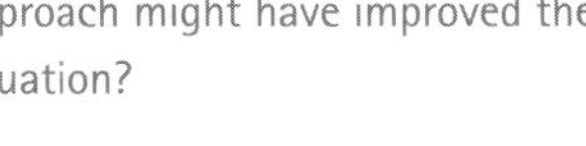

How do you think such an unusual approach might have improved the situation?

2.4 Economic growth

Economic growth occurs when the productive capacity of the economy increases. It can be illustrated by a shift to the right of the production possibility curve as shown in Figure 1. It is difficult to measure changes in **productive capacity**. So, as you saw in section 2.2, the main indicator of economic growth is taken to be the rate at which real GDP is changing.

Definitions

Productive capacity: the maximum possible output than can be produced with existing resources and technology.

Capital goods: goods that are used to produce other goods and services.

Labour productivity: output per worker/hour.

Causes of economic growth

For economic growth to be achieved there must be an increase in either the quantity and/or the quality of resources. For example, a country may be able to produce more because it has more **capital goods** and/or because the capital goods it has are of a higher quality, incorporating advanced technological features.

The size and quality of the labour force may also increase. Possible causes include net immigration, a rise in the retirement age and greater incentives for, say, more lone parents entering the labour force.

The two main causes of a rise in the quality of the labour force are improvements in education and training. A more educated and better-trained labour force will increase **productivity**.

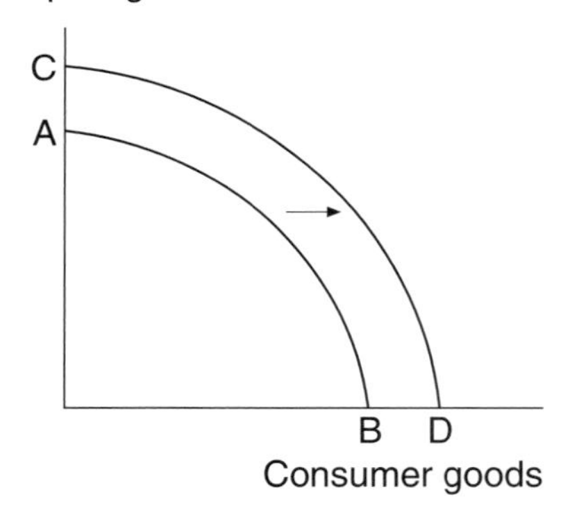

Figure 1: Economic growth

Trend growth

In practice, the productive capacity of most economies increases each year. In industrialised economies, this is due mainly to improvements in education standards and advances in technology. In some developing economies it is also due to rises in the size of the labour force.

Trend growth is the expected increase in potential output over time. It is a measure of how fast the economy can grow without generating higher inflation. In late 1999, the UK government revised upwards the economy's trend rate of economic growth from 2.25 per cent to 2.5 per cent, largely due to an increase in productivity growth.

Output gap

When the annual growth in real GDP equals the economy's trend growth, unemployment is unlikely to change. This is because the higher total demand can be matched by increases in output resulting from, say, improvements in technology.

However, when there is a slow rise in total demand, actual output is likely to grow more slowly than potential output. In this case, there will be an **output gap**. Figure 2 shows the growth in potential and actual output over time. The distance ***ab*** represents the output gap. The economy is capable of

Definition

Output gap: the gap between potential and actual output.

producing more goods and services than it is making. As firms, with their current resources, are able to make more products than they can sell, they are likely to reduce the number of workers they employ.

When the economy has been producing below its potential output, it is possible that its actual output will grow at a faster rate than its potential output, narrowing the output gap.

For short periods of time, the high levels of total demand may push rises in output above the trend growth rate. Some of the extra output may be achieved by workers working overtime and machines working flat out (with no pauses for maintenance). However, this cannot be sustained and is likely to lead to inflation.

The distance ***cd*** in Figure 2 shows an output gap, with actual output exceeding potential output, and the economy overheating. When the economy is in a recession unemployment increases, so actual output is below potential output. In contrast, in a boom actual output may be above potential output.

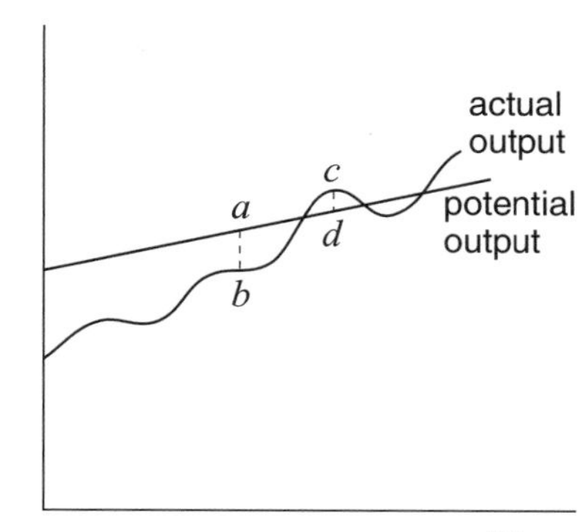

Figure 2: Growth in potential and actual output

Benefits and costs of economic growth

The main benefit of economic growth is likely to be a rise in people's material standard of living.

- If real GDP per head rises, the population can enjoy more products.
- Economic growth enables poverty within an economy to be reduced without having to redistribute existing income.
- Higher income raises tax revenue without having to increase tax rates. Some of this can be used to help to improve public services – for example, education and health care.

However, economic growth can also generate costs. In the short run, if the economy is operating at its productive capacity, there will be an opportunity cost (see section 1.2). Some resources will have to be switched from making consumer to capital goods.

If economic growth is achieved in a way that is not sustainable – for instance, in a way that causes pollution – there will be damage to the environment. There is also the risk that economic growth may result in the depletion of non-renewable resources and increased stress resulting from rapid change.

Making connections

Explain why economic growth is a macroeconomic objective.

Hot potato

'An increase in the quantity of goods and services available to people always improves the quality of their lives.' Do you agree? Think about the reasons for your answer.

Quickies

1 Identify two causes of economic growth.
2 What is meant by trend growth?
3 When is there an output gap?
4 What is the main benefit of economic growth?

Exam hint

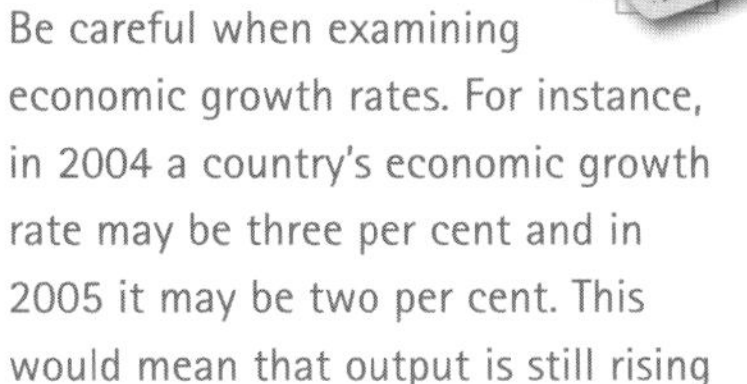

Be careful when examining economic growth rates. For instance, in 2004 a country's economic growth rate may be three per cent and in 2005 it may be two per cent. This would mean that output is still rising but at a slower rate – but it is not falling.

Inflation

Prices change all the time. Inflation, though, is a sustained rise in the general (average) price level. If, for example, the lower price of PCs is accompanied by a rise in price of most other goods and services, the average change in price will be upwards and inflation will occur. When inflation takes place, the value of money must fall. Each unit of the currency (for example, each pound) will be able to buy less than before.

Research task

Using *Economist* magazine or any other appropriate source, compare the UK's inflation rate with that of the USA, France and Japan. Then consider the significance of the differences you find.

Causes of inflation

There are two main types of inflation: **demand-pull** and **cost-push**.

Demand-pull inflation

This arises from total (aggregate) demand increasing at a faster rate than total (aggregate) supply. When the economy is producing at its productive capacity, increases in aggregate demand will pull up the price level.

Inflation can also occur when output is approaching its productive capacity (see section 2.4). This is because as output rises, shortages of skilled workers and capital equipment begin to build up. Firms wanting to expand compete with each other for these scarce resources by bidding up their prices. So increases in aggregate demand can have an effect on costs of production. However, the starting point of the inflation is an excessive growth of aggregate demand.

Cost-push inflation

This is an increase in costs of production. It is a rise in the general level that occurs independently of any change in aggregate demand. A common cause of cost-push inflation is a rise in wage rates above increases in productivity. Such a rise increases costs of production. This can set off inflation as the higher wages are also likely to cause an increase in aggregate demand. This, in turn, may cause a rise in costs of production and so the process continues.

Definitions

Hyperinflation: a situation where the general price level is rising very rapidly.

Menu costs: costs involved in changing prices in, say, catalogues due to inflation.

Shoe leather costs: time and effort involved in reducing holdings of cash and seeking the highest rate of interest.

The effects of inflation

A high rate of inflation can cause many problems. During a period of **hyperinflation**, people can lose confidence in the value of money and it can be difficult for an economy to operate. Even when inflation is not at hyperinflation but at levels that would be regarded as high, it can still impose costs on an economy. These include **menu**, **shoe leather** and administrative costs such as adjusting accounts and negotiating with unions about wage rises.

In addition, inflation creates an effect called **inflationary noise**. If the price of, say, one model of television rises, and there is no inflation, you might conclude that the TV is relatively more expensive than others on the market. However, with inflation you would be uncertain whether the rise in price actually reflects a relative price rise or whether it is in line with inflation.

Unanticipated and anticipated inflation

Some costs can arise if the future inflation rate is not correctly anticipated. These costs may include some people experiencing a fall in their real income. For example, if the rate of interest does not rise in line with inflation, the real rate of interest will fall and lenders will not be able to buy as much with the interest they receive. Some workers may not get wage rises that keep pace with inflation.

But some people will gain from inflation – for example, home owners (because the value of property tends to rise by more than the rate of interest), other borrowers and workers with strong bargaining power. The government is also likely to gain from inflation. This is because it is usually a large net borrower and if tax rates are not adjusted in line with inflation it may gain extra tax revenue – this is known as **fiscal drag**.

One of the most serious disadvantages of unanticipated inflation is the uncertainty it creates. For example, if firms are uncertain what their costs will be and what prices they will be able to gain, they may be reluctant to invest. This in turn, will slow down economic growth. However, when inflation is correctly anticipated, tax rates, pensions and wages can be adjusted in line with inflation.

Whether inflation is anticipated or not, it can have a harmful effect on a country's international trade position. What is important here is the country's inflation rate relative to other countries' inflation rates. If the country's inflation rate is above that of its main competitors, its goods and services will become less price competitive. This could result in fewer exports being sold and more imports being purchased.

Quickies

1. What is the difference between demand-pull and cost-push inflation?
2. What is meant by inflationary noise?
3. Why is unanticipated inflation more harmful than anticipated inflation?
4. Identify two groups who may benefit from inflation.

Definitions

Inflationary noise: the distortion of price signals caused by inflation.

Fiscal drag: when inflation increases people's money incomes, dragging them into higher tax brackets.

Inflation favours those selling houses

Thinking like an economist

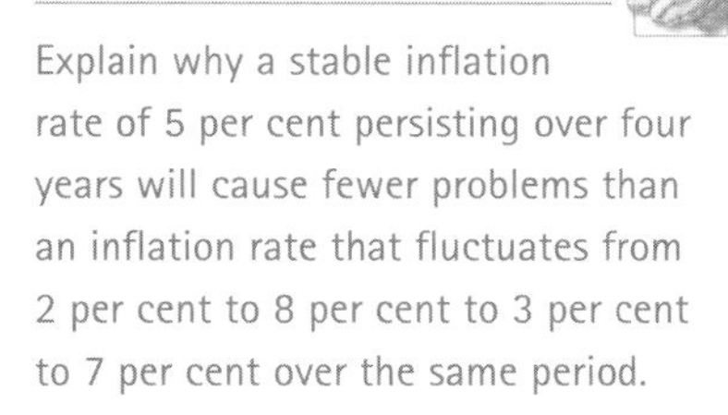

Explain why a stable inflation rate of 5 per cent persisting over four years will cause fewer problems than an inflation rate that fluctuates from 2 per cent to 8 per cent to 3 per cent to 7 per cent over the same period.

2.6 Employment and unemployment

Unemployment and employment are closely linked, but not always as strongly as people might think. Loss of jobs can have significant adverse effects on the economy and even more so on the unemployed.

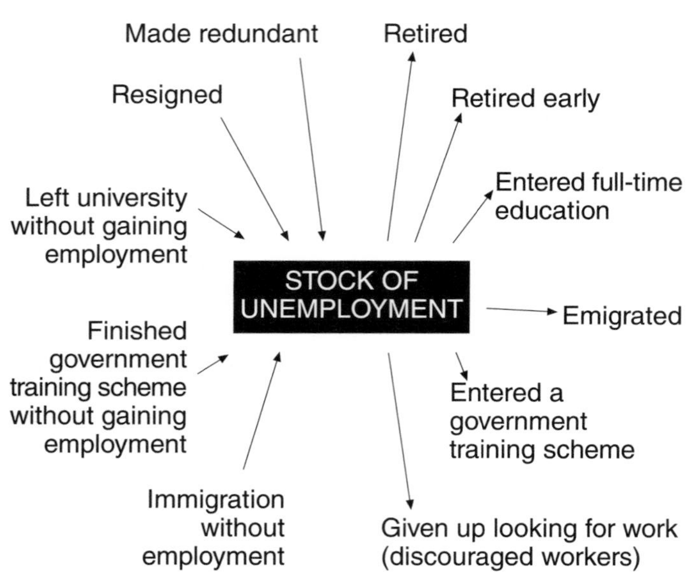

Figure 1: Inflows and outflows of unemployment

Unemployment and employment

When the number and rate of people unemployed goes down, the number and rate of people employed usually increases. Similarly, when employment falls, unemployment usually increases.

However, this does not have to occur and while (in practice) the figures usually move in opposite directions, they frequently do not move proportionately. For example, unemployment may fall by 30,000 one month, while employment rises by only 25,000. This situation can occur because there are several reasons why people cease to be unemployed, as shown in Figure 1. Unemployment increases whenever the inflow into unemployment exceeds the outflow from it.

Duration of unemployment

The government is also concerned with how long people are out of work, because the longer the period, the greater the costs involved. An unemployment rate of six per cent with people being out of work on average for two years will create more problems than an unemployment rate of nine per cent with people being unemployed for an average of two months.

Definition

Aggregate supply: the total amount a country's producers supply at a given price level.

The causes of unemployment

Large-scale unemployment occurs when aggregate demand is below the full employment level of **aggregate supply** (see section 2.9). In this case, output is below the level that could be produced with all the labour force in work.

Over time if aggregate demand grows more slowly than the increase in the productive capacity of the economy, there will be unemployment. There are several reasons why aggregate demand may rise more slowly or even fall – including:

- consumers becoming pessimistic about the future, and
- the country's products becoming less internationally competitive.

One cause of an increase in the country's productive capacity is an increase in the labour supply. If, for instance, more lone parents enter the labour force, the country will be capable of producing more goods and services. However, the effect a rise in the labour force has on employment and unemployment will depend on what is happening to aggregate demand, and therefore the demand for labour.

Also, firms will not want to employ people, even if aggregate demand is high and rising, if they lack the appropriate skills and mobility.

The main cost of unemployment

The main cost of unemployment to an economy is the opportunity cost of lost output – a potential output that is lost forever. When an economy has unemployed workers it is not producing at its productive capacity level. Figure 2 shows the production possibility curve of an economy experiencing unemployment. Due to unemployment, it is producing inside the curve at **a**. With full employment it could produce at **b**, **c** or any other point on the curve.

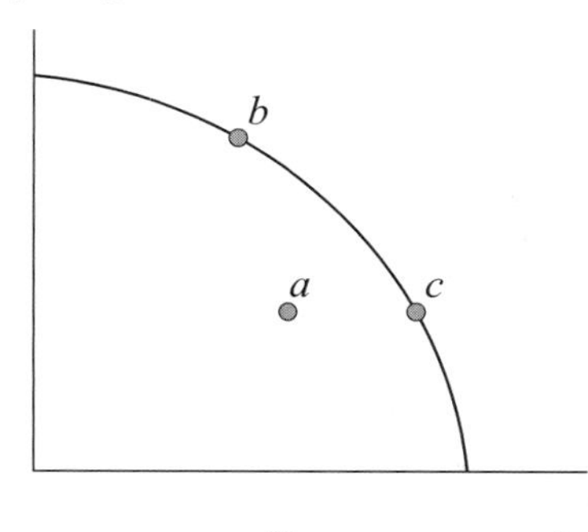

Figure 2: The opportunity cost of unemployment

When people are out of work they spend less, so the government receives less revenue from indirect taxes such as VAT. Total income will also be below what it would be if there was full employment, and so revenue from income tax will be lower than its potential level.

While tax revenue will be less, government expenditure will have to be higher because it will have to spend more money on Jobseeker's Allowance. If there was less unemployment, the government could spend more on other areas such as education or have lower tax rates.

When people are out of work, the worry about financial loss and loss of status can contribute to poor physical and mental health. In severe cases, the result of this can be the breakdown of families, or even suicide. Fall in income can reduce the health and educational performance of the children of the poor, with long-term implications for health-care needs and the quality of the labour force. Unemployment can therefore increase government expenditure on, for example, supporting lone parents and providing health-care.

Of course, those who bear the main burden of unemployment are the unemployed themselves. Apart from the problems listed above, the longer people are unemployed, the more they miss out on training, updating and promotion and, as a result, the more difficult they will find it to gain employment.

Research task

Research the effect that a rise in the school leaving age and a consumer boom is likely to have on unemployment.

Quickies

1. What would explain a rise in employment being accompanied by a rise in unemployment?
2. Why would improved training be expected to reduce unemployment?
3. Use a production possibility curve to explain the effect of a reduction in unemployment on output.
4. Why would a rise in employment be likely to raise tax revenue?

2.7 Balance of payments

The current account is a key section of the balance of payments. It consists of:

- trade in goods
- trade in services
- investment income
- transfers.

Trade in goods

The UK often earns more from its exports of oil, chemicals and capital goods than it spends on imports. However, in other categories (such as consumer goods, food, beverages, tobacco, and finished manufactured goods), it spends more on imports than it earns from exports. In recent years, the UK has had a deficit in trade in goods.

Trade in services

Services include, for example, travel (tourism), insurance, financial (banking), and computer and information services. The UK performs well in services. Since 1966, it has recorded a surplus every year. However, the surplus is usually smaller than the deficit in trade in goods, giving an overall trade gap.

Investment income

The UK usually has a surplus of investment income. This means that its residents earn more in terms of profits, interest and dividends on their assets held in other countries than foreigners earn on their investments in the UK.

Transfers

This covers transfers of money made and received by the government and individuals, and includes:

- government payments to and from the EU
- foreign aid payments
- money sent to UK families by UK workers abroad
- money sent out of the UK by foreigners working in the UK.

Causes of a current account deficit

A deficit on the current account occurs when the country's expenditure abroad exceeds its revenue from abroad. This situation can arise because the country has spent more on goods or services and/or there has been a net outflow of investment income. In the UK's case the most common reason for the current account to be **in the red** is for there to be a deficit on the trade balance.

- That deficit may arise because the country is importing raw materials. This may be self-correcting, as the raw materials may be converted into finished goods, some of which are exported.

Definition

In the red: being in debt as a result of expenditure exceeding income.

- It may also arise because the purchasers of the country's goods and services are experiencing economic difficulties and are not able to buy as many goods and services. When their economies improve the deficit may disappear.
- In contrast, the domestic economy may be booming and the high demand may suck in more imports, causing goods and services to be diverted from the export to the home market.
- What is more serious is if the deficit is caused by a lack of price or quality competitiveness. In this case, the deficit will not be corrected without steps to improve the performance of the country's firms.

Thinking like an economist

Why might a fall in incomes in the USA have an adverse effect on the UK balance of payments?

Effects of a current account deficit

The effects of a current account deficit will be influenced by its cause, its size and its duration. A small, self-correcting deficit is obviously of less concern than one that is large and that results from poor performance. When a country spends more than it earns, it is enjoying a higher living standard than it can afford. This may have to be financed by borrowing.

Making connections

Consider the effect of a rise in the country's inflation rate on its current account position.

Causes of a current account surplus

A surplus on the current account is experienced when a country's revenue from abroad is greater than its expenditure abroad. It may occur due to the country's revenue from exports exceeding expenditure on imports and/or because it is a net earner of investment income.

Care has to be taken in interpreting a surplus arising from export revenue exceeding import expenditure. This is because it may arise from the strength or weakness of the economy. The country is likely to have a surplus if its products are very internationally competitive. But it may also have a surplus if the country is in a recession. This is because its citizens will not spending their money on home products or imports, and because its firms, finding it difficult to sell at home, may be competing more vigorously in the export market.

Exam hint

In assessing a current account deficit or surplus, remember to consider its causes, sizes and duration.

Effects of a current account surplus

A surplus will mean that more money is entering the country than leaving it and will make a positive contribution to aggregate demand. However, it may also involve a net outflow of goods and services.

Quickies

1 What is meant by investment income?
2 Which section of the current account is most commonly in deficit?

2.8 Aggregate demand

In exploring what determines the level of economic activity in a country and in examining economic problems and issues, economists make frequent use of what is called aggregate demand and aggregate supply analysis. Here we will explore aggregate demand. Section 2.9 looks at aggregate supply.

Aggregate demand is the total demand for a country's goods and services at a given price level. Demand comes from:

- people buying products such as clothing – **consumption** (C)
- firms buying capital goods such as machines – **investment** (I)
- the government buying goods and services such as educational materials – government spending (G)
- foreigners buying the country's goods and services (X) minus domestic demand for foreign goods and services (M) – **net exports** (X–M).

Aggregate demand (AD) is often expressed as: AD = C + I + G + (X–M).

Definitions

Consumption: household spending on goods and services.

Investment: spending on capital goods.

Net exports: the value of exports minus the value of imports.

Consumption

Consumption is the largest component of aggregate demand. The main influence on consumption is income. As income rises, consumption is likely to increase – although the proportion spent usually declines when people become richer because they are able to save a higher proportion of their income.

Other influences on consumption include the age structure of the country, inflation, the rate of interest and expectations about the future. For example, a fall in the rate of interest will encourage some people to spend more. This is because they will gain less from saving, it will be cheaper for them to borrow and they will have more money left to spend when they have made their mortgage payments.

People can either spend or save some of their income. So decisions on savings also affect consumption. Factors likely to increase the amount saved are a rise in income, a higher interest rate, tax incentives and the development of more ways in which people can save.

Investment

This is the component of aggregate demand that fluctuates the most. Again, the main influence is income. When income is increasing, demand for consumer goods and services is also likely to be rising. So firms are likely to want to expand their capacity to meet this higher demand.

Investment is also influenced by expectations with firms investing more when they are optimistic about future consumer demand.

Firms are likely to invest more when profits are high. They will have the finance and incentive to purchase extra capital goods in order to expand capacity. A fall in the rate of interest should stimulate investment. It will reduce the cost of borrowing funds to spend on capital goods and will reduce the opportunity cost of using retained profits for investment purposes. Firms will also be encouraged to buy capital goods if they fall in price and if advances in technology make them more productive than existing ones.

Government spending

The amount a government spends depends on several factors, including:

- views on the extent of market failure, and the ability of state intervention to correct it
- the electorate's demand for health, education and roads
- the level of activity in the economy.

Net exports

Demand for a country's exports, relative to its demand for its imports, is influenced by, for example, the price and quality competitiveness of its goods and services, incomes at home and abroad, marketing and the exchange rate.

The aggregate demand curve

The aggregate demand (AD) curve shows the total quantity demanded at different price levels – see Figure 1. The curve slopes down from left to right because a fall in the price level will:

- make the country's goods and services more price competitive at home and abroad, so net exports will rise
- increase the amount people's wealth can buy; this will encourage them to spend more and so raise consumption (sometimes referred to as the wealth effect)
- cause interest rates to fall; lower interest rates encourage a rise in consumption and investment.

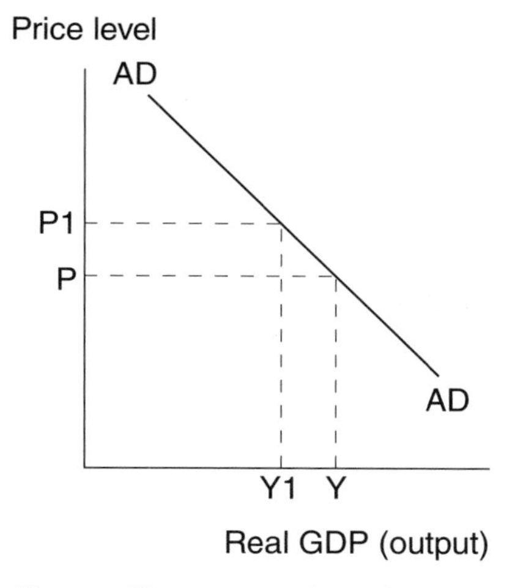

Figure 1: The aggregate demand curve

Shifts in aggregate demand

If the aggregate demand curve shifts to the right it means total demand has increased for some reason other than a change in the price level. A shift to the left represents a decrease in aggregate demand as shown in Figure 2.

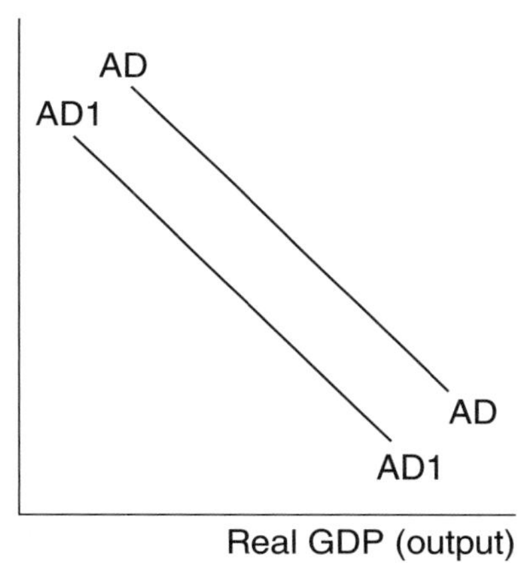

Figure 2: A decrease in aggregate demand

You have already encountered some reasons for components of aggregate demand changing. For example, advances in technology will encourage firms to demand more capital goods. Other causes include changes in the size of the population and in the money supply.

Exam hint

Be very careful with the labelling of AD diagrams. Remember, it is the price level on the vertical axis, real GDP on the horizontal axis and the curve shows aggregate demand. You will not get any marks for micro labels.

Quickie

Explain whether you would expect the following to shift the aggregate demand curve to the left or right.

(a) A fall in income tax. (b) A world recession.

2.9 Aggregate supply

Aggregate supply is the total quantity of goods and services that the country's firms and government concerns produce at a given price level. An aggregate supply (AS) curve shows the quantity of goods and services that would be produced at different price levels. Economists distinguish between:

- **short run aggregate supply**, and
- **long run aggregate supply.**

Short run aggregate supply

Short run aggregate supply is the total quantity that will be supplied at different price levels when the prices of factors of production are assumed not to be changing. Figure 1 shows a short run aggregate supply (SRAS) curve.

Figure 1: The short run aggregate supply curve

This curve slopes up from left to right. There are two ways of looking at this.

- One is to explain why the price level rises when output goes up. The reason is because while the wage rate, for example, is assumed not to be changing, marginal costs may rise with output. This is because to increase output, overtime rates may have to be paid and machinery may have to be worked at a faster rate, leading to more breakdowns.
- The other is to explain why aggregate supply should rise when the price level goes up. If prices do increase while the prices of factors of production remain constant, production becomes more profitable.

Shifts in short run aggregate supply

A movement to the left of the SRAS curve shows a decrease in aggregate supply, whereas a shift to the right shows an increase. Figure 2 illustrates an increase in short run aggregate supply. The main causes of changes in short run aggregate supply are:

- changes in import prices
- changes in the productivity of factors of production
- changes in taxation on firms.

These, of course, all change firms' costs of production.

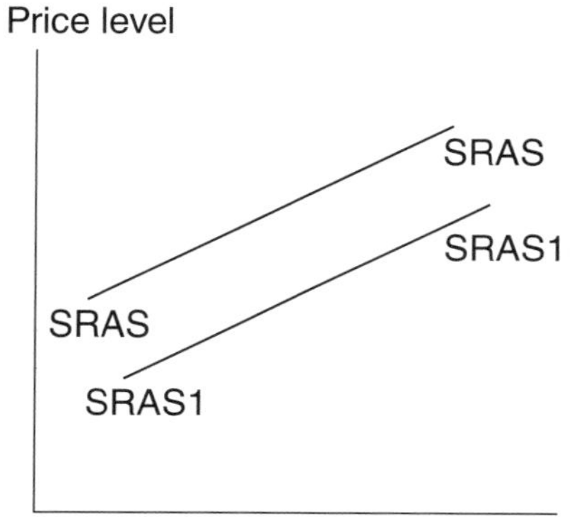

Figure 2: An increase in short run aggregate supply

Long run aggregate supply

In the long run, factor prices can change. Long run aggregate supply is the output that can be produced with the full employment of resources. So the long run aggregate supply (LRAS) curve shows the productive capacity of the economy.

Shifts in long run aggregate supply

An increase in long run aggregate supply is illustrated by a shift to the right of the LRAS curve and a decrease by a shift to the left. A move to the right of the LRAS curve, as shown in Figure 3, shows that the productive potential of the economy has increased. With its resources fully employed, an economy is capable of producing more goods and services. There are two main reasons why LRAS could increase.

- One is an increase in the quantity of resources. For instance, an increase in married women's participation in the labour force will increase the supply of potential workers and net investment will increase the quantity of capital goods available. Changes in benefit levels and tax rates can also affect the quantity of labour and enterprise on offer.
- Another is an increase in the quality of resources. So, for example, advances in technology, improvements in educational achievements, and geographical and occupational mobility will increase the quality of capital and labour and thereby raise their productivity.

Of course, a shift to the left of the LRAS curve represents a decrease in long run aggregate supply and therefore a reduction in productive capacity. This can be caused by either a decrease in the quantity and/or quality of resources. For instance, a country experiencing net emigration may have a decreasing labour force.

Quickies

1. What effect would a rise in the price level have on short run aggregate supply?
2. How would a fall in raw material costs affect the SRAS curve?
3. What does a shift to the right of the LRAS curve illustrate?
4. What effect would improved training have on long run aggregate supply?

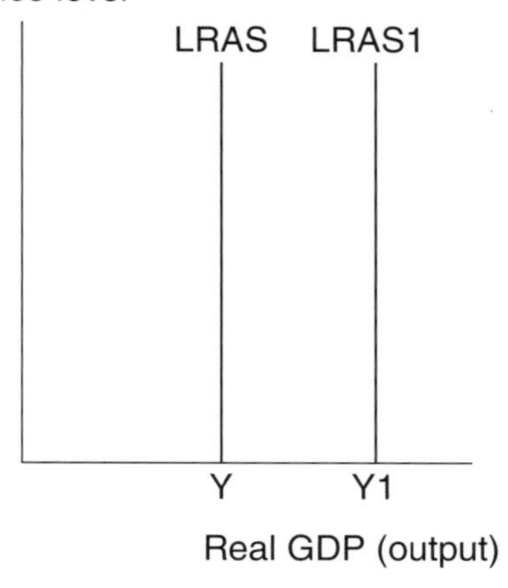

Figure 3: An increase in long run aggregate supply

Thinking like an economist

Raising the retirement age would be politically unpopular but the UK government is thinking of raising it to 70. By considering the effect on LRAS, identify a benefit to society of such a move.

Making connections

Compare the LRAS curve with the production possibility curve. All the factors that would shift a production possibility curve to the right would also shift the LRAS curve to the right.

Exam hint

As with AD diagrams, be very careful with the labelling of AS diagrams – price level on the vertical axis, and real GDP on the horizontal axis.

2.10 Changes in aggregate demand and aggregate supply

Having examined aggregate demand (section 2.8) and aggregate supply (section 2.9), you will now consider how they combine to determine output and the price level, and how changes in aggregate demand and aggregate supply affect the economy.

Definitions

Macroeconomic equilibrium: a situation where aggregate demand equals aggregate supply.

Macroeconomic disequilibrium: a situation where aggregate demand and aggregate supply are not equal.

Equilibrium output and price level

Equilibrium output and price level occur where aggregate demand and aggregate supply are equal (**macroeconomic equilibrium**). In this case, there is no reason for output or the price level to change. However if, for example, aggregate demand is greater than aggregate supply, there will be **macroeconomic disequilibrium.** This situation is likely to lead to an increase in price level and output at least in the short run. In contrast, if aggregate supply exceeds aggregate demand, there will be a tendency for the price level and output to fall.

Economic growth

Aggregate demand and aggregate supply are frequently changing. Over time, the productive capacity (see sections 1.9 and 2.4) of the economy tends to increase. Figure 1 shows the economy experiencing economic growth as the LRAS curve shifts to the right from **LRAS** to **LRAS1** and output increases from **Y** to **Y1**.

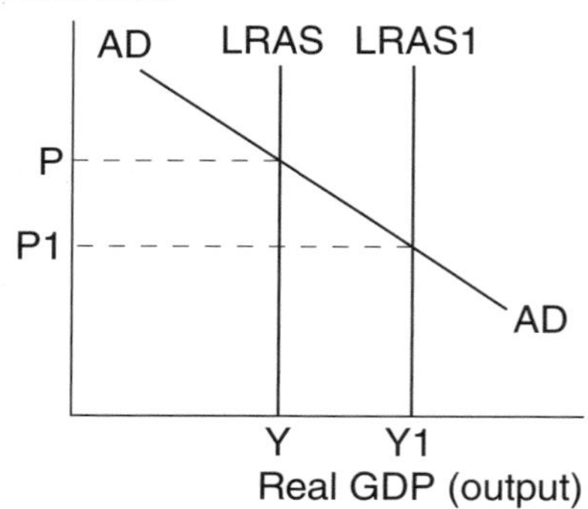

Figure 1: Economic growth

Over time, as well as aggregate supply tending to increase, aggregate demand also tends to increase. Figure 2 shows the growth in long run aggregate supply matching the growth in aggregate demand. When this occurs there tends to be no upward pressure on the price level and so no inflationary pressure.

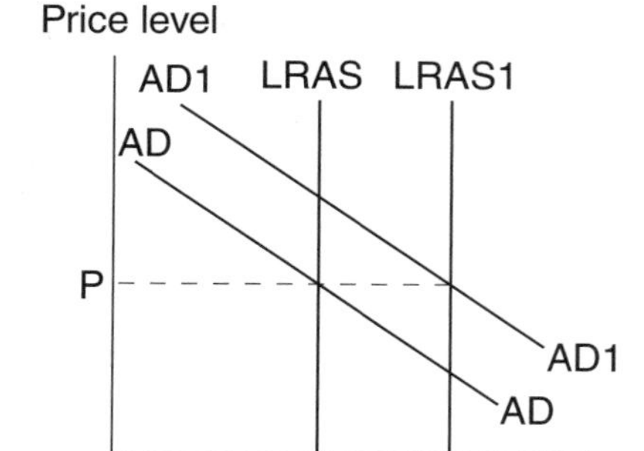

Figure 2: Growth in long run aggregate supply matching the growth in aggregate demand

Inflation

As you will remember from section 2.5, inflation can be either cost-push or demand-pull in nature. Increases in the costs of production will shift the SRAS curve to the left. Figure 3 shows the SRAS curve moving from **SRAS** to **SRAS1**. This causes the price level to rise from **P** to **P1** and may set off a period of inflation.

Higher aggregate demand will move the AD curve to the right. Figure 4 shows demand-pull inflation occurring with the price level being pulled up from **P** to **P1**. In this case, actual output exceeds potential output and there is an output gap, which can be referred to as an inflationary gap. Inflation will also occur if aggregate demand increases more rapidly than the trend rate of growth of output, as shown in Figure 4.

Unemployment

Unemployment can occur if aggregate demand falls below the productive potential output. Figure 5 shows the aggregate demand curve shifting to the left. The reduction in aggregate demand causes output to fall from Y to Y1.

Actual output is now below potential output. There is an output gap, which may be referred to as a recessionary gap. Such a fall in output is likely to result in some workers losing their jobs. Again, if the growth of aggregate demand is less than the underlying trend rate of growth of output, unemployment is likely to rise. There will be insufficient extra demand to make full use of the growth in productive capacity.

The balance of payments

If an economy has a current account deficit, with import expenditure exceeding export revenue, an increase in import expenditure will cause that deficit to grow in size. A larger deficit will, in turn, cause aggregate demand to fall. In the short run, a fall in aggregate demand will cause a fall in output and the price level.

In contrast, a reduction in a current account deficit, or a move from a deficit to a surplus or from a surplus to a larger surplus, will increase aggregate demand.

Investment

Investment is important because it will increase not only aggregate demand in the short run but also probably aggregate supply in the long run. This can enable output and living standards to increase without any significant inflationary pressure.

If the capital goods produced add to the capital stock (net investment), the productive capacity of the economy has obviously been increased. Even if the capital goods produced are being purchased just to replace worn-out and outdated capital goods (replacement investment) the productive capacity may still increase. This is because the new capital goods are likely to embody advances in technology. Today's computer and printing equipment is much more productive than that of ten or even five years ago.

Quickie

Use an aggregate demand and aggregate supply diagram to illustrate the effect of net investment.

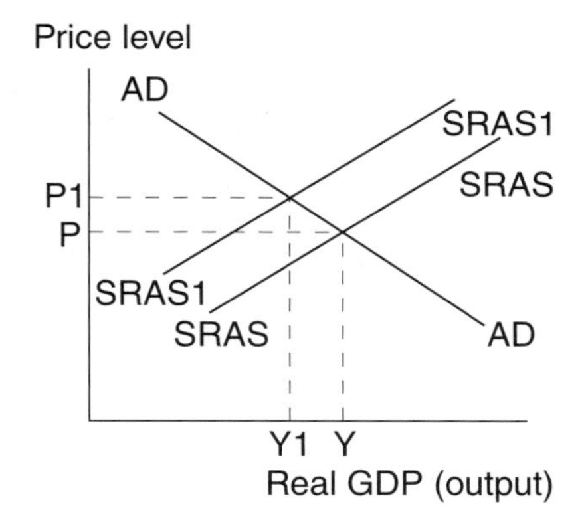

Figure 3: Cost-push inflation

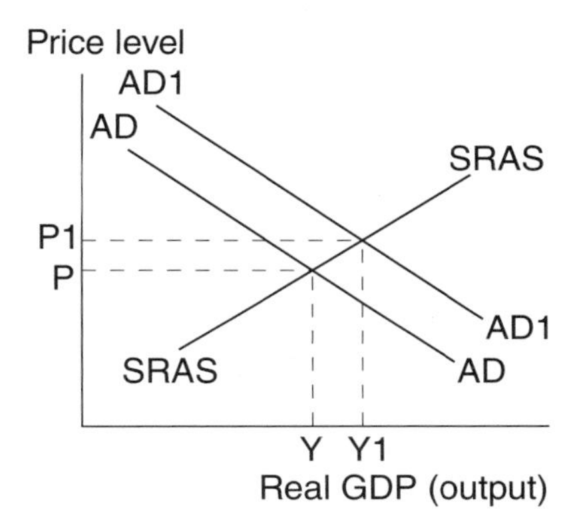

Figure 4: Demand-pull inflation

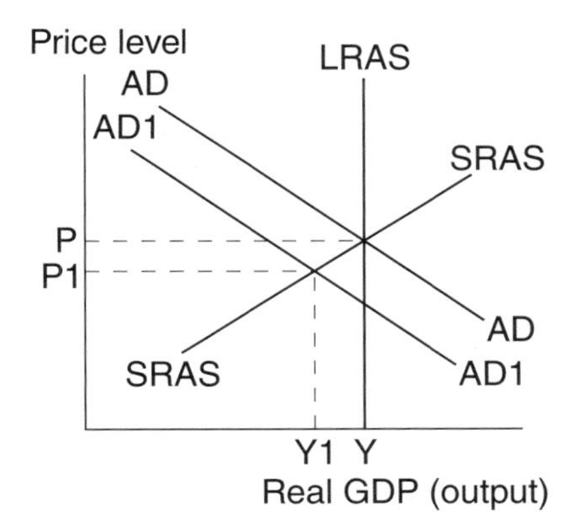

Figure 5: A recessionary gap

Exam hint

When analysing macroeconomic problems and issues, make use of aggregate demand and aggregate supply diagrams. These will help you to work through what will happen to output and the price level and why.

2.11 The multiplier effect

The **circular flow of income** is an economic model that illustrates how the macroeconomy works. As you will see in this section, it can be used to analyse the causes and consequences of changes in economic activity. It can also be used to explain how initial changes in aggregate demand result in greater final changes in aggregate demand.

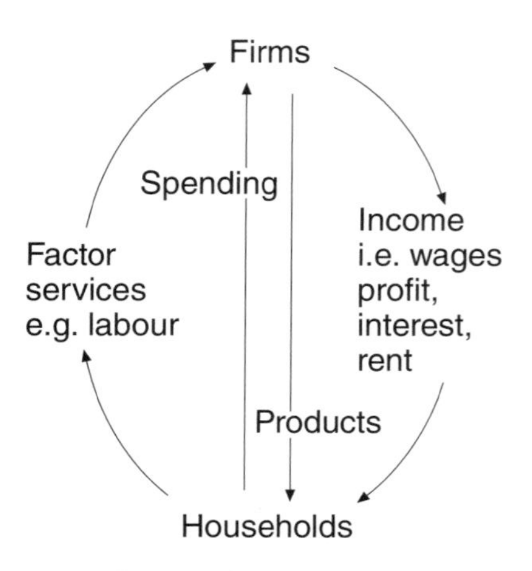

Figure 1: Circular flow of income

Definitions

Leakages: withdrawals from the circular flow.

Injections: additions to the circular flow.

Thinking like an economist

Using an AD and AS diagram, explain what effect an increase in expenditure on imports would have on output, employment and the price level.

The circular flow of income

In the simplified version of the circular flow of income model shown in Figure 1, there are two sectors:

- households, and
- firms.

Between these sectors flow income, spending, products and factor services. Households provide factor services – for example, labour and enterprise. In return, households receive incomes. They use these incomes to buy products produced by firms.

Leakages and injections

In practice, not all income earned is spent and there are additional forms of spending that do not arise from the circular flow. Income that is not spent on domestic output leaks out of the circular flow. There are three **leakages** (which are also known as withdrawals):

- taxation
- savings, and
- spending on imports.

Leakages reduce aggregate demand. In contrast, **injections** increase aggregate demand. Again, there are three:

- investment
- government spending, and
- exports.

These are additional forms of spending arising outside the circular flow of income. When the value of injections equals the value of leakages, output will not be changing and there will be macroeconomic equilibrium.

The multiplier effect

When injections exceed leakages, aggregate demand will increase. This rise will have a greater final effect on the economy, because when households, firms and the government spend money, that expenditure becomes the income of those who sell them the products. They, in turn, will spend some of the money they receive. So there is a knock-on effect with aggregate demand rising by more than the initial amount.

For example, if the government increases the value of pensions, the pensioners are likely to spend more on, say, heating, housing and holidays. Those selling these products will receive more income. Some of this income will be spent and some will leak out of the circular flow. Spending will continue to rise until leakages match the initial injection.

Of course, the **multiplier** effect works in reverse. A rise in income tax, for instance, reduces disposable income (see section 1.5) and therefore reduces consumption. Lower spending causes firms to cut back on production and reduces income. In turn, the lower income reduces aggregate demand further.

Definition

Multiplier: the process by which any change in a component of aggregate demand results in a greater final change in real GDP.

The significance of the multiplier effect

The existence of a multiplier effect means a government has to recognise that any change in its spending or taxation will have a knock-on effect on the economy. So, for instance, if the government wants to raise real GDP by £10 billion and the multiplier has been estimated at two, it would have to raise its spending by £5 billion.

Quickies

1. What are the three possible injections into the circular flow?
2. Why is saving a leakage from the circular flow?
3. In what sense does spending create income?
4. What would it mean if a country has a multiplier of three?

Hot potato

The size of the UK multiplier is thought to be lower than most countries' at 1.33. What is the significance of this?

Puzzler

Why do governments often miscalculate the size of the multiplier?

2.12 Fiscal policy

Fiscal policy is changes in taxation and government spending. It is one of the key economic policies that governments use to influence economic activity and achieve their macroeconomic objectives.

Definition

Fiscal policy: changes in government spending and taxation.

Taxes

Taxes can be categorised in two main ways.

1 **Direct tax** (for example, on the income of people and firms) and **indirect tax** (for example, VAT and excise duty).
2 Progressive tax (which takes a higher percentage from the income of the rich), proportional tax (which takes the same percentage from the income of all income groups) and regressive tax (which takes a greater percentage from the income of the poor).

Government spending

The main items of government spending are:

- social security (including spending on pensions and Jobseeker's Allowance)
- health
- education
- defence.

In recent years there have been a number of pressures on governments to spend more. One significant pressure is the ageing population. With people generally living longer, there is an increasing demand for NHS treatment, pensions and residential care.

The Budget

The Chancellor of the Exchequer outlines government spending in its spending reviews and taxation plans in the annual Budget. A budget deficit arises when government spending exceeds tax revenue, whereas a budget surplus occurs when tax revenue is greater than government spending.

Fiscal policy and aggregate demand

The government can raise aggregate demand by increasing its own spending and/or by reducing taxes. Government spending is a component of aggregate demand. Government spending on, for example, computers in schools will directly increase aggregate demand. This higher spending will also have a multiplier effect causing aggregate demand to rise even higher.

Cuts in income tax will increase people's disposable income (see section 1.5). This will raise consumption and again have a multiplier effect. Rises in government spending and cuts in taxes are referred to as reflationary, loose or expansionary fiscal policy.

Making connections

Consider an appropriate fiscal policy measure that could be used to reduce demand-pull inflation.

In contrast, deflationary, restrictionist or tight fiscal policy involve measures that reduce aggregate demand – that is, cuts in government spending and rises in taxes. Figure 1 illustrates the effect of deflationary fiscal policy.

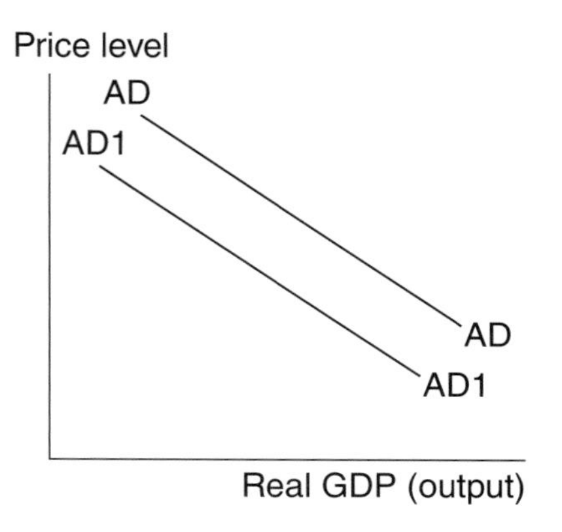

Figure 1: The effect of deflationary fiscal policy

Fiscal policy and the pattern of aggregate demand

Fiscal policy can also change the pattern of aggregate demand. A rise in government spending on pensions, financed by a rise in corporation tax, would be likely to raise consumption and may reduce investment.

Fiscal policy and aggregate supply

Changes in taxes and government spending can also affect aggregate supply. A cut in Jobseeker's Allowance and income tax rates, for instance, will alter economic incentives that in turn may change the supply of labour. Government spending on education and training and investment grants may shift the LRAS curve to the right, as shown in Figure 2, if they succeed in improving the quantity of the labour force and the quality of capital goods.

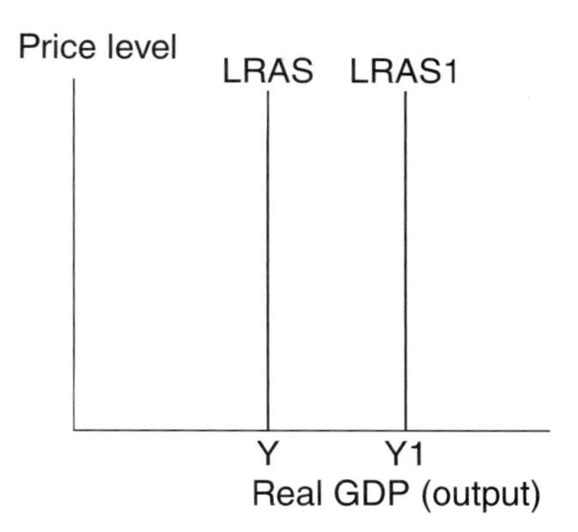

Figure 2: The effect on LRAS of an increase in government spending on training

Effectiveness of fiscal policy

Fiscal policy can be used to influence the performance of individual markets and the economy as a whole. Some forms of government spending and taxation, including cuts in corporation tax and training grants, have the potential to increase both aggregate demand and aggregate supply. A number of taxes and forms of government spending adjust automatically to offset fluctuations in real GDP. For instance, government spending on unemployment benefits rises without any change in policy when real GDP falls.

However, fiscal policy also has several drawbacks. Changes in government spending and tax rates are not often made and they take time to have an effect on the economy. A number of forms of government spending are inflexible. For instance, it is difficult to cut spending on health care and pensions.

It is difficult to estimate the effects that changes in taxation and government spending will have on the economy. A rise in taxation designed to reduce inflation may cut aggregate demand too far and cause a rise in unemployment. On the other hand, it might have little effect on aggregate demand if households and firms do not change their spending and investment plans despite the higher taxes.

Exam hint

In examining the effects of fiscal policy measures, it is useful to illustrate your analysis with AD and AS diagrams.

Quickies

1. What are the two instruments of fiscal policy?
2. Distinguish between a progressive and regressive tax.

2.13 Monetary policy

Monetary policy measures include changes in:
- the money supply
- the rate of interest, and
- the exchange rate.

These measures are used to affect the economy by influencing aggregate demand.

Definition

Monetary policy: government changes in the money supply, the rate of interest and the exchange rate.

Changes in the money supply

An increase in the money supply is likely to increase aggregate demand. If the government prints more money or makes it easier for banks to lend more money, people will have more money to spend. This will increase aggregate demand.

Exam hint

Most questions on monetary policy concentrate on interest rate changes.

Changes in the rate of interest

The main monetary policy measure currently used is changes in the rate of interest. The Monetary Policy Committee (MPC) of the Bank of England sets its interest rate with the objective of keeping inflation close to the government's target level for CPI of 2 per cent.

If the MPC believes that aggregate demand is going to rise above the trend growth rate and therefore cause an increase in the inflation rate, it will raise the rate of interest.

- A higher rate of interest is likely to reduce consumption, investment and possibly net exports.
- A higher rate of interest raises the cost of borrowing and the opportunity cost of using retained profits to finance investment. This higher cost and expectation of lower sales is likely to reduce investment.
- A higher rate of interest may also encourage foreigners to buy the currency so they can place money into the country's financial institutions and earn a high rate of return. Higher demand for the currency would raise its value. When the price of a currency increases, the country's exports rise in price and its imports fall in price. A change in prices of exports and imports may reduce export revenue and increase import expenditure and so lower net exports.

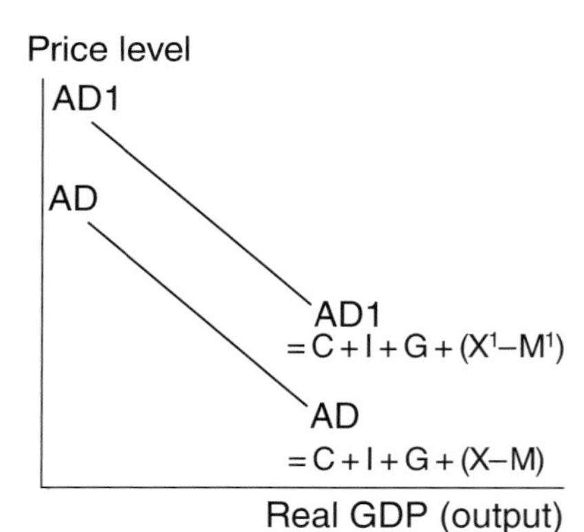

Figure 1: The effect of a reduction in the exchange rate

Changes in the exchange rate

As we already know, a change in the exchange rate affects aggregate demand by altering export and import prices. If a government wants to raise aggregate demand to reduce a deflationary gap, it may try to reduce the exchange rate. This reduction would increase the price competitiveness of the country's products and therefore increase exports and reduce imports as shown in Figure 1. A government's central bank can reduce the value of its currency by lowering its interest rate or selling its currency.

The effectiveness of monetary policy

The main policy measure currently being used to influence short-term economic activity is changes in the rate of interest. This measure offers the opportunity to change it relatively quickly, as the MPC meets every month. Changes not only in interest rate but also in the exchange rate and money supply can have a significant impact on aggregate demand.

However, it can take time for monetary policy measures to influence aggregate demand. For instance, it is estimated to take 18 months before a change in the rate of interest will alter consumption and investment plans.

In the 1970s and 1980s it was difficult to control the money supply – especially as banks have a strong profit motive to increase bank lending. In the early 1990s the government found it difficult to maintain the value of the pound within set margins.

Hot potato

The MPC has been criticised for being too concerned with inflation. When deciding whether to change the rate of interest, some argue that more consideration should be given to the impact on employment and economic growth. What do you think?

Undesirable effects

Monetary policy measures may have undesirable side effects. A rise in the exchange rate, designed to reduce inflationary pressures, may worsen the balance of payments position and increase unemployment. Households and firms may also not react in the way expected. Lowering the rate of interest to stimulate rises in consumption and investment will not work if households and firms are pessimistic about future economic prospects.

The effects of monetary policy also tend to be more concentrated on certain groups than changes in income tax, for example, tend to be. For instance, a rise in the rate of interest will hit firms that export a high proportion of their output more than other firms. This is because they will be affected not only by higher costs but also by a likely fall in demand resulting from a rise in the exchange rate.

In addition, a government's ability to change its interest rate is limited by the need for it to remain in line with other areas and countries' interest rates – most notably the EU's and the USA's – unless it is prepared to experience an inflow or outflow of funds.

Making connections

Compare monetary policy and fiscal policy in terms of how they work and their effectiveness.

Research task

Each month, check on the MPC's decision on the rate of interest – what it has decided to do and why. This decision is usually announced in the middle of the month and good articles usually appear in the broadsheet papers. Also read the minutes of the monthly meetings of MPC on the Bank of England's website. Go to www.heinemann.co.uk/hotlinks to access this site.

Quickies

1. What are the three instruments of monetary policy?
2. What effect is a fall in the rate of interest likely to have on the exchange rate?
3. Identify two limitations of monetary policy.

2.14 Supply-side policies

Supply-side policies seek to increase aggregate supply by raising the efficiency of markets and so increase aggregate supply. The term covers a range of measures, some of which are examined below.

Definition

Supply-side policies: policies designed to increase aggregate supply by raising the efficiency of markets.

Education and training

Improvements in education and training should raise productivity of labour. Output per worker/hour will increase and the productive capacity of the economy will rise. This will shift the long run aggregate supply curve to the right as shown in Figure 1.

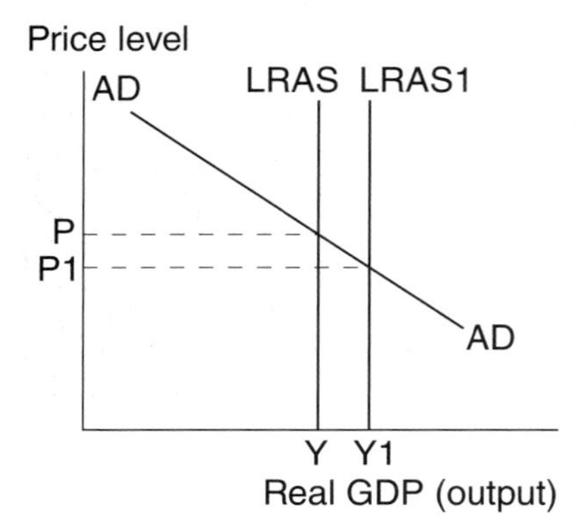

Figure 1: The effect of improvements in education and training

Reduction in direct taxes

As well as increasing aggregate demand, lower direct taxation may also increase aggregate supply. This would be achieved by increasing incentives to firms, workers and potential workers. A cut in corporation tax will increase the funds that firms have available to invest and the return from any investment undertaken. If investment does increase, the productive capacity of the economy will rise.

- Some economists think a cut in income tax might encourage existing workers to work overtime, be more willing to accept promotion and stay in the labour force for longer. In addition, they believe it will persuade more of the unemployed to accept employment at the going wage rate, as their disposable income will rise.
- Others economists argue that lower income tax rates may encourage some workers to take more leisure time, as they can now gain the same disposable income by working fewer hours. They also argued that what stops the unemployed from gaining employment is not a lack of willingness to work at the going wage rate but a lack of jobs.

Reduction in unemployment benefit

- Those economists who believe market failure is a significant problem and favour government intervention do not support a cut in Jobseeker's Allowance. They believe this would reduce aggregate demand, output and employment.
- However, supporters of free market forces argue that lowering Jobseeker's Allowance will, by widening the gap between employment and benefits, force the unemployed to seek work more actively and accept employment at lower wage rates.

Reduction in trades union power

- Those economists who favour the operation of free market forces believe that reductions in **trades union** power will reduce imperfections in the labour market. They say that trades unions reduce employment by pushing wage rates above the equilibrium level and encouraging workers to engage in restrictive practices. They suggest that reducing the power of trades unions will increase labour productivity and reduce the cost of employing labour. As a result, firms will be encouraged to employ more workers and raise output.

- Others argue that trades unions act as a counterbalance to the market imperfection of very powerful employers. They also claim they reduce firms' costs by acting as a channel for communication between employers and workers on issues and because it is cheaper to negotiate with one body than with individual workers.

Privatisation and deregulation

- Supporters of a **free market approach** argue that government intervention in the economy should be reduced. They believe that firms are in the best position to make decisions about what to produce, how to produce and what to charge. This is because they are subject to the discipline of the market. If they do not provide products that consumers want at competitive prices, it is argued, they will go out of business. So these economists favour the removal of rules and regulations on firms (**deregulation**) and the transfer of firms from the public to the private sector (**privatisation**).
- However, some economists (supporters of an **interventionist approach**) argue that rules, regulations and/or government ownership of firms are beneficial in several circumstances where there is a high risk of market failure.

Virgin Rail – an example of privatisation

The effectiveness of supply-side policies

Supply-side policies are now widely used. They have the advantage that they are selective, targeted at particular markets and are designed to raise efficiency.

- Economists agree that if the supply-side performance of the economy can be improved, it will be easier for a government to achieve its objectives. Increasing aggregate supply enables aggregate demand to continue to rise over time without inflationary pressures building up. A higher quality of resources should also make domestic firms more price and quality competitive and so improve the country's balance of payments position.
- But as we already know, there is disagreement about whether a free market or interventionist approach should be adopted with differences of opinion about, for instance, how potential workers respond to cuts in benefits and whether firms operate more efficiently in the public or private sector. Some of the policies also take a relatively long time to have an effect.

Hot potato

What do you think is the best way of encouraging lone parents to enter the labour force?

Quickies

1. Define supply-side policies.
2. Identify two supply-side policies that should increase the quality of resources.
3. Explain what is meant by deregulation.
4. Identify one strength and one limitation of supply-side policies.

2.15 Policies to reduce unemployment

There are many policy measures that a government can use to reduce unemployment. The choice of measures is influenced by the cause of unemployment, the rate and duration of unemployment, and the state of the other key macroeconomic objectives. In the short run, unemployment may be reduced by measures that increase aggregate demand. In the long run, supply-side measures may be more effective.

Short run

In the short run, with an economy operating below its productive capacity, unemployment may be reduced by increases in aggregate demand. In this situation, expansionary fiscal and monetary policy can be used to create jobs. A government, using fiscal policy, could increase its spending and/or cut tax rates to raise aggregate demand.

In practice, a rise in government spending could have more impact on aggregate demand (and therefore unemployment) than tax cuts. This is because some of the rise in disposable income that will result from lower taxes may be saved and some may be spent on imports.

A fall in interest rates and/or an increase in the money supply should stimulate consumption and investment and so raise aggregate demand. It may also raise net exports if it causes a fall in the exchange rate.

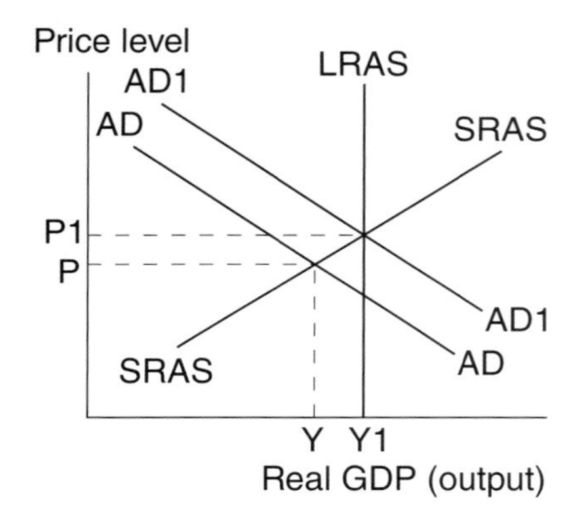

Figure 1: The effect of an increase in AD

Figure 1 shows the effect of a rise in aggregate demand on real GDP. Expansionary fiscal and monetary policies may have undesirable side-effects. One consequence may be a rise in the price level as the economy approaches the full employment level. The higher level of spending may also increase any existing deficit on the current account of the balance of payments.

Long run

In the long run, if there is no shortage of aggregate demand, the cause of unemployment will lie with supply-side problems. Those out of work when aggregate demand is high and there is no shortage of job vacancies are likely to:

- be between jobs
- be lacking the appropriate skills
- be geographically or occupationally immobile
- have family circumstances that restrict their ability to work
- lack the incentive to move off benefits and find employment.

There are several factors that determine such unemployment.

- The time people spend finding a job after they have left another job is influenced by the quantity of information they have about job vacancies.
- Many of the long-term unemployed lack qualifications, have poor communication skills and are geographically immobile.
- Some may have lost the work habit.
- Some may have difficulty affording child-care or overcoming prejudice.
- Some may believe they are better off on benefits.

In these circumstances, it is unlikely that raising aggregate demand will succeed in reducing unemployment. What is needed is an increase in the attractiveness of work to the unemployed and an increase in the attractiveness of the unemployed to employers. Supply-side policies are likely to be more effective in achieving these objectives than demand-side policies.

Supply-side polices

Supply-side policies (see section 2.14) can be implemented to increase economic incentives and the quality of the labour services offered to the unemployed.

Such measures include the provision of information, improved education and training, the provision of work experience, financial support for child care, and a widening gap between the income received from employment and that received in benefits. The latter measure can include, for instance, a reduction in the **marginal tax rate.**

The New Deal

The need to tackle the problems of long-term unemployment and youth unemployment lay behind the introduction of the New Deal by the Labour government in 1998. This scheme provides help and advice to the unemployed in seeking a job during the first four months of unemployment. After this, the unemployed have four options:

- to take the offer of a job subsidised by the government
- to take a place on an educational or training course
- to undertake voluntary work
- to undertake work with an environmental task force.

The intention behind these options is to develop skills, confidence and work experience.

Unemployment and the full employment level

When the unemployment percentage is close to the full employment level, it is increasingly difficult to reduce unemployment further. If, however, policy measures succeed in reducing the time people spend in between jobs and in particular long-term unemployment, the unemployment percentage at the full employment level may be reduced.

Quickies

1. Identify two policy measures a government could implement to increase aggregate demand.
2. Explain two reasons why someone may be unemployed.
3. Identify two supply-side policies that could be used to reduce unemployment.
4. What is the New Deal?

Web link

See the homepage of the Institute of Fiscal Studies by visiting www.heinemann.co.uk/hotlinks and clicking on this section.

Definition

Marginal tax rate: the proportion of extra income that is taken in tax.

Making connections

Discuss the benefits that would be experienced as a result of a fall in unemployment.

Policies to control inflation

If a country is experiencing inflation, the measures it implements will be influenced by what is thought to be causing the inflation. As well as tackling any current inflation, governments also implement measures that they hope will ensure long run price stability.

Short run cost-push

There are several policy measures a government can take to control inflation in the short run. If it believes inflation is caused by excessive increases in wage rates, it may try to restrict wage rises.

It can control wages in the public sector directly by restricting increases in government spending allocated to public sector wage rises. It can also restrict wage rises in both the public and private sectors by introducing an **incomes policy**. For instance, a government may place a limit on wage increases of five per cent or £2000 a year. This measure does seek to reduce inflation without causing unemployment.

In practice, a number of problems arise with the operation of incomes policies – including the fact that employers and employees often find ways round the limit (by, say, changing job titles in order to award higher-than-permitted wage rises). A limit on wage rises also introduces a degree of inflexibility in labour markets, with firms wanting to expand and attract more labour being unable to raise wage rates as much as they would like.

These and other problems have discouraged UK and many other governments using incomes policies in recent decades.

Web link

See the Bank of England's website by visiting www.heinemann.co.uk/hotlinks and clicking on this section.

Short run demand-pull

To reduce demand-pull inflation, a government may adopt deflationary fiscal and/or monetary policy measures. These are ones that seek to reduce inflation by decreasing aggregate demand, or at least the growth of aggregate demand. A government could, for instance, raise income tax. This would reduce people's disposable income and their ability to spend.

The main short run anti-inflationary measure employed in the UK is currently changes in interest rates. Higher interest rates are likely to reduce aggregate demand by reducing consumption, investment and possibly net exports.

Mervyn King, a member of the MPC and Governor of the Bank of England from July 2003

The Monetary Policy Committee

The MPC of the Bank of England sets the rate of interest with the main objective of achieving the government's target rate of inflation of 2 per cent, as measured by the CPI. Subject to meeting that objective, it has been instructed to support the economic policy of the government, including its objectives for employment and economic growth.

Monetary policy stance

A tight (or restrictionist) monetary policy is one that aims to reduce aggregate demand, or at least the growth of aggregate demand, usually in a bid to lower inflation or improve the balance of payments position. In contrast, an expansionary monetary policy approach (loose monetary policy) is one that seeks to stimulate a growth in aggregate demand. So reducing the rate of interest would be regarded as an expansionary approach.

Long run

In the long run, a government is likely to seek to reduce the possibility of inflationary pressure by increasing long run aggregate supply. If the productive capacity of the economy grows in line with aggregate demand, with shifts in the aggregate demand curve being matched by shifts in the LRAS curve, the economy can grow without the price level rising. This will enable people to enjoy more goods and services without the economy experiencing inflationary and balance of payments problems.

As we saw in section 2.14, the policies used to increase long run aggregate supply are supply-side policies. Improvements in education, training, increased incentives and other measures, if successful, should increase the quantity and quality of resources and therefore increase the maximum output the economy is capable of producing.

Supply-side policies are a long run approach to controlling inflationary pressure, as they take time to have their full impact on productive capacity. Nonetheless, there is the advantage that they do not run the risk of the adverse short run side effects on employment and output that deflationary fiscal and monetary policy may pose.

Quickies

1 Identify a government policy measure that could be adopted to reduce cost-push inflation.
2 What is meant by deflationary fiscal policy?
3 What is currently the main short run anti-inflationary measure being used in the UK?
4 Explain a possible disadvantage of deflationary monetary policy.

Making connections

The MPC consists of nine members drawn from employees of the Bank of England, including the Governor of the Bank of England and four economists nominated by the Chancellor of the Exchequer. It meets monthly to review evidence on the performance of the economy and indicators of changes in inflationary pressure. This information includes figures on the current and predicted growth of the money supply, the exchange rate, wage rates, employment, productivity, retail sales and surveys of business and consumer confidence. If the MPC believes that the information points to a risk that inflation will rise above the target it will raise its interest rate.

Thinking like an economist

Explain three reasons which may lead the MPC to believe that the inflation rate will rise in the future.

2.17 Policies to promote economic growth

Here you will examine the policy measures a government may use to increase output in the short run, and long run measures that can be implemented to increase economic growth. You will also examine why governments seek to achieve stable economic growth and the nature of **economic cycles**.

Short run

Increases in output in the short run can occur due to increases in aggregate demand if the economy is initially producing below its productive capacity. During low economic activity, aggregate demand may be stimulated by expansionary fiscal and/or monetary policy. Some measures of fiscal and monetary policies have the advantages that they may increase both aggregate demand and, in the long run, aggregate supply. For instance, a lower rate of interest is likely to stimulate consumption, but also higher investment will raise long run aggregate supply. Increases in some forms of government spending – for example, spending on education – will also shift the long run aggregate supply curve to the right.

Long run

In the long run, increases in output can continue to be achieved only if the productive capacity of the economy increases. This is why changes in long run aggregate supply are so important. So for economic growth to occur, the quality and/or quantity of resources have to increase. Supply-side policies seek to achieve such an outcome. For instance, measures that raise investment will increase long run aggregate supply.

The extent of the increase will depend on the amount of investment, its type and how efficiently it is used. Capital deepening (which involves increasing the amount of capital per worker) will be more effective than capital widening (which occurs when investment increases to keep up with increases in the supply of labour).

Definition

Human capital: education, training and experience that a worker possesses.

To use capital efficiently it is important to have educated and healthy workers. Investment in **human capital** should increase the productive capacity of the economy, but again the extent to which this occurs is influenced by the appropriateness and the quality of the investment. For example, the function of training and one of the functions of education should be to develop the skills needed in the competitive world market. These include not only numeracy and literacy but also communication, interpersonal skills and literacy and computer technology skills.

While increases in the quality and quantity of training and secondary education in a number of countries, including the newly industrialised countries, have received praise, the UK has been criticised for its low levels of training, education standards and staying-on rates. UK employers have been critical of skill levels (particularly communication and interpersonal skills) of the school leavers they employ. They, in turn, have been criticised in several reports for the poor quantity and insufficient training they provide.

Stable growth

In seeking to promote economic growth, most governments aim for stable growth. Their objective is for actual growth to match trend growth and for that trend growth to rise over time.

They try to avoid aggregate demand increasing faster than the trend growth rate permits, since this can result in the economy overheating, with inflation and balance of payments difficulties arising. They also try to stop aggregate demand rising more slowly than the trend growth rate, since this would mean an output gap developing with unemployed resources. So what most governments try to avoid is destabilising fluctuations in economic activity. When it was elected in 1997, the Labour government gave as one of its objectives, the end of 'boom and bust'.

One way the Labour government is seeking to achieve greater economic stability is by creating stability of economic policy. For instance, it:

- has given the Bank of England independence to determine interest rates (subject to its need to meet the government's inflation target)
- sets three-year spending plans for government departments
- has put limits on the level of government debt.

Making connections

Discuss four supply-side policies that could be implemented to promote economic growth.

Effects of economic cycles

Economic cycles (sometimes known as business cycles), describe the tendency for economic activity to fluctuate outside its trend growth rate, moving from a high level of economic activity (boom) to negative economic growth (recession).

Governments seek to dampen these cyclical fluctuations because of the harmful effects they can have on the performance of the economy. Uncertainty that aggregate demand will continue to rise will tend to discourage investment. It may also mean that firms are reluctant to increase employment opportunities. During an upturn, some employers may be reluctant to take on more workers fearing that the increased level of activity will not last, while during a downturn some may hoard labour.

Exam hint

Emphasise the importance of supply-side policies in improving the potential capacity of the economy.

Quickies

1. Identify a fiscal policy measure that can increase both aggregate demand and aggregate supply.
2. Why are supply-side policies so important in promoting economic growth?
3. Why do governments aim for stable economic growth?
4. Distinguish between an economic boom and a recession.

2.18 Policies to improve the balance of payments

There are both short run and long run policy measures that a government can use to improve its balance of payments position. The short run measures tend to concentrate on demand, while the long run measures focus on improving the supply-side performance of the economy.

Short run

In the short run, there are three main policy measures a government can use to raise export revenue and/or reduce import expenditure in the case of a current account deficit:

- reduce the value of the currency (exchange rate adjustment)
- reduce domestic spending (demand management)
- increase import restrictions.

Each measure has the potential to improve the balance of payments position but also has its limitations.

Exchange rate adjustment

Definition

Depreciation: a fall in the value of the currency.

A country may seek to reduce its exchange rate if it believes that its current level is too high and is consequently causing its products to be uncompetitive against rival countries' products. A **depreciation** will cause export prices to fall in terms of foreign countries' currencies and import prices to rise in terms of the domestic currency.

However, to succeed in increasing export revenue and reduce import expenditure it is important that demand for exports and imports is price elastic, and that other countries neither devalue nor increase their import restrictions.

If the fall in the exchange rate increases demand for the country's products, it is likely that employment and output will also rise in the short run. However, by increasing demand for the country's products and raising import prices it may lead to inflationary pressures.

Demand management

To discourage expenditure on imports and to encourage some products to be switched from the home to the export market, a government may adopt deflationary fiscal and monetary policy measures. Domestic spending may be reduced by higher taxation, lower government spending and/or higher interest rates. However, there is the risk that the resulting reduction in spending may cause output to fall and unemployment to rise.

Import restrictions

Definitions

Tariff: a tax on imports.

Quota: a limit on imports.

A country may seek to reduce expenditure on imports by imposing import restrictions including **tariffs** and **quotas**. However, such measures may have inflationary side-effects. For example, imposing tariffs will:

- increase the price of some products bought in the country

- raise the cost of imported raw materials, and
- reduce competitive pressure on domestic firms to keep costs and prices low.

Placing restrictions on imports also runs the risk of provoking retaliation. In addition, membership of a trade bloc such as the EU and of the **World Trade Organisation (WTO)** limits the independent action a country can take on import restrictions.

Long run

If a deficit arises from a lack of quality competitiveness, lower labour productivity or higher inflationary pressure, then reducing the value of the currency, deflationary policy measures and import restrictions will not provide long-term solutions. In this situation, the most appropriate approach would be to implement supply-side policies.

Supply-side policies

To raise international competitiveness, there are several supply-side policies a government may take, including:

- cutting corporation tax to stimulate investment
- cutting income tax to encourage enterprise and effort
- privatising industries if it is thought that firms will operate more efficiently in the private sector
- deregulating markets to promote competition
- promoting education and training to increase productivity and reduce labour costs.

The success of these measures depends on their appropriateness – for example, the type of training provided, and how firms and workers respond to the incentives provided. The measures also can take a relatively long time to have an effect.

Current account surplus

A balance of payments disequilibrium may also arise because of a current account surplus. A government may seek to reduce or remove a surplus in order to avoid inflationary pressures and to raise the amount of imports it can enjoy. To reduce a surplus, a government may seek to raise the value of its currency, introduce reflationary fiscal and monetary policy measures and/or reduce import restrictions.

Quickies

1. Identify two factors that will influence the success of a depreciation in improving the current account position.
2. Explain a disadvantage of imposing import restrictions.

Definition

World Trade Organisation (WTO): an international organisation that promotes free international trade and rules on international trade disputes.

Web link

To see the website for the World Trade Organisation (WTO) go to www.heinemann.co.uk/hotlinks and click on this section.

Making connections

Explain how a government could seek to reduce the value of its currency.

2.19 Activities: the performance of the UK economy and government policy objectives

See sections 2.2 to 2.7.

Activity 1

Answer the following objective test questions.

1 Which of the following is a government macroeconomic objective?
   (a) Balance of payments equilibrium.
   (b) High unemployment.
   (c) Unsustainable economic growth.
   (d) Zero inflation.

2 Which item is included in the RPI measure of inflation but not the RPIX?
   (a) VAT.
   (b) Council tax.
   (c) Foreign holidays.
   (d) Mortgage interest payments.

3 What is the main opportunity cost of unemployment to society?
   (a) Output.
   (b) Higher crime levels.
   (c) Jobseeker's Allowance.
   (d) Health care expenditure.

4 What must occur as a result of inflation?
   (a) Fiscal drag.
   (b) A fall in the value of money.
   (c) A transfer of income from savers to borrowers.
   (d) A reduction in the country's international price competitiveness.

5 The information below shows changes in a country's economy. What happened between 2003 and 2004?

	Money GDP (£ million)	Population (millions)	Index of prices
2003	50,000	20	100
2004	60,000	22	120

   (a) Money income per head remained constant.
   (b) Money income per head fell.
   (c) Real income per head fell.
   (d) Real income per head rose.

6 Which of the following would indicate that an economy is in a recession?
   (a) A fall in the balance of payments deficit on current account over a period of a year.
   (b) A fall in real GDP over a period of six months or more.
   (c) A rise in the rate of inflation over a period of six months or more.
   (d) A rise in the number of unfilled job vacancies over a period of a year.

7 Which of the following would indicate that economic growth is occurring?
(a) An increase in the inflation rate.
(b) A rise in the productive capacity of the economy.
(c) A decrease in the rate of employment.
(d) A move of the production possibility curve to the left.

Activity 2

Year	RPIX
1995	2.9
1996	3.0
1997	2.8
1998	2.6
1999	2.3
2000	2.1
2001	2.1

Table 1: Inflation (RPIX) % changes on a year earlier

Use the data in Table 1 to compare the actual rate of inflation between 1995 and 2001 with the government's 2.5 per cent inflation target.

Activity 3

Compare the UK's and France's changes in output over the period shown. See Figure 1.

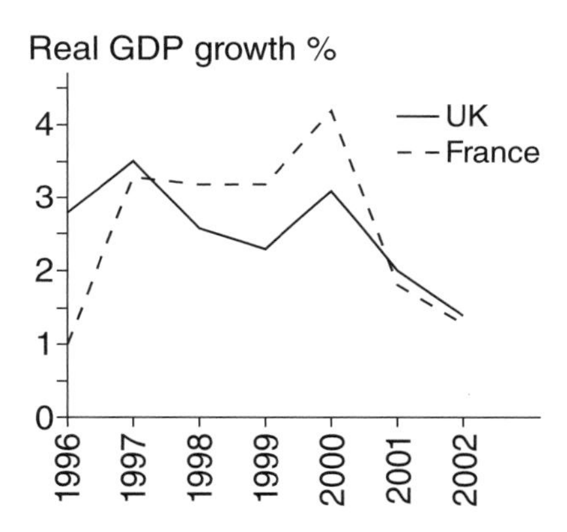

Figure 1: Comparison of UK and French growth rates, 1996–2002

Activity 4

	Exports	Imports
1996	167,196	180,918
1997	171,923	184,265
1998	164,056	185,869
1999	166,198	193,722
2000	188,085	218,108

Table 2: Total trade in goods 1996–2000, £m

1 Calculate the trade in goods balance for each of the years shown.
2 Comment on the trend in the trade in goods balance for the period shown.

2.20 Activities: how the macroeconomy works

See sections 2.8 to 2.11.

Activity 1

Answer the following objective test questions.

1 What would result in a shift to the right of the short run aggregate supply curve?
 (a) A decrease in wage rates.
 (b) A decrease in labour productivity.
 (c) An increase in indirect taxes.
 (d) An increase in income tax.

2 Which of the following would cause an increase in aggregate demand?
 (a) A decrease in net exports.
 (b) A decrease in the rate of income tax.
 (c) An increase in the labour force.
 (d) An increase in the rate of interest.

3 Figure 1 shows the aggregate demand and supply curves for an economy. What could have caused the increase in output from **Y** to **Y1**?
 (a) A decrease in income tax.
 (b) An increase in the exchange rate.
 (c) A decrease in the money supply.
 (d) A fall in consumer optimism.

4 Figure 2 shows the aggregate demand and supply curves for an economy in the short run. Which of the following could have caused the shift in aggregate supply from **SRAS** to **SRAS1**?
 (a) A decrease in wage rates.
 (b) A decrease in the rate of interest.
 (c) An increase in labour productivity.
 (d) An increase in raw material costs.

5 Which of the following must be occurring if an economy is producing on its long run aggregate supply curve?
 (a) The country is experiencing a current account surplus.
 (b) The country is operating at its full capacity level of output.
 (c) The country is experiencing an economic boom.
 (d) The country is encountering rising inflation.

6 What is an economy likely to experience if the rate of growth of aggregate demand is less than the trend rate of growth of output?
 (a) An increase in inflation.
 (b) An increase in unemployment.
 (c) A decrease in productive capacity.
 (d) A decrease in output.

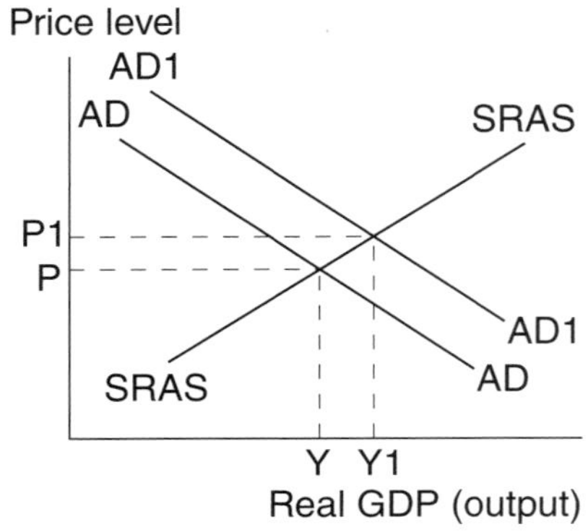

Price level
AD1
AD
SRAS
P1
P
AD1
AD
SRAS
Y Y1
Real GDP (output)

Figure 1: Aggregate demand and supply curves for an economy

Price level
SRAS1
AD
SRAS
P1
P
SRAS1
SRAS
AD
Y1 Y
Real GDP (output)

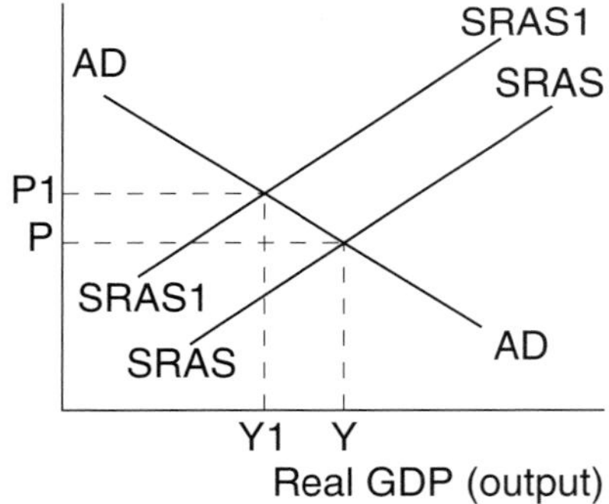

Figure 2: Aggregate demand and supply curves for an economy in the short run

7 What effect would a decrease in aggregate demand have on output and the price level in the short run?

	Output	Price level
(a)	reduce	reduce
(b)	leave unchanged	reduce
(c)	reduce	leave unchanged
(d)	leave unchanged	leave unchanged

Activity 2

A country's consumption is € 200 billion, investment is € 60 billion, government spending is € 80 billion, exports are € 90 billion and imports are € 120 billion. Calculate:

1 net exports, and
2 aggregate demand.

Activity 3

It has been said that increased investment allows an economy to grow without experiencing problems of inflation.

1 What is meant by investment?
2 Explain how increased investment can allow 'an economy to grow without experiencing problems of inflation'.

Activity 4

A country experiences a rise in its general price level.

1 What effect will this have on aggregate demand?
2 Explain one reason why the AD curve is downward sloping.

Activity 5

An economy moves temporarily from a position of equilibrium to disequilibrium as a result of a fall in consumption.

1 What would have been the relationship between aggregate demand and aggregate supply when the economy was in disequilibrium?
2 Explain the forces which would have caused the economy to return to equilibrium.

2.21 Activities: the main instruments of government macroeconomic policy

See sections 2.12 to 2.18.

Activity 1

Answer the following objective test questions.

1 What is the aim of supply-side policies?
  (a) To shift the LRAS curve to the left.
  (b) To increase economic incentives and market efficiency.
  (c) To increase the supply of money.
  (d) To shift the SRAS curve to the left.

2 A government wants to employ fiscal policy to reduce inflation. Which of the following measures is it most likely to implement?
  (a) A reduction in interest rates.
  (b) A reduction in the exchange rate.
  (c) An increase in the size of the budget deficit.
  (d) An increase in tax rates.

3 A country is experiencing a high rate of unemployment. Which of the following measures is likely to increase output both in the short run and long run?
  (a) Increased government spending on training.
  (b) An increase in the exchange rate.
  (c) A reduction in the money supply.
  (d) A reduction in investment subsidies.

4 Which of the following is an expansionary fiscal policy measure?
  (a) An increase in government expenditure.
  (b) An increase in taxation.
  (c) A decrease in interest rates.
  (d) A decrease in the exchange rate.

5 Which of the following could cause unemployment in the short run?
  (a) An increase in government spending.
  (b) An increase in the exchange rate.
  (c) A decrease in taxation.
  (d) A decrease in interest rates.

6 Which of the following is most likely to be effective in reducing a balance of trade surplus?
  (a) A reduction in the value of the currency.
  (b) A reduction in the money supply.
  (c) An increase in government spending.
  (d) A move from a budget deficit to a budget surplus.

7 Which of the following situations could result in inflation?
  (a) A budget surplus.
  (b) An increase in the exchange rate.
  (c) Workers gaining wage rises below the increase in labour productivity.
  (d) The rate of growth of aggregate demand exceeding the trend rate of growth of output.

Activity 2

The rate of inflation, as measured by RPIX, rose to 2.3 per cent in the year to October compared with expectations of an increase to 2.2 per cent. The increase led to discussion among economists about whether the MPC would raise interest rates.

In its inflation report, the Bank of England stated that inflation might overshoot the target rate due to high pay rises, particularly in the public sector. However, it also stated that it might undershoot its target because of a slowdown in global growth and domestic consumption rising more slowly.

1 Explain how:
   (a) a rise in interest rates may reduce inflation
   (b) pay rises might increase inflation.
2 Discuss the possible effects of a rise in UK inflation.

Activity 3

In September 2002, unemployment fell to its lowest level in 27 years, largely as the result of a consumer boom. With a jobless total of 5.2 per cent, unemployment in the UK was among the lowest in the industrialised world.

The fall in unemployment came despite significant job losses in traditional manufacturing and hi-tech sectors. It was the creation of extra jobs in call centres, leisure services and retailing that ensured that unemployment was declining. There was some concern, though, that tight labour market conditions were pushing up wage rates and posing an inflationary threat.

1 Explain:
   (a) how a consumer boom could reduce unemployment
   (b) two other causes of a fall in unemployment.
2 Discuss a policy measure the government could adopt to reduce both inflation and unemployment.

Activity 4

In the third quarter of 2001, US real GDP fell for the first time in eight years and at the fastest rate for a decade. In response, President George W Bush approved an economic stimulus package, which included a rise in government spending. The Federal Reserve, the central bank of the USA, also cut interest rates.

1 Explain what may cause real GDP to fall.
2 Discuss how a rise in government spending and a cut in interest rates may increase:
   (a) real GDP
   (b) economic growth.

2.22 Exam practice

Objective test questions

1 Which of the following would cause a rightward shift in the long run aggregate supply curve?
(a) An increase in consumption.
(b) An increase in imports.
(c) An increase in investment.
(d) An increase in exports.

2 What is a budget surplus?
(a) An excess of export revenue over import expenditure.
(b) An excess of tax revenue over government expenditure.
(c) An excess of aggregate supply over aggregate demand.
(d) An excess of investment over saving.

3 Which of the following would cause a rise in the Retail Price Index (RPI) but not the RPIX?
(a) An increase in the rate of VAT.
(b) An increase in food prices.
(c) An increase in petrol prices.
(d) An increase in mortgage interest rates.

4 Which of the following would be most likely to increase aggregate demand?
(a) An increase in the rate of interest.
(b) An increase in government spending.
(c) An increase in the rate of income tax.
(d) An increase in the exchange rate.

5 What is the most likely effect of an increase in inflation?
(a) A reduction in government revenue.
(b) A reduction in the nominal value of interest paid to savers.
(c) An increase in menu costs.
(d) An increase in the value of money.

6 What are supply-side policies designed to do?
(a) Alter the money supply.
(b) Raise aggregate supply.
(c) Finance government provision of goods and services.
(d) Reduce the supply of labour in order to reduce unemployment.

7 Which of the following are features of a reflationary monetary policy?

	Money supply	Interest rates
(a)	increase	increase
(b)	increase	reduce
(c)	reduce	reduce
(d)	reduce	increase

8 Figure 1 shows a country's production possibility curve. Production is initially at point *y*. What would enable the economy to move to point *z*?
(a) The attainment of full employment.
(b) An increase in the rate of interest.
(c) An improvement in the existing level of technology.

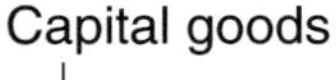

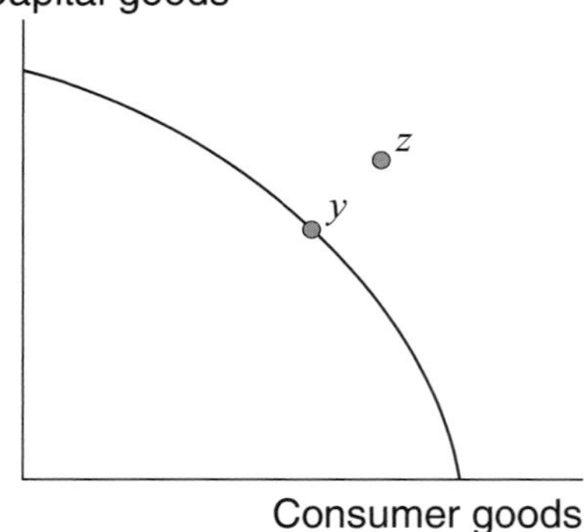

Figure 1: A country's production possibility curve

(d) A reduction in the rate of inflation.

9 An aggregate demand curve slopes down from left to right. This can be partly explained by the effect of a change in the price on
(a) the budget deficit
(b) the rate of interest
(c) the labour force
(d) the productive capacity of the economy?

10 A country experiences an increase in real GDP per head. In what circumstances would such a rise understate the change in a country's standard of living?
(a) There was a rise in the size of the population.
(b) The rate of inflation increased.
(c) There was an increase in negative externalities.
(d) The average number of hours worked declined.

Data response question

Study Table 1 and Extract 1, then answer all the questions that follow.

Year	Economic growth rate (%)
1997	3.2
1998	3.3
1999	2.2
2000	3.1
2001	1.8
2002	1.0

Table 1: Economic growth, 1997–2002

Extract 1

In his pre-Budget speech in November 2002, the Chancellor of the Exchequer revised down his forecast for economic growth in 2002 from 2–2.5 per cent to 1.6 per cent. This followed a pronounced slowdown in the growth of output at the start of the year. Aggregate demand had been growing more slowly with the main driving force being increases in consumption. The Chancellor stated that the output gap has varied in recent years and was actually zero in 1999.

(a) Explain two possible reasons why the economic growth rate may slow down. (4 marks)

(b) Describe the main changes in economic growth rate as shown in Table 1. (6 marks)

(c) Discuss the policies the government should adopt if it wishes to increase the rate of economic growth. (15 marks)

2.23 Exam guidance

Exam hint

Do not rush your answers for the multiple-choice questions. Read the questions and the options carefully. Consider what you think is the correct answer, but also make sure that the other options could not be correct.

Answers to objective test questions

1 Answer (c)
A rightward shift in the LRAS curve represents an increase in productive capacity. Such an increase would be caused by a rise in the quantity or quality of resources. An increase in investment would increase the stock of capital goods and so increase the maximum amount the economy can produce. Answers (a), (b) and (d) would cause a change in aggregate demand and therefore a shift of the AD curve.

2 Answer (b)
A budget surplus arises when a government raises more in tax revenue than it spends. Answer (a) describes a trade surplus, (c) macroeconomic disequilibrium and (d) a situation where an injection exceeds a leakage.

3 Answer (d)
Mortgage interest payments are included in the RPI but omitted from the RPIX. Answers (a), (b) and (c) are included in both inflation measures.

4 Answer (b)
Government spending may increase aggregate demand directly by, for example, increasing demand for school equipment, or indirectly by, for example, raising pensions and therefore allowing pensioners to spend more. Answers (a), (c) and (d) would all be likely to decrease aggregate demand.

5 Answer (c)
An increase in inflation will require firms to alter their prices in, for example, catalogues. Government revenue is likely to rise due to fiscal drag and the nominal rate of interest is likely to rise during inflation, although the real rate is likely to fall and the value of money will fall.

6 Answer (b)
Supply-side policies seek to increase LRAS and so productive capacity. Answer (a) relates to monetary policy and (c) to fiscal policy; (d) would reduce productive capacity.

7 Answer (b)
Reflationary monetary policy seeks to increase aggregate demand. An increase in the money supply and a reduction in the rate of interest would be likely to stimulate a rise in consumption, investment and possibly net exports.

8 Answer (c)
To move to point *z* the economy's productive capacity would have to increase. Answer (c) would enable the economy to produce more goods and services. Answer (a) would cause a movement from inside to on the production possibility curve. Answer (b) may reduce investment and so cause a leftward shift in the production possibility curve.

9 Answer (b)
The rate of interest tends to move in line with the price level. So when the price level falls, the rate of interest also tends to fall – which stimulates investment and consumption.

10 Answer (d)
Real GDP per head does not take into account the number of hours worked. If the average number of hours worked declines while incomes are rising, the quality of people's lives is likely to be improving. Answer (c) would reduce the quality of people's lives and, as externalities are not included in GDP figures, it would mean that real GDP figures would overstate the change in a country's living standards. Answers (a) and (b) are reflected in real GDP per head figures.

Answers to the data response question

(a) You need to consider what can cause economic growth, then relate this to a possible slowdown in the economic growth rate. Important causes may be a slowdown in investment, advances in technology, and/or the size or quality of the labour force. Identify two causes, then explain how each would result in the productive capacity of the economy increasing more slowly.

(b) You need to explain the information in the table, analyse it and draw some conclusions. In this case, you would start by stating that output rose throughout the period shown. Then you could mention that the rate at which it rises varies throughout the period and that output was rising more rapidly at the start than at the end of the period. Finally, you could conclude that in three of the years the economic growth rate exceeds the trend growth rate, for three it is below it, and the average growth rate (2.4 per cent) comes close to the trend growth rate.

(c) Here you should recognise what are appropriate policy measures to increase output and achieve economic growth. You would need to recognise that for output to continue to rise in the future it is necessary for the productive capacity of the economy to increase. You should mention that while measures to increase aggregate demand may raise output in the short run if the economy is operating below full capacity, in the long run to achieve economic growth it is necessary to implement supply-side policies. You also need to explain how supply-side policies may raise LRAS. You should explain and evaluate supply-side policies, discussing the differences between free market and interventionist approaches, and the strengths and limitations of supply-side policies.

Exam hint

The last question part is marked on the basis of levels. To achieve the highest level (Level 5) you need to be able to apply relevant concepts, show good understanding and make use of evidence and analysis to evaluate the issues/arguments identified. (Indeed without evaluation you can only gain a maximum of 7 marks.)

Further reading

2.2

C. Bamford & S. Grant. *The UK Economy in a Global Context*. Heinemann, 2000. Chapter 2.

2.3

C. Bamford & S. Grant. *The UK Economy in a Global Context*. Heinemann, 2000. Chapter 2.

2.4

C. Bamford & S. Grant. *The UK Economy in a Global Context*. Heinemann, 2000. Chapter 7.

S. Grant. *Economic Growth and Business Cycles*. Heinemann, 1999. Chapter 4.

2.5

C. Bamford & S. Grant. *The UK Economy in a Global Context*. Heinemann, 2000. Chapter 6.

M. Russell & D. Heathfield. *Inflation and UK Monetary Policy*, 3rd edition. Heinemann, 1999. Chapters 1–5.

2.6

C. Bamford & S. Grant. *The UK Economy in a Global Context*. Heinemann, 2000. Chapter 6.

G. Hale. *Labour Markets*. Heinemann, 2001. Chapter 5.

D. Smith. *UK Current Economic Policy*, 2nd edition. Heinemann, 1999. Chapter 5.

2.7

C. Bamford & S. Grant. *The UK Economy in a Global Context*. Heinemann, 2000. Chapter 2.

2.8

C. Bamford & S. Grant. *The UK Economy in a Global Context*. Heinemann, 2000. Chapter 1.

2.9

C. Bamford & S. Grant. *The UK Economy in a Global Context*. Heinemann, 2000. Chapter 1.

2.10

C. Bamford & S. Grant. *The UK Economy in a Global Context*. Heinemann, 2000. Chapters 1, 6 & 7.

2.11

C. Bamford & S. Grant. *The UK Economy in a Global Context*. Heinemann, 2000. Chapter 1.

2.12

D. Smith. *UK Current Economic Policy*, 2nd edition. Heinemann, 1999. Chapters 3-4.

2.13

M. Russell & D. Heathfield. *Inflation and UK Monetary Policy*, 3rd edition. Heinemann, 1999. Chapters 6-9.

2.14

C. Bamford & S. Grant. *The UK Economy in a Global Context*. Heinemann, 2000. Chapter 3.
M. Cook & N. Healey. *Supply-side Policies*, 4th edition. Heinemann, 2001. Chapters 3–7.
D. Smith. *UK Current Economic Policy*, 2nd edition. Heinemann, 1999. Chapter 2.

2.15

C. Bamford & S. Grant. *The UK Economy in a Global Context*. Heinemann, 2000. Chapter 3.

2.16

C. Bamford & S. Grant. *The UK Economy in a Global Context*. Heinemann, 2000. Chapter 6.
M. Russell & D. Heathfield. *Inflation and UK Monetary Policy*, 3rd edition. Heinemann, 1999. Chapter 8.
D. Smith. *UK Current Economic Policy*, 2nd edition. Heinemann, 1999. Chapter 4.

2.17

C. Bamford & S. Grant. *The UK Economy in a Global Context*. Heinemann, 2000. Chapter 7.
S. Grant. *Economic Growth and Business Cycles*. Heinemann, 1999. Chapters 2–4.
D. Smith. *UK Current Economic Policy*, 2nd edition. Heinemann, 1999. Chapter 6.

2.18

C. Bamford & S. Grant. *The UK Economy in a Global Context*. Heinemann, 2000. Chapter 4.

PART 3

MARKETS AT WORK

3.1 Markets at work

This is the final part of study for the AS section of your A level examination. You need to have completed modules 1 and 2 before tackling this, but if you have been well organised you will have been aware of the demands of this module from the start of your course. What is required is simple. You need to apply what you have learned about micro- and macroeconomics to one of three markets:

- housing
- the environment
- sport and leisure.

This is illustrated by the spider diagram on page 129.

AQA is very clear in its specification that you don't need to learn new theory to do this module, but it pays to familiarise yourself with the particular characteristics of each market. At the beginning of this book (see pages 14–17), you were advised to choose one of these markets, then build up a file of relevant notes, stories and applications. If you have done this, read through the notes on your chosen market and get plenty of practice answering exam questions. If you have yet to choose your market, do so now. The following might help you to make up your mind.

Housing

Housing is the most popular option and probably the easiest market to find out more about. Estate agents and local councils are very useful sources of information, and there are a number of voluntary organisations like Shelter, which also produce useful facts, figures and opinions. The housing market contains a mix of market provision and government intervention. Some houses are allocated by the price system, while others are meant to be allocated to those in greatest need. As housing is a major budget item for many, changes in the housing market can have an impact on the whole economy.

The environment

Although you are not required to know additional theory, studying the environment as an option means that you need to have a good grasp of the detail associated with negative externalities and how they might be treated. If you are interested in green issues, then choose this market to study.

Again, you'll find it easy to obtain information, especially as issues like global warming are crucial to all of us.

Sport and leisure

In some ways, this is the hardest option because there are so many different markets that encompass sport and leisure. Of course, this area does include, for example, football and music. But it also includes other things like holidays, travel, film, plus a range of different entertainments. This makes it harder to predict questions and can provide traps for the unwary. Being an Arsenal FC fan is not enough to ensure success; you have to know about a whole range of markets.

Content of each section

Part 3 comprises of three main sections:

- Housing (sections 3.2–3.5)
- The environment (sections 3.6–3.9)
- Sport and leisure (sections 3.10–3.13).

Each of these sections has a general overview of the market, plus further information on micro- and macroeconomic aspects. Part 3 concludes with sample questions, exam practice and guidance.

The examination

The examination, known as Unit 3, lasts for one hour. You will have to choose one data response question drawn from each of the three markets listed above. You don't have to choose before you go into the exam room but it is a good idea to have pre-chosen one or, at the most, two of the above areas. If you are leaving your choice to the last moment, read the questions before the data. This will help you to make a quick choice because time in this exam is limited. You need to make sure you have enough time to tackle the higher-scoring questions, which will come at the end of your paper.

The markets at work paper will give you 30 per cent of your marks for AS and 15 per cent of your final total for A level, so it is worth marginally less than the other two parts. It is worth remembering, however, that *all* your marks count. So make sure you do as well as you can in this paper. It will ease the pressure if you choose to complete the A level.

Revision tactics

The best approach, as has been said earlier, is to decide at the beginning of the course which option you are going to choose. Make sure your teacher gives you lots of examples of how economic concepts can be applied to your option, and build up a file of news cuttings, electronically if you wish.

If this is the first time that you have thought about the module 3 then the preceding advice is less useful. If you are risk adverse (jargon for someone who doesn't like taking chances) then choose the Housing option and make sure you know the sections which follow thoroughly. Go and talk to local estate agents, your local district or unitary council and people from charities like Shelter. Ensure that you have a grip on current issues. Go through the contents pages for the first two parts of this book and note which concepts have most relevance to housing.

Don't let this put you off doing The Environment or Sport and leisure options but in both cases remember this is an economics exam – not sport studies, or geography, or about football or even less about rock and roll.

Whichever option you choose, spend the last few weeks before your exam practising past papers. Work through the three revision sections (3.14–3.16) after you have completed module 3 – *Markets at work*.

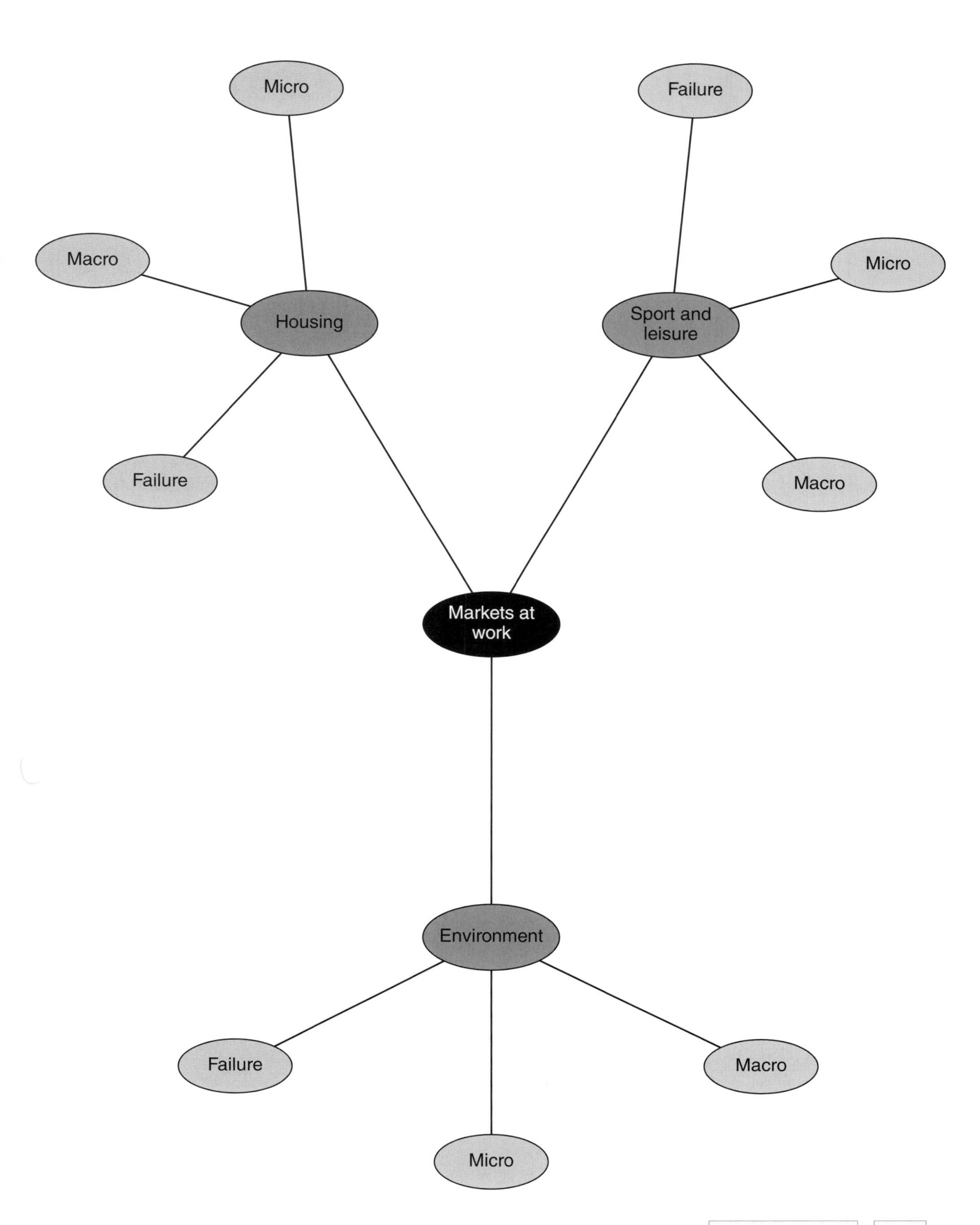
Micro
Failure
Macro
Micro
Housing
Sport and leisure
Failure
Macro
Markets at work
Environment
Failure
Macro
Micro

3.2 Housing: an overview

This section describes the main markets that make up the housing market as a whole. Sections 3.3 to 3.5 show how economic concepts introduced in Parts 1 and 2 can be applied to the housing market. Housing is usually broken down into three interconnected markets:

- owner occupation
- private renting
- **social housing.**

The demand for owner-occupation

This is the most common form of housing ownership in the UK. In 2000, 70 per cent of households in the UK were owner-occupied. For most people, buying a house represents the largest individual item they are likely to purchase in their lifetime. The overwhelming majority of house purchases are financed by **mortgages**, which are a form of long-term lending. Repayment of mortgages is usually monthly, and the main influence on the size of repayments is the interest rate. If the mortgage holder fails to keep up his or her payments, the bank or building society that lent the money can repossess the property, sell it and use the proceeds to repay the outstanding loan.

It should be obvious from the above that many factors affect the demand for owner-occupied houses – not least the interest rate and consumer confidence. It is possible to argue that, *ceteris paribus*, the demand for houses will be greater if prices are low and vice versa. Hence, the demand curve for owner-occupied houses will slope downwards from left to right.

Web link

For up-to-date property news see the Hometrack website by visiting www.heinemann.co.uk/hotlinks and clicking on this section.

The supply of homes for owner-occupation

There are two interconnected subsets of this sector:

- newly built houses, and
- second-hand properties.

The production of new houses for owner-occupation is dominated by nationally known companies such as Bovis, Wimpy and Westbury, which are in business to make profits.

However, the majority of properties coming onto the national housing market are second-hand. They are almost exclusively owned by their current occupiers, whose motivations in deciding whether or not to offer their property for sale are very complicated. Anticipated sale price is a key factor, and recent trends indicate that rising house prices are associated with greater preparedness to sell.

The suppliers of both new and second-hand houses are likely to be more willing to supply houses if prices are relatively high and less willing if prices are low. Hence the supply of housing slopes upwards from left to right.

Thinking like an economist

Estate agents are key players in the housing market. Analyse their activities in terms of helping to make parts of the housing market work.

The price of owner-occupied houses

Although this is a complex market, the price of owner-occupied houses will be determined by interaction of demand and supply, as shown in Figure 1.

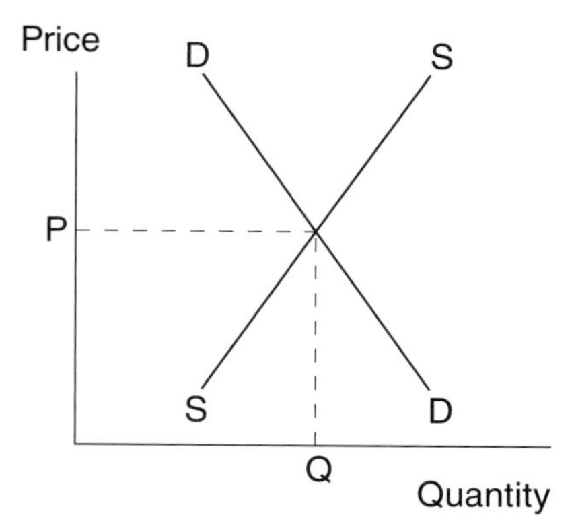

Figure 1: Demand and supply of owner-occupied houses

The private rented sector

In the UK, about 10 per cent of households are part of this sector (which is significantly lower than most other European countries). This sector tends to be one of extremes, consisting at one end of luxurious accommodation and at the other of some of the worst housing in the UK. The demand for the latter comes from those excluded from other housing sectors. For the whole market, the price (rent) will be determined by demand and supply.

Social housing

'Social housing' is the name now given to both local authority-owned and housing-association owned housing. Both sub-sectors are, or have been, government funded and exist to compensate for the failure of the other two markets (owner occupation and private renting) to ensure an adequate supply of affordable housing.

Early examples of social housing, which was provided by various charitable trusts, go back about 100 years. This work was continued by local authorities between the 1920s and the 1980s, which undertook extensive provision of council houses, flats and estates to replace slums and raise living standards for the less well off. Conservative governments in the 1980s encouraged tenants to buy their council houses. Housing associations developed in the 1960s as charitable trusts to modernise and improve old houses as another means of providing decent housing to those in need.

Social housing is not a market in the way that other markets have been described in this book. In most cases, the needs of potential tenants are assessed and points are given according to various criteria – for example, the number of children in a family and the state of existing accommodation. Available housing is then (theoretically) allocated to those in greatest need, and normal demand and supply analysis is not appropriate.

Quickie

What will happen to the price of owner-occupied housing if:

(a) income tax is cut

(b) interest rates are raised

(c) the supply of privately rented properties is cut

(d) land prices increase?

Hot potato

'There is no good reason for the government to intervene in the housing market.' Do you agree with this assertion? Give reasons for your answer.

Exam hint

Remember, for module 3 you can choose to answer questions on one of three markets. Ensure you have a clear strategy before the exam. You can just concentrate in advance on one market, but if you really want to be prepared look at the questions before the stimulus material.

The housing market and microeconomics

A number of microeconomic concepts are especially important in helping you to understand how housing markets work. These include:

- price elasticity of demand and supply
- income elasticity of demand
- externalities
- equity.

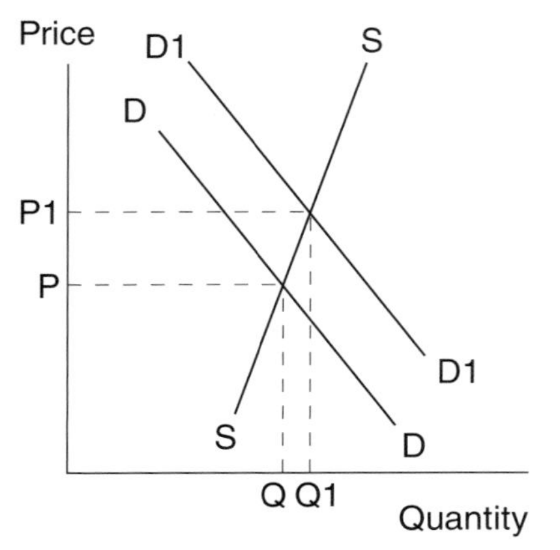

Figure 1: Demand and supply elasticity of the housing market

Price elasticity of demand and supply

All the different measures of demand and supply elasticity can be applied to the housing market, and it is possible to argue that both the price elasticity of demand and the elasticity of supply for housing in general are relatively inelastic. Spending on housing takes up a relatively large share of most people's income. Additionally, there are no real substitutes for housing (see section 1.4), and the supply of housing cannot be easily changed in the short run. This is illustrated in Figure 1.

It follows that any disturbance to this market is likely to have a much greater effect on prices rather then sales. For example, if it becomes easier to get a mortgage, shown by the shift in demand to **D1**, there is likely to be a relatively big jump in the price of houses, shown at **P** to **P1**.

Income elasticity of demand

The demand for particular types of housing in many parts of the country is highly sensitive to changes in income. Mortgage offers are usually worked out as multiples of an individual or couple's income. Typically building societies will lend around 3 times a person's annual income; thus, someone earning £25,000 a year would be able to borrow £75,000. A rise in salary will, therefore, increase their buying power, and moving to a bigger or more luxurious house is seen by many people as being socially desirable, making this kind of housing a superior good. On the other hand, poor-quality housing is likely to be regarded as an inferior good. Indeed, significant numbers of houses in some northern cities in the UK continue to remain empty or can be brought at a very cheap price.

Externalities

The existence of positive externalities associated with good housing and negative externalities associated with poor housing were first identified in the mid-nineteenth century.

- Employers such as the Cadbury family, who cared greatly about the well-being of their workers, provided decent housing for them because they recognised that well-housed workers were more productive. In this way, housing could be seen to be a merit good.
- On the other hand, bad housing was, and is, associated with illness and disease, which imposes negative externalities and additional costs on the rest of society.

For these reasons, the provision of housing by the private sector has been seen to be a source of market failure, giving a rationale for the intervention of local and national governments and the voluntary sector.

The housing market can also be said to fail because there is a fundamental imbalance between demand and supply. There are more households in the UK than there are, in the jargon, housing units. This is becoming an increasing problem as more marriages end in divorce, creating an even greater demand for housing.

Research task

How will you meet your housing needs in ten years time?

Equity

The existence of significant externalities coupled with an imbalance between demand and supply of housing has created significant inequalities within housing markets. In the UK, there has been a long-term under-supply of housing in those areas in which needs are greatest.

- This contributes to the use of bed-and-breakfast accommodation as emergency housing and to the considerable problem of homelessness.
- On the other hand, the well-off can afford to live in large, under-utilised and luxurious accommodation.

Some would argue that the existence of such inequalities is not morally justifiable.

Quickie

Why can housing be described as both a merit and a demerit good?

Puzzler

Why do house prices in the UK tend to be more volatile than the prices of other commodities?

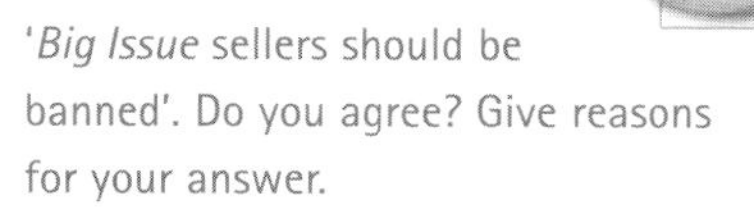

Hot potato

'*Big Issue* sellers should be banned'. Do you agree? Give reasons for your answer.

3.4 Government intervention in the housing market

Some would argue that some housing markets fail. In very crude terms, the supply of housing never seems to keep up with the demand, and some groups of people can't afford what is provided by market forces. Moreover, there are significant external benefits that accrue from the provision of decent housing. Finally, some people would argue that decent housing should be regarded as a merit good. For all these reasons most governments in the world intervene in housing markets. In an effort to save these failing markets, the UK government has used:

- subsidies
- tax relief.
- rent controls

These policies have not always worked and have resulted in government failure.

Subsidies

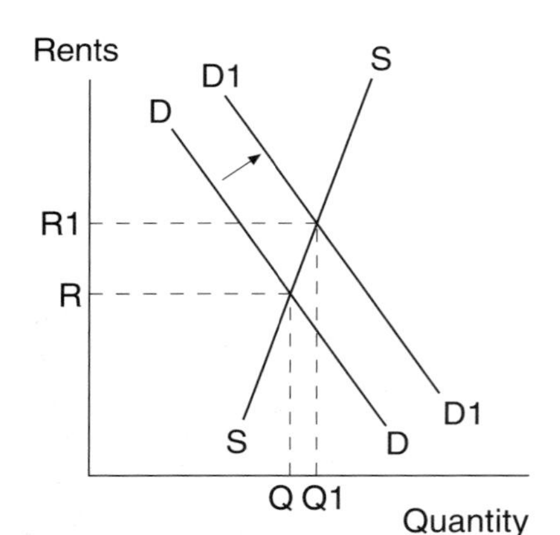

Figure 1: The effect of housing benefits on the rented sector

Poor people tend to have the greatest problems in buying or renting decent quality accommodation and UK governments have used a variety of approaches to make housing more affordable. Currently, two different approaches are used to increase the supply of affordable housing:

- housing benefits
- low-cost government loans.

Housing benefits

These are an additional welfare payment that can be paid to tenants on low incomes in both social housing and that provided by private landlords. The effect of these is to boost low incomes to enable poor people to afford rents, which are market determined. This is analysed in Figure 1, which shows higher rents and an increased supply of housing.

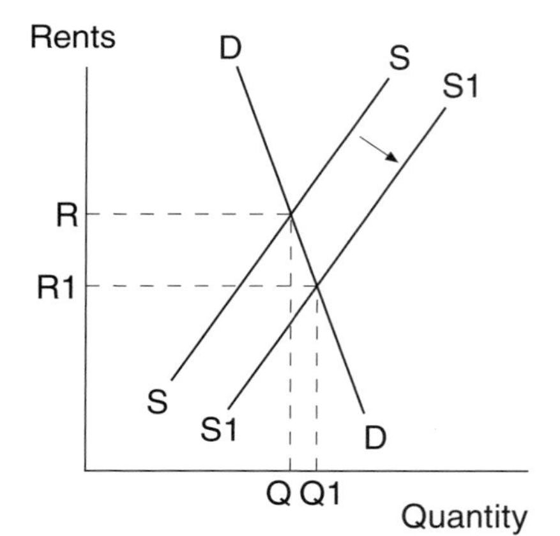

Figure 2: The effect of low-cost loans from government on the supply of housing

Low-cost government loans

The government provides these to housing associations, which are then used to build or renovate houses to an acceptable standard. The theoretical effect is to increase the supply of housing and push down rents, as shown in Figure 2.

Rent controls

The rents of social housing provided by both local councils and housing associations are not directly set by market forces. If this were the case, rents would rise until demand equalled supply and those on low incomes would be left homeless.

Rents are set at what is called an 'economic level'. This means that the total revenue earned is meant to be equal to the total costs of providing such housing. As indicated earlier, some tenants are given additional income to help them pay such rents, and housing associations may be able to borrow funds at discounted rates. The effects of these interventions can be modelled using demand and supply analysis.

Tax relief

In order to encourage people to buy their own homes, until very recently the UK government gave **tax relief** to those using a mortgage to buy their own homes. The effects of this can be analysed in the same way as the effects of housing benefit. In this case, the demand for owner-occupation would have been boosted, but the effect would be to force up prices.

Research task

To find out what housing conditions were like in the 1960s in the UK, watch *Cathy Come Home* (a drama that was originally made for TV). Contact your local Shelter office to find out where you can get a copy.

Government failure

To some extent, all these policies have led to examples of government failure in which the outcomes of intervention have not been as planned and have arguably made things worse.

This is vividly illustrated in the outcomes of the major slum clearance schemes undertaken in the 1950s and 1960s. Local councils were given subsidies to demolish large areas of sub-standard housing in inner cities and replace them with new housing estates, including tower blocks. Some estates were built without facilities like shops, while others were not adequately maintained. Resettling people into the new estates involved great social change, and family and friendship patterns were disrupted. These changes resulted in effects that were never anticipated – for example, vandalism, social isolation and crime. Some of these estates are now being demolished and planners are reverting to more traditional housing designs, which are meant to promote a greater sense of community.

Terraced housing such as this illustrates a shift back to traditional housing designs

In some ways, giving tax relief to help people buy their own homes has been a greater source of government failure. These tax allowances were payable to all income earners irrespective of their income or housing need. Greater amounts were paid in these subsidies than were granted to local authorities to build council houses. The effect was effectively to push up the price of houses and the real beneficiaries were the house sellers, not those for whom the intervention was designed.

Finally, until the 1980s, governments tried to limit the rents payable to private landlords. The effect of this in some areas, especially where housing was in short supply, was to create an unofficial market. One form of this was called 'key money', and in order to rent a flat or even a room, prospective tenants had to pay the landlord or agent large sums of money. Those who refused or fell into rent arrears were often forced out of their homes.

Quickie

The supply of housing tends to be inelastic. Analyse the affect on price and sales of the abolition of tax relief to mortgage holders.

Housing and macroeconomics

Although the housing sector of the economy is made up of several markets that can be most usefully analysed using microeconomics, spending on housing is so significant that changes in housing markets have an impact on the whole economy. Macro aspects of the housing markets include relationships with:

- national income
- inflation
- investment.

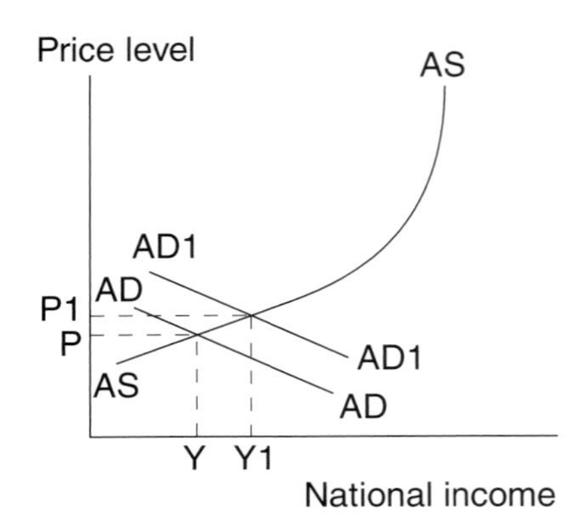

Figure 1: The positive effects of a booming house market

Research task

Undertake a joint research project into housing provision in your area. Assess the extent of each sector of the local housing market. Analyse how each market works in order to equate demand and supply. Judge each market in terms of productive efficiency, allocative efficiency, externalities, equity and government intervention. What recommendations would you make to improve housing provision in your area? What would be the implications of these recommendations? What conclusions can you make?

National income

Spending on housing is often the largest individual item of expenditure for many UK households. Any change in spending on housing is likely to have an effect on consumption – which could be positive or negative.

Positive effects

If there is an increase in demand for housing, *ceteris paribus* there will be an increase in consumption. If consumption increases, aggregate demand will shift upwards to the right. This will have an effect on national income (real GDP) and/or the price level. If there are unemployed resources available in the economy, national income will rise and we will all become better off.

Changes in the housing market are also thought to be a significant influence on consumer confidence and spending on other goods or services. Thus, if house prices are rising, home owners feel better off, find it easier to borrow money and are more likely to demand other goods. The positive effects of a booming housing market are illustrated in Figure 1.

Negative effects

The housing factor described above can also work in the opposite direction. There was a massive housing boom in the late 1980s and house price rises outstripped increases in the prices of other goods. Rapid increases in interest rates in 1989 led to a collapse in the housing market and house prices fell. Over 1 million households ended up with '**negative equity**' – that is, they owed more on their mortgages than their houses were actually worth. This had a dramatic negative effect on consumer confidence. Householders were reluctant to borrow, and consumer spending took a long time to recover. Gradually, increasing house prices have removed most people from the negative equity trap.

Inflation

An increase in demand for housing could also, depending on the availability of unused resources, lead to significant increases in inflation. For this reason the Monetary Policy Committee of the Bank of England takes a close interest in the performance of housing markets in making judgements about desirable levels of interest rates. The possible link between a booming housing market and the price level is illustrated in Figure 2, where increasing activity in the housing market might lead to an increase in aggregate demand. If resources are not available to meet that demand, prices will rise from P to P1 representing a significant acceleration in inflation.

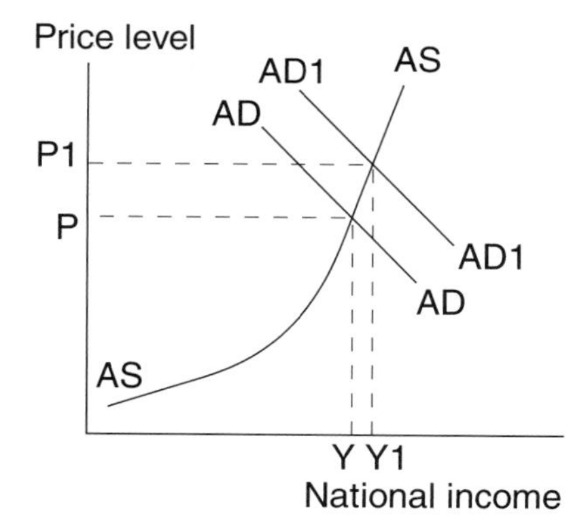

Figure 2: Possible links between a booming housing market and the price level

Investment

Investment is another key macro concept that refers to increases in the capital stock. Home ownership in the UK is given a greater priority than in other countries. Many other Europeans are more content to rent housing than is the case in the UK.

It follows that we tend to invest more in home ownership and some economists have argued that this results in lower levels of economic growth in the UK. Investment in plant and machinery can have the effect of increasing the productive capacity of the whole economy, leading to the possibility of long-term increases in national income and living standards. Less direct benefits follow from investment in the housing stock; there is not such a direct link between improving the housing stock and rising economic growth. This possibility can be modelled using production possibility curves as shown in Figure 3. Point ***b*** on the production possibility curve is more likely to lead to an outward shift than point *a*.

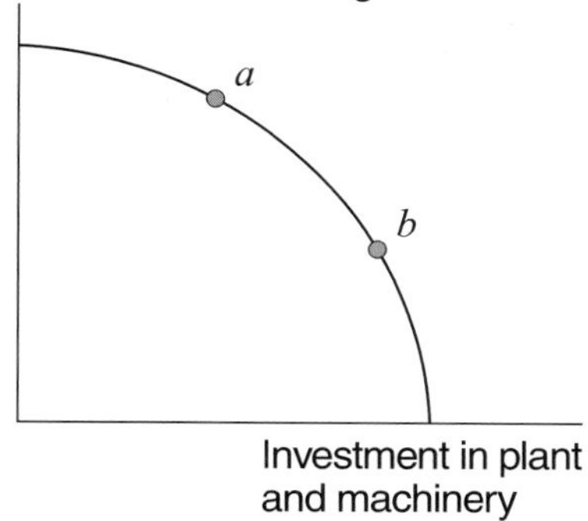

Figure 3: Production possibility curve

Quickie

Use the AD/AS model to explore the impact of a collapse of the housing market on:

(a) national income
(b) inflation.

Exam hint

Make sure you don't get confused between AD/AS diagrams and those involving supply and demand in micro markets. This is a very common error at AS and it tells the examiner straight away that you have not revised thoroughly.

3.6 The environment: an overview

This section describes the impact of environmental issues on the economic problem, and applies the concept of negative externalities to environmental issues. Sections 3.6 to 3.9 show how economic concepts introduced in Parts 1 and 2 can be applied to the environment market.

The economic problem revisited

You should remember this – threes into two won't go! The demand for the world's resources exceeds their supply. Hence societies have to find ways of sorting out who gets what, which resources are used to produce which goods and services, and how these things are produced. We tend to rely on markets to answer these complicated questions. However, you will be aware that markets don't always work in the way that they were intended to or in the best interests of a society. Environmental economics takes this analysis forward by distinguishing between **renewable** and **non-renewable resources.**

- Fossil fuels such as oil and coal take millions of years to be formed. As far as we are concerned, once they are used up they cannot be replaced – that is, they are non-renewable.
- On the other hand, resources like timber and other agricultural products can continue to be produced (albeit some more easily than others) – therefore they are renewable.

The more we rely on using up non-renewable sources, the greater the threat to the survival of the planet as we know it. Alternatively, if we can find ways of making better and more extensive use of renewable sources, the more optimistic the outlook for our future and that of our children.

The economic/environmentalist debate

There is a major debate as to whether or not market systems can take account of these global dimensions to the economic problem.

- Economists who believe in the free market argue that concerns about global survival are misplaced. They reason that if a non-renewable resource is in short supply, its price will rise, rationing its use and encouraging the development of alternatives, possibly renewable.
- However, some environmentalists say that these arguments are naive, and that if left to the market non-renewables will be consumed more quickly than the development of alternatives consumed.

This debate continues and finding out more about environment economics will at least help you to understand the complexity of the issues involved.

Research task

Consider any local economic activity and assess its environmental impact. Is it sustainable? Are there positive or negative externalities? Are there global implications? Does the price paid for the product or service reflect its full environmental costs?

Negative externalities

As you will see in section 3.9, traditional economic analysis tends to mirror economic behaviour in that commodities such as air, water and even the land itself were regarded as free goods. As our understanding has developed, we now recognise that nothing is free. The world is full of examples that show the limits of such short-term thinking – rivers, lakes and seas that can no longer sustain life because they have been used to cool, wash and clean without thought for the consequences. Sections 1.19 and 1.22 on negative externalities and market failure, provide a means of trying to analyse these unplanned third-party effects of economic activity. You need to revise your knowledge of these, and the following should provide a start.

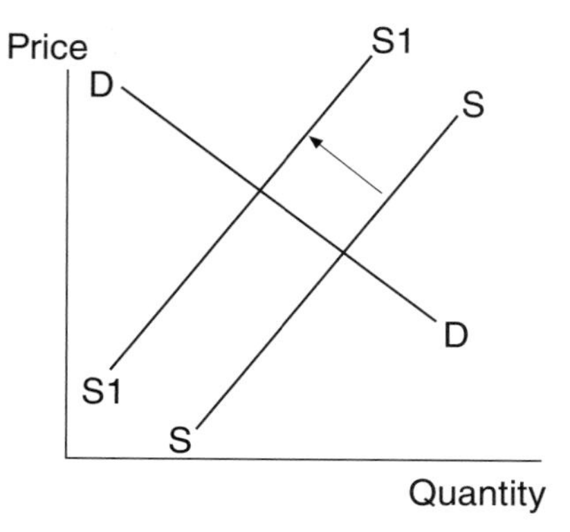

Figure 1: The costs of safely disposing of used nuclear fuels

We now know that the original producers of nuclear power for electricity generation underestimated the costs of safely disposing used nuclear fuels. This is illustrated in Figure 1, in which **D** represents the demand for nuclear-generated electricity. **S** illustrates the supply of this form of energy without full account of disposal costs. **S1** is meant to represent the full social costs of producing electricity in this way. Clearly, the price that does not incorporate the possible negative externalities is much lower than would be the case if producers were fully responsible for all their costs.

The realisation in the 1980s that nuclear-generated electricity had been effectively underpriced had a significant effect on the industry. From being one of the cheapest sources of electricity, the nuclear industry became one of the most expensive. The costs of disposing of spent radioactive fuel had been underestimated, and British Nuclear Fuels, the privatised company responsible for the generation of nuclear electric power, only survives to this day because of large government subsidies.

Exam hint

Don't forget, for module 3 you can choose between answering questions on housing, the environment, or sport and leisure. Make sure you have a clear strategy before you go into the exam room. If you decide to concentrate on the environment, don't worry with the other two. If you want to hedge your bets, look at the questions before you look at the stimulus material – whatever your approach stay cool and focused.

Finally ...

One of the challenges to economists when dealing with environmental issues is to devise ways of fully accounting for the impact of economic activity on the environment. Does the price paid by consumers for equatorial hardwoods accurately reflect the possible long-term costs that may arise from erosion, the destruction of species and possible climate change? Similarly, does the price paid by motorists include the long-term costs of global warming?

Hot potato

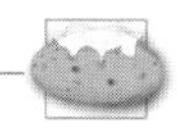

Do you agree that capitalism will save the planet?

3.7 Government intervention

The association of significant negative externalities and other aspects of market failure linked to environmental economics has provided governments with a rationale for market intervention. The analysis in section 1.22 is useful in helping to assess the likely effectiveness of different policies designed to correct possible market failures. As you might remember, there are three main approaches for governments to consider:

- the price mechanism
- direct controls
- tradable permits.

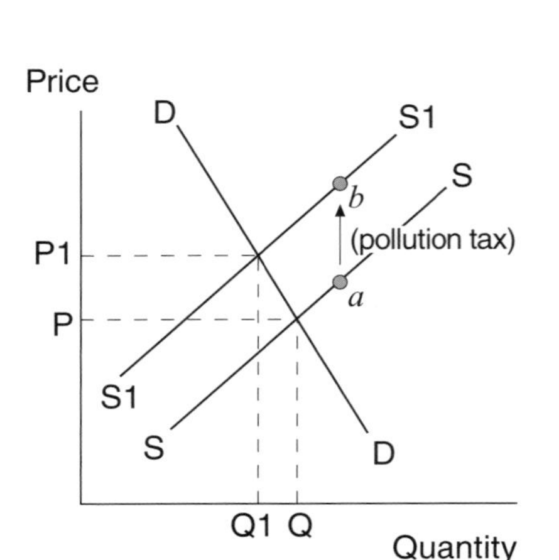

Figure 1: Taxing away negative externalities

Price mechanism

This approach can be illustrated diagrammatically as shown in Figure 1.

If a government is able to calculate accurately the external costs attributed to a polluting company, it could introduce a tax equal to the vertical distance ***ab***. This would force consumers of this product to pay a price that represented the full costs to society of its production. Output would be reduced to **Q1** and the government would actually use the price mechanism to cure market failure.

This approach is very attractive, as it is based on the premise that the polluter should be made to pay for the costs of the negative externalities that have been generated. In theory, tying additional taxes to the external costs gives the greatest incentive to bad polluters to clean up their business, while companies who do not pollute would escape the additional taxation.

However, successful introduction of pollution taxes will depend on the ability and competence of a government to calculate the extent of negative externality. Then it is faced with the challenge of ensuring the tax is paid. There is clear scope for government failure, especially if the pollution tax is not set at an appropriate level. Alternatively, firms enjoying market power may choose to pass on the additional costs to consumers, who, if faced with no substitutes, would effectively pay the tax, leaving production and pollution close to its original levels.

Direct controls

Because of the problems of setting and collecting pollution taxes, governments may prefer to use direct controls. Thus, in the UK emissions of potentially dangerous chemicals are controlled by various regulations.

Advertising by the tobacco industry is limited and car safety is promoted by annual car tests. There are literally thousands of regulations designed to ensure that businesses do not create negative externalities.

The effectiveness of direct controls is sometimes hard to assess. Some are readily accepted – for example, the statutory obligation for firms to take out public liability insurance. But others, such as regulations covering driving hours and breaks for truck drivers, are sometimes ignored. The main problem is that direct controls have to be policed and, if broken, courts are expected to impose sanctions or fines. Sometimes the latter are set too low, limiting the possible effectives of this approach.

Tradable permits

The US approach to economics and pollution has inspired a different market-based approach in the UK, which involves the government giving or selling permits to polluters to emit a certain amount of waste. These permits can then be bought and sold. If a company chooses to cut pollution by more than the limit set by the government, it could sell the unused part of its permit to a company that is having problems meeting the government targets. In this way, the company producing the lower emissions would gain and the heavier polluter would be forced to pay. By setting an overall limit to how much pollution is allowed, governments could reduce this negative externality, but it would be left to market forces to determine where emissions would be reduced.

In the USA, market-based solutions have been developed further, whereby the government's Environmental Protection Agency auctioned air pollution permits that put a price of between US$122 and US$450 on the right to release 1 tonne of sulphur dioxide into the environment. A special futures market has been developed in which pollution permits can be brought and sold.

The possible limitation to the effectiveness of these policies is similar to those that apply to the imposition of pollution taxes and to direct controls. Governments have to get things right. They need to set pollution limits at appropriate levels, with the net effect of trade in permits being reduced emissions. If levels are too low, there might be problems of evasion. If they are too high, there is unlikely to be much effect on emissions of pollution. The trading of permits can mean that the state of that specialised market can lead to other factors influencing demand and supply and price of permits rather than that level which will have the most favourable environmental impact.

Research task

Find out about and evaluate Professor Coase's contribution to dealing with negative externalities. A search on the Internet might be a good place to start.

Hot potato

Do you agree with the contention that markets can be used to deal with pollution problems?

3.8 Environmental issues and macroeconomics

There are important links between macroeconomics and environmental issues – including:

- conflicts with macroeconomic policy objectives
- changing how we measure national income
- inter-government co-operation.

Conflicts with macroeconomic policy objectives

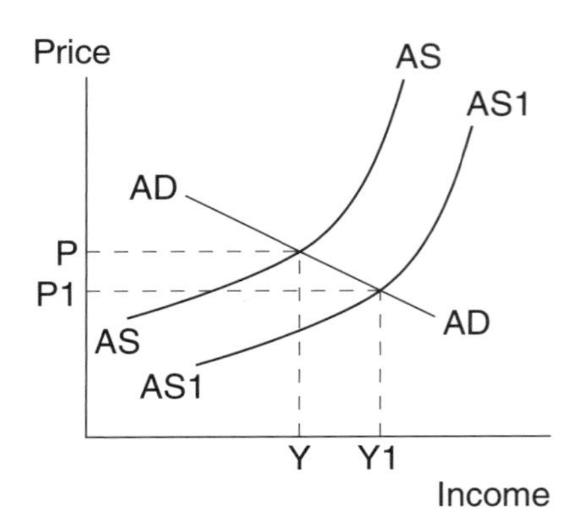

Figure 1: Expanding the productive capacity of an economy

In traditional economic theory, economic growth is seen as very desirable. As you can see in Figure 1, expanding the productive capacity of an economy shifts the aggregate supply curve to the right. The effect of this is to both increase national income as shown by the increase from **Y** to **Y1**, and reduce inflationary pressures as shown in the possible reduction in the price level from **P** to **P1**. Thus, it is possible to combine increasing the standard of living and reducing inflationary pressures.

However, some economists have long argued that economic growth should not be uncritically regarded as a good thing. If growth is associated with large-scale negative externalities caused by the **depletion** of non-renewable resources, economic growth may be undesirable. Moreover, resource **degradation** arising from the treatment of air, water and other natural resources as free goods, is another possible negative aspect of economic growth.

Growth and sustainability

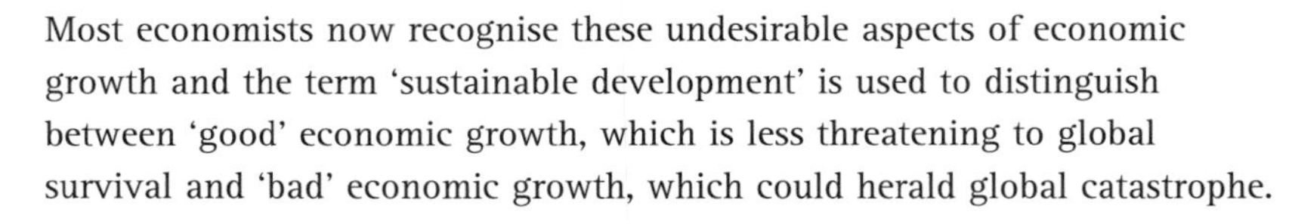

Most economists now recognise these undesirable aspects of economic growth and the term 'sustainable development' is used to distinguish between 'good' economic growth, which is less threatening to global survival and 'bad' economic growth, which could herald global catastrophe.

Definitions

Don't get depletion and degradation mixed up.

- **Depletion** refers to the using up of non-renewable resources.
- **Degradation** relates to the effects of pollution spoiling the quality of all available resources.

However, this tension between growth and sustainability is very common. The USA has refused to sign up to the **Kyoto Agreement**, which limits the emission of greenhouse gases, because its government argues that these limitations will result in lower economic growth and higher unemployment in the USA. For poorer countries, sacrificing economic growth for environmental concerns can mean the difference between life and death for those struggling to survive.

Making connections

What are the macroeconomic implications of limiting economic growth?

Changing how we measure national income

The traditional, and still commonly used, measure of macroeconomic performance, real gross domestic product (GDP), aggregates the money values of all final goods and services produced in the domestic economy during a year and excludes valuation of most environmental goods.

Traditional economics has made analysis of the environmental impact of economic activity even harder, as depleting a stock of natural resources (for example, oil, minerals and forests) increases GDP, since it results in increased output. One response to the failure of traditional methods of measuring economic growth has been to adjust GDP to account for the depletion of natural resources – 'green GDP'. Thus economists have recalculated Indonesia's growth rate to include the consumption of natural capital. Allowing for the degradation of resources, such as timber, lowers the growth rate from seven per cent to four per cent.

Similar changes have been suggested to change the way that we measure our standard of living to include the net balance of externalities. GDP is the usual measure that is used, as once allowances are made for price levels, this gives an indication of the value of the goods and services we are able to consume. More complex measures try to take account of 'quality of life' factors, which are very difficult to quantify.

Exam hint

Beware – some of you will get quite worked up about environmental issues. Whether you are pro or anti, try not to let your views get in the way of showing your understanding of economic concepts and your ability to make reasoned judgements.

Inter-government co-operation

Environmental issues are not limited by political boundaries and the emergence of world rather than national markets has increased the pressure on the world's resources. This makes finding solutions even harder, as international co-operation is required if possible solutions are to be given the chance to work. Increased air travel and the growth of global tourism have made the world a smaller, but also more fragile, place in terms of sustainability.

Pollution knows no boundaries and there are many examples of negative externalities being created in one country affecting others. It has been argued in northern Europe for many years that sulphur emissions from UK power stations have been carried by prevailing winds to create acid rain in Scandinavia and Germany, in turn destroying large areas of woodland as well as poisoning lakes and rivers. Similarly, competition for dwindling fish stocks in the North Sea has resulted in threats to the survival of several species such as cod.

Strategies to try to deal with these situations require international (inter-governmental) co-operation. This is often very difficult, as national interests have to be subordinated to those in the best needs of everyone.

Hot potato

'International tourism should be severely restricted.' Do you agree? Give reasons for your answer.

Quickie

How might the pursuit of greener economic policies conflict with:

(a) inflation targets

(b) the balance of payments

(c) employment?

3.9 Other environmental considerations

Environmental economics is newly emerging as an important area of study and research. It began to develop in the 1960s. Prior to this, economists tended to ignore the environmental effects of economic activity. Resources like air and water tended to be regarded as free goods. Notions of non-renewable resources were ill-developed. Environmental economics attempts to compensate for the shortcomings of traditional approaches, some of which are included in this section.

Research task

Find out all you can about the effectiveness of London Council's attempts to limit private vehicle access to Central London and thereby reduce congestion and pollution. The Internet might be a good place to begin your research.

Cost benefit analysis

One of the challenges to economists when dealing with environmental issues is to devise ways of fully accounting for the impact of economic activity on the environment. Does the price paid by consumers for equatorial hardwoods accurately reflect the possible long-term costs that may arise from erosion, the destruction of species and possible climate change? Similarly, does the price paid by motorists include the long-term costs of global warming?

One method that has been used for many years in an attempt to place a monetary value on the environmental effects of any economic activity is **cost benefit analysis**. This involves distinguishing between the private costs of, say, building a road (that is, buying land, and paying for raw materials and labour costs), and the external costs such as additional noise and air pollution. Added together, these represent the full social cost of building a road, and this is set against the full social benefit that might follow the building of that road. Although it is hard to place a value on some environmental impacts such as particular plants or animals that may be faced with extinction, cost benefit analysis provides a means by which both environmental costs and benefits can be assessed.

Microeconomic tools of analysis

Another way of accounting for environmental considerations is by adapting a simple input/output model to take account of the production of waste. This in turn is subdivided into that which can be absorbed by the environment, that which causes damage and that which can be recycled. This is illustrated in Figure 1.

Extraction
Basic processing
Consumption of product
Non-product outputs
Recycling
Waste
Assimilated by environment
Damage to environment
* Use of primary material and energy inputs

Figure 1: Input and output analysis applied to environmental degradation

Input and output analysis applied to environmental degradation

Not all economists agree with approaches that attempt to account for the environmental effect of economic activity. Some economists have argued that devoting resources to environmental regulations distorts the market system and diverts inputs from the production of output to other goals, such as reducing emissions. Since environmental benefits are not measured in GDP, diverting resources leads to a fall in GDP and economic growth, as traditionally measured, slows. Some US economists have estimated that environmental regulations have caused a 2.6 per cent to 6 per cent reduction in US GDP.

Ken Livingston introduced the London Congestion Charge in 2003, against much opposition to the scheme

Consumer responses

Perhaps the most interesting aspect of environmental economics is trying to gauge how consumers are likely to respond to concerns about issues such as global warming, species loss and possible policy conflicts with other goals of economic policy. These issues are especially relevant in trying to develop strategies to deal with some of the harmful by-products of expanding car ownership.

Most people now accept that we would all be better off if the use of public transport were increased and that of private cars reduced. However, there have been violent reactions to government efforts to raise fuel duty to discourage private motorists, and attempts to limit the access of cars to city centres have not been well received. Such has been consumer resistance that the UK government appears reluctant to try more radical approaches to dealing with the negative externalities that are linked to private motoring.

Exam hint

It may sound simple, but make sure you can use demand and supply diagrams to analyse the possible effects of government use of pollution taxes to limit negative externalities. Make sure you think about the elasticity of demand for the good or service in question.

Summary

Environmental economics is one of the fastest growing research areas, especially as other scientists produce gloomy forecasts of future pollution levels, ozone depletion and global warming. The existence of such issues provides a challenge to economists and their traditional ways of working. The inter-disciplinary nature of approaches to trying to deal with ensuring the planet survives provides another challenge to compartmentalising thinking and analysis between particular disciplines. Nonetheless, economists are likely to have an increasing role to play in devising strategies that promote sustainable development.

Quickie

How might the government use taxation, controls or tradable permits to limit private car use?

Hot potato

'We would all be far better off if we invested more in deriving fuels from agricultural products than from reliance on fossil fuels.' Do you agree with this statement? Give reasons for your answer.

3.10 Sport and leisure: an overview

The economics of sport and leisure is a developing area of applied economic study. It includes holidays and travel, film, TV, the theatre and other forms of entertainment. Over the last decade this has been one of the fastest growing sectors of the economy. This market differs from the two that you have just studied in that it is hard to define where the leisure market begins and ends.

Defining leisure itself is relatively easy. Some economists suggest it is any time when we are not in paid employment. In other words, sleeping, eating, watching TV and so on can all be defined as leisure. For this reason you need to make sure you can apply demand and supply analysis to a range of different markets. Applying earlier theory involves consideration of the four variables thought to have the most impact on demand:

- price
- price of other goods
- incomes
- tastes.

Price

The demand for sport and leisure activities is partly a function of price. Many sport and leisure activities are provided by competitive markets in which supplies seek to gain the best possible return in relation to other objectives. Thus, price becomes an important factor affecting the demand for a whole range of sport and leisure goods.

However, it is important to note that a whole range of sport and leisure services are consumed in what we would not normally describe as markets. The desire or otherwise to walk, play netball or go sailing may be partly influenced by the price of the required materials or equipment, but price alone is probably not that important. Sport and leisure industries embrace a whole range of activities for which non-monetary incentives, such as personal fitness or devotion to a particular team or band, are important.

One consequence of this is that normal economic measures such as the amount of consumer spending probably do not apply. However, a whole range of businesses depend on the growth and development of these non-monetary sectors and efficient planning of production means that assessments have to be made as to whether or not, say, walking, train-spotting or painting and decorating are growing or contracting markets.

Price of other goods

Some sport and leisure markets, such as that for sportswear or fast food, appear to be highly competitive; special offers and emphasis on price in marketing and promotion probably indicate that customers are price sensitive. But not all sports and leisure goods and services are regarded as close substitutes. Even though there may be little to distinguish one football or rugby club from another, spectator sports and the entertainment business are notorious for the extent to which individual fans develop brand locality. This is exploited by major football clubs and music promoters who currently charge around £25 to see a match or a gig – far more than is charged for other forms of entertainment lasting around 90 minutes.

The existence of a wide range of complementary goods is another characteristic of most sports and leisure markets. Those people who are considered fans of particular activities can appear almost oblivious to the price of various add-ons. Replica football shirts are a good example.

Nike is an example of a strong sporting brand. Are there any close substitutes to Nike?

Incomes

The sport and leisure industry as a whole is increasing in significance as a sector in the economy because for most people it is a normal good, and for many a superior good. Although it is a major generalisation and simplification of customer behaviour, those on low incomes are more likely to spend larger proportions of their income on housing and food, while expenditure on these tends to decline relative to increases in income. For example, 50 years ago foreign holidays were the preserve of the very rich. Similarly, the suppliers of fitness centres, restaurants, home improvements and so on try to tap into the fact that there can be a highly positive income elasticity of demand for such services.

This aspect of the demand for leisure and sport is magnified because, as incomes rise, people are able to work less. This creates the time and space to be involved in leisure and sport.

Hot potato

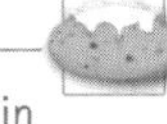

Can the mobile phone market in the UK continue to grow?

Tastes

Another feature of these markets is that they are growing and developing in response to the development of more varied and diverse consumer tastes. Food, travel, music and the arts have all become far more differentiated. This is partly a function of rising incomes over time but it can also be explained in sociological terms as individuals seek to use and display their growing wealth in ever more diverse ways. These changes pose particular problems for companies who rely on mass marketing to create demand for their products. However, those chasing profits and expansion are able, at least, to create the illusion of greater customer choice by creating ranges of options and building in obsolescence to stock products like cars, mobile phones and clothing.

Research task

Find out how your parents and grandparents listened to music.

3.11 The supply of sport and leisure services

This section deals with some special supply conditions that may apply to sport and leisure – including:

- price fixed short run supply
- price barriers to entry
- price monopoly power.

Fixed short run supply

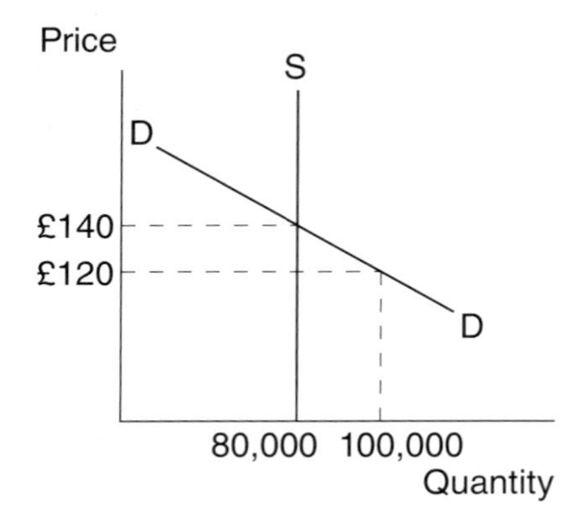

Figure 1: Setting a price for tickets to Glastonbury Festival

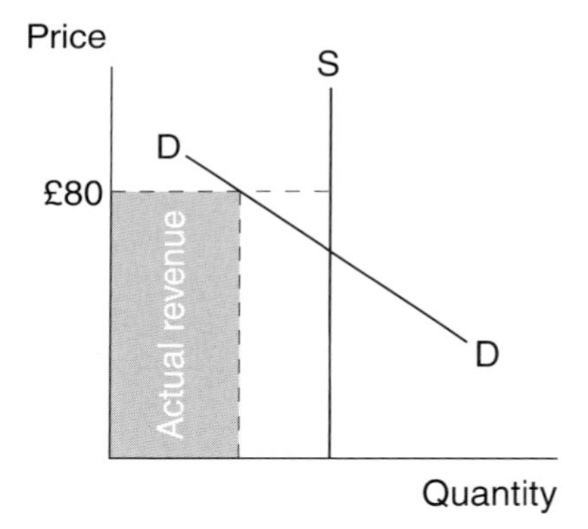

Figure 2: What would happen if prices of tickets to Glastonbury were set about the equilibrium

The supply of sports and leisure services is often totally inelastic in the short run. This has particular implications when it comes to pricing decisions. For example, the capacity of sporting and entertainment venues is almost always limited. Thus, in recent years the relevant local authorities have limited sales to the Glastonbury Festival to 80,000 tickets. Prices have been set at about £120. This is illustrated in Figure 1.

Could the organisers have set a higher price? In 2003 tickets sold out on the first day they went on sale, which indicated that the demand could have been something like D. In this case it would have been possible for the organisers to set a price around £140 a ticket. According to the diagram, 20,000 more fans wanted to go. The effect of setting a price below the market clearing equilibrium resulted in both an unofficial market in tickets, which were being sold for up to £250 each, and doubtless ingenious attempts to gain entry without paying.

On the other hand, if the price were set above the equilibrium the promoters would find that their sales revenue would be drastically reduced. This is illustrated in Figure 2.

The Glastonbury example highlights a common feature of many sport and leisure related industries. Short run supply is very often totally inelastic. Hotels have a fixed number of beds. Stadiums have a fixed number of seats, as do planes and trains. Within such fixed capacities, the marginal or extra cost of attracting another punter or passenger is often close to zero.

This means that suppliers are often very inventive in creating pricing structures that aim to maximise the use of capacity for the particular service. Thus, it is usually cheaper to book hotel rooms at weekends because business users are fewer. Companies such as EasyJet have been tremendously successful, because they use very flexible pricing structures to ensure that their planes run at or near to capacity.

Barriers to entry

Sport and leisure consist of many linked and inter-related markets. Competition and barriers to entry vary widely. It is relatively easy to form a band, for example, but the next stages in building a career get progressively harder.

- The supply of bands usually exceeds the availability of suitable venues, which means that promoters can get away with paying virtually no money to newly formed bands.
- Getting airtime or signing a recording contract is even further down the line, making the barriers to entry to the big time really hard to get through.

But if you do make it, much of the competition drops away and in some cases power shifts from the record label to the artist. For example, Robbie Williams recently extracted a £20 million (plus) contract from the record label EMI on the premise that he will help them break back into the lucrative US market.

The difference between Robbie and all the wannabe bands is illustrated in Figure 3, where **S1** represents the virtually elastic supply of new bands and **S** the special characteristics that make Robbie (to enough people) unique. Add a special Robbie demand curve **D**, compared to **D1** for lesser-known bands, to Figure 3 and you have an explanation for his world-breaking record deal.

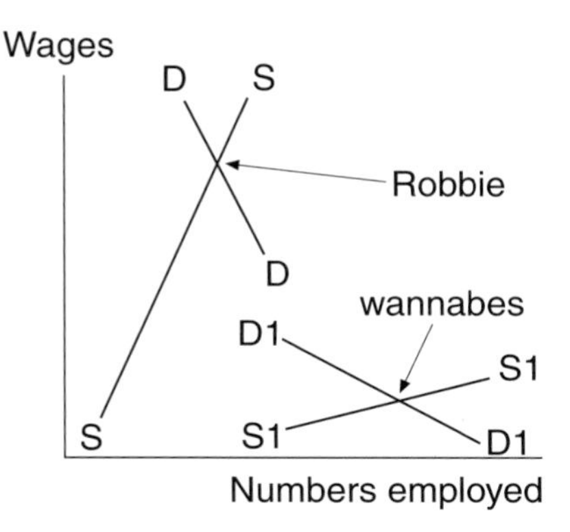

Figure 3: The difference between Robbie Williams and the wannabes

Monopoly power

The name of the game in sport, as with many business areas, is to create a monopoly. Success in sport can involve the creation of immense economic power. There is a special relationship involving the uniqueness of successful entertainers or sporting teams, and once this has been established, monopoly power can ensure that enormous revenues can be earned. The building of Manchester United as a brand is an example of how what was seen not long ago as a rich man's hobby – running and supporting a football club – has been transformed into multi-million pound business. They are able to charge high prices to see games, negotiate lucrative TV contracts, and sell club mechanise at inflated prices.

Hot potato

'Manchester United will be the death of league football.' Do you agree? Give reasons for your answer.

Quickie

Use demand and supply analysis to investigate the impact of the Internet on CD sales.

3.12 Market failure and government intervention

Most governments actively intervene in some sport and leisure markets, and this is at least partly a response to market failure in four possible forms:

- limiting monopoly power
- trying to compensate for negative externalities
- the provision of public goods
- providing merit goods.

These interventions can result in government failure.

Monopoly power

Monopolists potentially force up prices, restrict competition and limit consumer choice. As we know, sporting and leisure sectors of the economy contain highly individual talents, and in some ways these become natural monopolies. Individual bands, clubs, orchestras and theatre companies are effectively monopolies, but the UK government appears to prefer to rely on self-regulation of the bodies and trusts like the Football Association and The National Opera in order to protect the public interest. Although these organisations are large multi-million pound businesses, their aims often include a wider range of social objectives than would be the case with more commercial organisations. This complicates issues associated with the regulation of monopoly power.

In the UK, the government has used the Competition Commission to regulate, or at least keep an eye on, the operation of those parts of the sport and leisure industries that are more obviously run for clear commercial objectives. Thus, the government has taken a keen interest in the acquisition of monopoly positions within the media industry – for example, the dominance of Rupert Murdoch's News Corporation of satellite TV provision.

Similar attention is paid to the activities of other media owners and such diverse activities as the motorsport industry. In some cases, it can be argued that some of these monopoly interests have more power than the government. For example, the UK government appeared to back off from forcing the owners of Formula 1 motorsport to find forms of sponsorship other than from the tobacco industry.

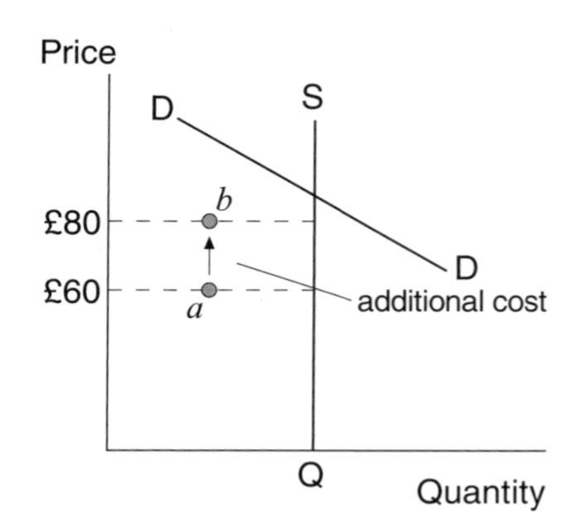

Figure 1: Internalising negative externalities at Glastonbury Festival

Negative externalities

Sport and leisure activities can attract significant numbers of participants and spectators, and large concentrations of people almost inevitably cause negative externalities. Festivals such as Glastonbury are a good example, especially in terms of policing and disturbance to those living near to the festival site.

Various approaches are used to try to internalise these negative externalities. The festival organisers are required to meet some of the additional policing costs and are required to employ specialist security teams. The additional costs are passed on to festival-goers in terms of higher ticket prices. The effect of this is modelled in Figure 1, in which the vertical distance ***ab*** represents the additional policing and security costs actually passed on to the punters. As long as demand for £80 tickets exceeds Q, all the additional costs will be paid by the festival-goers.

Public goods

The countryside, which often provides the backdrop to a wide range of leisure and sporting activities, is used by economists as a classic example of a public good. It is hard to determine who should pay for the upkeep of areas of outstanding national beauty, hard to exclude beneficiaries and in general terms it can be argued that the consumption of national beauty by one person does not preclude the same by another. Many living in such beautiful areas of the country would like to find a way of charging tourists for the privilege of enjoying the countryside, but this has yet to happen.

Merit goods

Governments have been deeply involved in subsidising and directly providing some types of sport and leisure goods because of the perceived social benefits that would be lost if markets were left to provide sport and leisure facilities. The most powerful arguments are those that depend on the link between active participation in sports and leisure and improvements in health. Fitter, stronger, healthier individuals are less likely to be a burden to the state in terms of, say, health care and more likely to be productive in the workplace. It might also be argued that national sporting success can raise public confidence, thereby contributing to higher levels of productivity.

For these reasons, the government spends around £2 billion a year in direct support of sport in the UK, uses lottery proceeds to support arts and sport, and works through local authorities to ensure that sport and art are provided through education and community programmes.

Hot potato

Is the opera a merit good?

Exam hint

Leisure and recreation facilities are often provided by the government because it is both a merit and a public good. Merit goods are judged by society for some reason to be desirable, while public goods are those for which it is difficult to directly charge the user.

Summary

Does all this work? Not always. UK governments tend to use subsidies for capital expenditure, and many sporting and creative arts activities run into difficulties creating enough revenue to cover running costs. Failures of this type can result in the waste of resources. Similarly, political interference can result in additional costs, as has been shown by the confusion surrounding a replacement for Wembley Stadium. All of these are good examples of government failure.

Quickie

Use demand and supply analysis to explain why public provision of leisure facilities is almost always cheaper than private provision.

3.13 Macroeconomic factors

There are a number of macroeconomic applications that are particularly relevant to the leisure and tourism industries – including:

- impact on inflation and employment
- the balance of payments
- economic regeneration and development.

Impact on inflation and employment

Spending on sport and leisure tends to increase as national income increases and it can be both a cause and effect of increasing national income. The impact of any increase in customer spending can be assessed using aggregate demand and aggregate supply analysis.

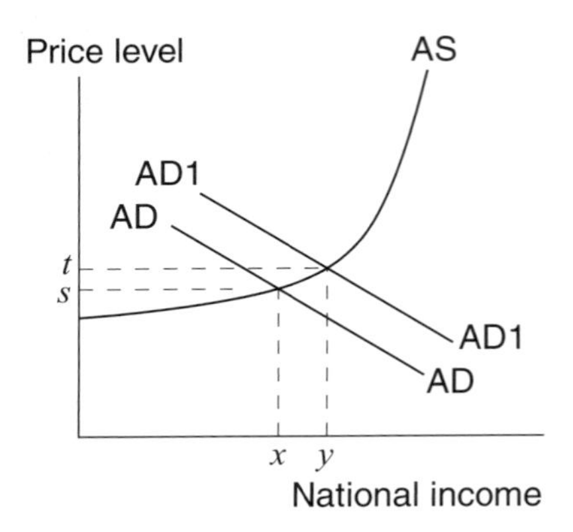

Figure 1: The effects of increased consumption caused by increased spending on sport and leisure

This is shown in Figure 1, where **AD1** represents the effects of an increase in consumption, caused by an increase in spending, on sport and leisure. The effects on national income will depend on the availability of unused resources within the economy. The primary impact will be on national income, as shown by the increase from x to y. In this context, the impact on the price level is minimal, shown by the small rise from s to t in the price level.

If demand were to increase further, shortage of available resources (represented by the more vertical section of the aggregate supply curve) indicates that prices will be pushed up relative to levels of national income.

Balance of payments

Spending on both sport and leisure can have significant impact on the balance of payments – especially if the latter involves tourism. Spending on travel and tourism counts as a trade in services and is treated as an 'invisible' good in terms of the balance of payments. Tourists coming to the UK or travelling on British-owned carriers make a positive contribution to the balance of payments. British travellers abroad and those using foreign-owned transport firms contribute to negative outflows.

As traditional seaside holidays in the UK can be considered to be an inferior good, while foreign travel tends to have a highly positive income elasticity of demand, tourism trends for UK residents are having an adverse effect on our balance of payments. The possible worsening of the balance of payments on the UK's current account has been partly compensated by increases in the number of American and Japanese tourists visiting the UK. However, the foot and mouth outbreak in UK, the events of September 11 (2001) in the USA and stagnation in the Japanese economy have limited these positive inflows.

Making connections

In which industries is there the greatest growth in number of job opportunities?

Economic regeneration and development

UK and other governments have used their spending on sport and leisure to promote urban regeneration. This is partly because of the positive externalities that are seen to be linked with the provision of this kind of merit good, and partly because of what are seen as the local multiplier effects of such forms of government spending.

Thus, support for large sporting events such as the Olympics brings vast numbers of new visitors, creates demand for local businesses and can provide facilities that will continue to meet social needs as well as encouraging regeneration. Government spending on the arts and environmental projects such as the Eden Project in Cornwall have been used to tackle regional unemployment. While this project has been a great success, there have been government failures, such as the Dome in London.

The popularity of different tourist destinations can be volatile. Changes in exchange rates can have a significant effect on flows of tourists to particular countries. A rise in the value of the US dollar compared to other currencies is more likely to make Americans take foreign holidays. A movement in the other direction is likely to have an opposite effect. A recent tourist study showed that 95 cents of every US dollar spent by tourists in Antigua in the West Indies flows out of the local economy.

Changes in the flows of tourists will, in turn, have an effect on those countries most dependent upon tourism. Nepal is one of the poorest countries in the world and receives most of its foreign earnings from tourism. Even a small fall in the number of tourists could have a damaging effect on living standards.

The Eden Project in Cornwall opened in 2001

Web link

Go to www.heinemann.co.uk/hotlinks and click on this section to see the website for the Eden Project in Cornwall.

Summary

Sport and leisure are fast-growing sectors of the economy, and this development has both micro and macro effects. Their growth provides many new jobs to replace those lost in declining sectors of the economy. The development of this sector has other implications, not least the impact of worldwide tourism on fragile economies and eco structures.

Hot potato

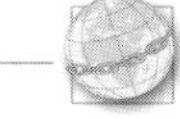

'Tourism is a failed strategy to promote economic growth.' Do you agree? Give reasons for your answer

Quickie

How might a fall in foreign visitors to the UK affect:

(a) the balance of payments
(b) the exchange rate
(c) employment levels
(d) inflation?

Exam hint

Don't forget to practise those AD/AS diagrams. You can almost be sure they will come in useful and nice, tidy diagrams impress examiners

3.14

Activities: markets at work

Activity 1

What are the special features of the housing market?

What are the differences between houses and other products on the market? Why are the activities of producing, selling and buying a house not quite the same things as producing, selling and buying something like a CD or a can of baked beans?

Consider, one by one, each of the following special features of the housing market. Write down a reason why each item in the list causes the market for houses to be different from the market for most other products (in other words, explain how each feature might affect aspects of the market such as supply, demand, price or elasticities).

1. Houses are not 'homogeneous' products. No two houses are identical.
2. Buyers and sellers have imperfect information.
3. The 'stock' of existing houses is large in relation to the 'flow' of new houses.
4. There is a large and important second-hand market.
5. Demand affects price in the short run, supply takes longer.
6. Expectations of future prices can be as important as current trends.
7. Buyers also tend to be sellers.
8. Existing home owners are in a very different position to first-time buyers.
9. Buying/selling involves large transaction costs (such as legal fees).
10. Houses are immobile; markets are regionalised/localised; excess demand and supply can exist at the same time in different places or for different types of house.
11. Externalities: Good housing is a merit good; bad housing a demerit good.
12. Public sector housing, in some shape or form, has an important role.
13. Income elasticity is probably more influential than price elasticity.
14. House-buying is a major decision, involving long-term considerations and borrowing. Consumer confidence is crucial.
15. House-buying is more a form of investment than consumption.
16. Housing is a capital asset: values affect the macroeconomy as well as the microeconomy.
17. Rising prices on the housing market are generally reported as 'good news'; falling prices as 'bad news'.
18. UK economic policy is transmitted through the housing market via the interest rate.

Activity 2

What contribution can economists make to debate on the environment?

Environment and microeconomics

1 What is the difference between money costs and opportunity costs?
2 Economics is all about the 'best use of resources'. In what way is this idea very relevant to the environment?
3 Explain the difference between private costs and social costs (refer to negative externalities or external costs).
4 Methods of internalising externalities:
  (a) Explain the differences between 'command and control' (or 'direct') methods and 'market-based' methods.
  (b) For each method consider and write down some:
    i. examples
    ii. advantages
    iii. disadvantages.

Environment and macroeconomics

If it is good for the environment is it bad for the economy?

1 Explain, with examples, ways in which economic growth might:
  (a) harm the environment
  (b) benefit the environment.
2 Explain with examples, how measures to improve the environment might:
  (a) harm the economy
  (b) benefit the economy.

Activity 3

What economic issues are raised by 'sport and leisure'?

Choose a sport and leisure issue (such as those mentioned in the margin) and consider it from both a microeconomic and macroeconomic point of view. For example, consider a big event such as an FA Cup Final at the Millenium Stadium in Cardiff.

1 From a microeconomic point of view:
  (a) what are the factors influencing supply of and demand for tickets?
  (b) what are the likely price, income and cross elasticities of demand?
  (c) is the market for tickets competitive or monopolistic?
2 From a macroeconomic point of view:
  (a) how might a big event affect tourism, spending, and hence inflation interest rates and exchange rates?
  (b) how might a big event be affected by influences such as aggregate demand or interest rates?
  (c) what are the multiplier effects of big events?

Exam hint

When revising for 'Sport and leisure' remember:

- the subject matter of 'sport' includes the 'usual suspects' (soccer, cricket, rugby) and big events such as FA Cup, Olympics, and Formula 1
- the subject matter of 'leisure' includes holidays, travel, film, television, music, theatre industries, tourist attractions, shopping as a leisure activity, gambling, the national lottery
- recurring issues include admission prices versus abolition of charges; effects of globalisation (e.g. satellite television): pay-per-view versus subscription versus public service broadcasting; the role of government in sport and leisure markets.

3.15 Exam practice

Housing

Study Extract 1 and Figure 1 and then answer the questions which follow.

Extract 1: The house owning economy

The stock market might be falling, but the housing market will not necessarily follow suit. The stock market might be driven by speculation, but the housing market reacts to the real economy. High interest rates and unemployment are both bad for the housing market. Conversely, as incomes rise, so the demand for housing rises.

When house prices rise, there is a 'wealth effect': house owners feel more wealthy, and more confident about borrowing. Some will borrow against the increased value of their houses ('equity withdrawal'). Thus mortgage borrowing is an important component of aggregate demand. Higher house prices can therefore have an upward multiplier effect on employment, but a strong housing market might worry the Monetary Policy Committee (MPC) of the Bank of England, and might encourage them to raise interest rates (or delay lowering them). Aggregate demand is more volatile than aggregate supply, since the components of AD change with wider fluctuations over shorter periods of time than the components of aggregate supply. Similarly, the demand for housing can change much more quickly than the supply of houses.

House prices and interest rates are also relevant to the 'north-south divide'. In a recession, when interest rates are high and exporting is difficult, exporters in the manufacturing regions suffer a disproportionate fall in demand for their outputs.

The Heinemann Examiner, 1 May 2003.

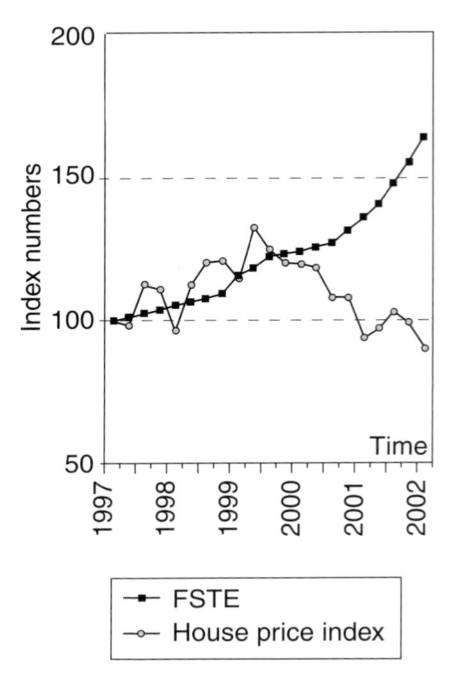

Figure 1: Movement of the Halifax house price index versus the FTSE share price index, 1997-2002

(a) What is meant by the term 'monetary policy'? (3 marks)

(b) Describe the trends in house and share prices shown in Figure 1. (4 marks)

(c) Explain how changes in the housing market can have both upward and downward multiplier effects. (8 marks)

(d) With the help of an aggregate supply and aggregate demand (AS/AD) diagram, predict how a fall in house prices would affect output and other prices in the economy. (10 marks)

(e) The Monetary Policy Committee (MPC) appears to pay a lot of attention to the housing market. Explain why it does this and discuss whether it is possible to pay too much attention to house prices rather than other economic indicators. (15 marks)

The environment

Study Extract 2 and Table 1 and then answer the questions which follow.

Extract 2: Permits to pollute

Shortly after becoming president in 2001, George W Bush announced that the USA would withdraw from the Kyoto Protocol, and declared that he would not support any measure that would harm America's businesses and the US economy.

The Kyoto summit sought to reduce carbon dioxide (CO2) emissions, which are estimated to cause over 60 per cent of global warming. The problem exists because burning fossil fuels such as oil, gas and coal creates costs, but the users only pay for the private costs of extraction and distribution. They do not necessarily pay the cost to the environment ('negative externalities') created when these fuels are burned. One way of internalising these externalities would be to tax the use of goods and services whose production entail the emission of greenhouse gases. More developed countries, like the USA, produce more emissions than less developed countries, and so they would need higher taxes.

Another method would be to introduce 'permits to pollute'. Power companies, for example, would have to purchase permits to enable them to release a certain amount of CO2 each year. The industry would then operate within a 'bubble' of permitted pollution. A market would be created in tradable permits, and 'carbon trading' would take place. If it wished to exceed its quota of pollution a 'dirty' firm would need to buy surplus permits from a 'clean' company. As time goes on the permitted 'bubble' could be reduced in size, forcing up the price of permits and creating an ever stronger incentive to invest in clean technology. At Kyoto the USA supported what it saw as the 'flexibility' of carbon trading, but other countries preferred direct, 'command and control' agreements to restrict emissions.

The Heinemann Examiner, 2 June 2003.

Source, by final user	1995	2000	2005
Industry and agriculture	56	58	62
Transport	41	45	49
Households	39	41	42
Commercial services and the public sector	23	26	30
TOTAL	159	170	183

Table 1: CO_2 emissions in the UK, as predicted in 1991 (millions of tonnes of carbon)

(a) What is meant by the term 'externalities'? (3 marks)

(b) Describe the changing pattern of carbon dioxide (CO2) emissions as shown in Table 1. (4 marks)

(c) Explain, with examples, how a policy of environmental taxation differs from a policy of 'command and control'. (8 marks)

(d) With the help of a supply and demand diagram explain how a market in tradable permits could assist in reducing CO2 emissions. (10 marks)

(e) Evaluate the view that what is good for the environment is bad for the economy. (15 marks)

Study Extract 3 and Table 2 and then answer the questions which follow.

Extract 3: The price of heritage

How much should you pay to see the world's heritage? Heritage sites which were previously free, or had very low admission charges, are suddenly becoming more expensive. In some old Italian cities you might have to pay to walk in the cobbled streets. This year the admission fee for foreign tourists at the Taj Mahal in India has risen by 6,000 per cent. Cheap airline flights to Barcelona have increased tourist arrivals into the airport tenfold since the 1992 Olympics. At the global level, by the year 2010 there could be an estimated billion tourist trips (approximately doubling since 1995). While the extra income and employment is naturally welcome, some destinations feel swamped by tourists.

Some tourists are very price conscious: haggling in the local market might be seen as part of the fun of tourism, but it is possible for locals to resent it. If you can afford to travel to Thailand or South America (even as a back-packer) then perhaps you can afford an extra 5p for a souvenir. This kind of money means more to locals than it does to you.

Less developed countries with world-class ancient monuments but with inefficient taxation systems are discovering foreign tourists as a source of government revenue. If prices are increased, there is more incentive for the conservation of places which, in a sense, belong to the whole world. While the price mechanism can be used to 'ration' access, in the UK heritage is increasingly being treated as a public good. The British government has given a subsidy to national museums and galleries to enable them to abolish entry charges altogether, and it remains to be seen how this policy develops when these subsidies end.

The Heinemann Examiner, 3 July 2003.

Site	Location	Price (sterling equivalent)	Visitor numbers per year
St. Mark's Basilica	Venice, Italy	Free, but £1 to see the altar, and £1.50 for the treasury, with discounts for students and seniors.	5,000,000
The Alhambra Palace	Granada, Spain	£4 with specific times on ticket for entry to busiest areas and an overall limit on the number of visitors per day (advance booking recommended for busy periods).	2,200,000
The Acropolis	Athens, Greece	Approx. £10, negotiable, for personal guide. Entry fee £3.50 (main site) and £3.50 (museum). Students and seniors half price. Free on Sundays.	500,000

Table 2: Examples of heritage attractions in Europe

(a) What is meant by the phrase 'public good'? (3 marks)

(b) Describe the extent to which Table 2 shows the use of prices to 'ration' access to heritage sites. (4 marks)

(c) Discuss possible reasons why it could happen that if prices are increased, there is more incentive for the conservation of important sites. (8 marks)

(d) Extract 3 mentions a price increase of 6,000 per cent. Using a demand diagram and the idea of 'elasticity' discuss the possible effects of increasing prices by such a large amount. (10 marks)

(e) Identify possible reasons for the British policy of enabling national museums and galleries to introduce free admission, and evaluate the effects of not charging for visitor attractions. (15 marks)

3.16

Exam guidance

Exam hint

Unit 3, question pattern:

(a) A definition: *3 marks*

Learn basic economic definitions so that you can answer this question clearly and accurately. If your definition is not a generally accepted one, the examiner will mark on a point-by-point basis, so make as many points as you can. Also, where relevant, give an example.

(b) A descriptive question: *4 marks*

You are usually asked to describe a trend shown in the data or to give a simple explanation of something stated in the text.

(c) An interpretive question: *8 marks*

You are asked to use a higher order skill, for example, to comment on a quote taken from the data, apply an economic principle to analyse part of the data, comment on an assumption made by the author, or identify a flaw in the data.

(d) A question with a diagram: *10 marks*

You will usually be asked to use a diagram to help explain something.

(e) An extended question: *15 marks*

In effect, this is a mini-essay. It should show how well you can take an overview of issues. Make sure you use the data and evaluate in order to help you reach the higher levels. One way of evaluating is to look at two sides of an argument and say which side is the stronger and why; or identify several issues and say which is the most significant.

Answers to the data response questions

Housing

(a) Mention interest rates, the role of the Monetary Policy Committee and the aim of policy (to control inflation).

(b) Describe the way that each line is moving; then comment on whether there is any obvious relationship between them. (There does not seem to be.)

(c) You don't need to go into the detail of multiplier theory (this is not on your AS specification). However, you need to explain that an increase in spending has a multiplier effect on the economy. One person's spending will increase another person's income; this person will in turn spend more, so that overall aggregate demand and employment will increase. Similarly, explain a 'downward' multiplier caused by reduced spending. When house prices rise people feel wealthier (the 'wealth effect') and might be encouraged to spend more.

(d) This follows on from part (c). The AD line shifts to the left, output falls, and so does inflation.

(e) Essential points here are the trade-off between inflation and employment, and the fact that house prices are regional; if there is a north-south divide, should people in the north suffer high interest rates because of an overheated housing market in the south-east?

The environment

(a) You could answer this question in terms of positive or negative externalities, or both. However, negative externalities are generally more relevant to environmental questions. Mention internal costs, external costs and social costs (which are the sum of the other two). Just for luck, give an example.

(b) Look across the rows (comment on the predictions over time) and down the columns (say which activities are the biggest polluters).

(c) Read the relevant sections of this book and make sure that you can compare and contrast the two classes of policy. Generally, command and control policies require a more active government, and policing is necessary to ensure that rules are obeyed. Market-based approaches are more difficult to evade, but they might take longer to work. Market-based policies are sometimes called 'polluter pays'. However, polluters might also end up paying under command and control, for example, if they are forced to use a certain piece of technology, or if they are fined for non-compliance.

(d) Show and explain how the supply of permits shifts to the left, increasing the price of pollution, and reducing the quantity of pollution over time.

(e) There is some overlap with part (c), but since this is a 'holistic' question, some repetition is only to be expected. Use plenty of examples. Environmental standards can be costly to business; however environmentally responsible businesses are likely, in the future, to have more loyalty from customers as they become more environmentally aware. Good practice therefore supports good profits.

Sport and leisure

(a) Mention non-excludability and non-rivalry - read the relevant sections of this book if unsure of these terms – and give an example.

(b) There appears to be some sort of 'demand curve' pattern working here, with cheaper attractions getting more visitors; but of course this is only a small sample, and all the attractions are very different to each other.

(c) Higher prices bring in higher revenues and therefore make a profit and support local jobs and living standards. If the sites are money-spinners, then locals are both more likely to want to preserve them, and have the money to spend on preservation.

(d) With such a huge percentage change in price, it is reasonable to suppose that demand is price inelastic. Your diagram does *not* need to include a supply curve, as you are told to draw a 'demand diagram'. Show a higher price, and shade the area on the diagram showing total revenue. With a 'steep' (relatively inelastic) demand curve, the higher price is a revenue earner.

(e) Use your knowledge of public goods theory, and expand on the terms you used in part (a). Refer to merit goods, as this is what the museums and galleries can be argued to be. Mention some of the practical problems and their solutions. The museums, for instance, will need alternative sources of income; but if they get a lot more visitors, they can sell more souvenirs and encourage people to use café facilities even if they are not necessarily going to view the exhibits. With free entry, whole families are more likely to visit, and people who might have visited only rarely might become regulars.

Exam hint

AQA Units 1–3 are all marked out of a maximum of 40 marks. In Units 1 and 2, the objective test item is marked out of 15 and the data response item is marked out of 25. In Unit 3, however, all 40 marks are for data response, and the question normally has five parts instead of three.

Exam hint

Achieving top marks in data response questions.

- If you have a choice of question, (i.e. if you have prepared for more than one topic for Module 3) choose carefully, on the basis of the *whole* question. Do not be put off a question because a small part of it is difficult and do not be attracted to it if a small part appears easy. Remember that the final part carries the most marks.
- Be aware of an 'incline of difficulty': as you move through the questions you should be using higher order skills. Also try to 'evaluate' in the longer answers. Use the data wherever possible, and refer to the data where appropriate.
- Use your pre-existing economic awareness. Have some pre-existing knowledge of ball-park figures. For instance the national product of the UK (in round numbers) is £1 trillion, the average growth rate of the UK economy is just over two per cent, and four per cent would be regarded as an inflation rate that is too high. Use these to set the given data in context.
- Analyse from different standpoints, e.g. producers/consumers; employers/employees; exporters/importers etc.

Glossary

Aggregate demand	The total demand for a country's goods and services at a given price level.
Aggregate supply	The total amount a country's producers supply at a given price level.
Allocative efficiency	Refers to who gets what. An economy would be allocatively efficient if everybody received exactly those goods and services for which they were prepared to pay the market price.
Balance of payments	A record of transactions between a country's residents and the rest of the world.
Barter	Where one group of people with a surplus of something, say, fish, swaps with another group able to produce, say, more grain.
Brand loyalty	A term often used in business to explain why customers stick to the same brand.
Buffer stocks	Stocks held by a government to smooth out changes in prices by the sale and purchase of stocks.
Capital goods	Goods that are used to produce other goods and services.
Ceteris paribus	Others things considered equal.
Circular flow of income	A model involving flows of income and goods meant to illustrate the way spending and incomes move around the economy.
Complements	Goods which tend to be purchased together.
Consumer sovereignty	The principle that the consumer ultimately decides what gets produced.
Consumption	The proportion of a households' income spent on goods and services.
Cost benefit analysis	Calculations involving social costs and benefits used to assess the viability of both private and public investments.
Cost-push inflation	A rise in the price level caused by increases in the costs of production.

Cross elasticity of demand	The elasticity of demand for one good in relation to changes in the price of another.
Degradation	The effects of pollution spoiling the quality of all available resources.
Demand curve	Shows the likely relationship between the price of a good or service and the quantity demanded. These curves usually slope downwards from left to right, showing either that as price falls demand is likely to rise, or that as price rises demand is likely to fall.
Demand-pull inflation	A rise in the price level caused by increases in aggregate demand.
Demerit goods	Goods which are considered to be socially undesirable.
Depletion	The using up of non-renewable resources.
Depreciation	A fall in the value of currency.
Deregulation	The removal of government restrictions and controls on business activity.
Direct tax	Tax on the income of individuals and firms.
Disposable income	Income after direct taxation has been deducted and state benefits have been added.
Division of labour	Breaking up the production process into individual jobs.
Economic cycles	Fluctuations in economic activity over time, often referred to as booms and busts.
Economies of scale	Factors which contribute to decreasing long run average costs.
Elastic	Responsive.
Equilibrium	When two forces are equal. Often refers to demand and supply.
Excess supply	Situation in which supply exceeds demand.

Externalities	Occur when there is a divergence between private and social costs and/or between private and social benefits.
Factor immobility	A situation in which factors of production do not move readily in responses to changes in their price.
Factor markets	Intermediate markets in which the factors of production are traded.
Factors of production	Land, labour, capital and enterprise which are used in varying proportions to produce goods and services.
Fiscal drag	When inflation increases people's money incomes, dragging them into higher tax brackets.
Fiscal policy	Changes in government spending and taxation.
Free market approach	Leaving markets to work without government or other external intervention.
Full employment	A situation where those wanting to work can gain employment at the going wage rate – often taken as an unemployment rate of three per cent.
Globalisation	The broadening of markets and production to a world wide scale.
Government administrations	Government regimes that run the length of a parliament e.g. the Labour Government 1997-2001.
Gross Domestic Product	Total output of the economy.
Human capital	Education, training and experience that a worker possesses.
Hyperinflation	A situation where the general price level is rising very rapidly.
In the red	Being in debt as a result of expenditure exceeding income.
Income elasticity of demand	Measures of the response in demand to changes in income.

Incomes policy	A government policy designed to control factor incomes, most commonly wages.
Indirect tax	Taxes levied on goods and services which households only pay if they buy those goods and services.
Inelastic	Not responsive.
Inferior goods	Goods for which the demand tends to fall as people's incomes rise.
Inflation	A sustained rise in the general price level.
Inflationary noise	The distortion of price signals caused by inflation.
Injections	Additions to the circular flow of income.
Interventionist approach	The process by which governments and other external agencies may intervene into the free working of markets, to promote efficiency.
Investment	Spending on capital goods.
Kyoto Agreement	International agreement to limit the emissions of greenhouse gases (not accepted by the US).
Leakages	Withdrawals from the circular flow in income.
Long run aggregate supply	Total supply that can be produced with the full employment of resources.
Macroeconomic disequilibrium	A situation where aggregate demand and aggregate supply are not equal.
Macroeconomic equilibrium	A situation where aggregate demand equals aggregate supply.
Marginal tax rate	The proportion of extra income that is taken in tax.
Market clearing	The price necessary for all stocks of goods to be sold and all consumers satisfied.
Menu costs	Costs involved in changing prices in say, catalogues, due to inflation.

Merit goods	Goods which if left to market forces would be under-consumed and which have positive externalities.
Mixed economies	Economies involving a mix of private and public provision of goods and services.
Monetary policy	Government changes in the money supply, the rate of interest and the exchange rate.
Monopoly	In theory, this is when one firm produces the entire output of an industry. In UK law, this is when one firm produces more than 25% of the total output of an industry.
Mortgages	Long term borrowing used to purchase property.
Multiplier	The process by which any change in a component of aggregate demand results in a greater final change in real GDP.
Natural conditions	Differing conditions of certain countries such as weather and landscape, which result in commodities that can be traded in areas not able to produce such things.
Negative equity	A situation in which property is worth less than any outstanding debts used in its purchase.
Negative externality	Additional costs faced by a third party caused by the production or consumption of a particular good or service.
Net exports	The balance arrived at by deducting the value of imports from that of exports. This can be a positive or negative amount.
Non-renewable resources	Natural resources, which when used up cannot be replaced.
Normal goods	Goods which increase in demand as incomes rise.
Opportunity cost	The best possible alternative that has to be given up as the result of a particular choice.

Output gap	The gap between potential and actual output.
Positive externality	Additional benefits enjoyed by a third party caused by the production or consumption of a particular good or service.
Price controls	The imposition, usually by governments, of maximum or minimum price levels for particular goods or services.
Price discrimination	Charging different prices to different customers for the same product.
Price elasticity of demand (PεD)	$\frac{\text{\% change in quantity demanded}}{\text{\% change in price}}$
Price elasticity of supply	$\frac{\text{\% change in quantity supplied}}{\text{\% change in price}}$
Price indexes	Measures of changes in the price level.
Price makers	Firms which have sufficient monopoly power to set prices.
Price mechanism	A means by which resources can be allocated between different and competing uses.
Private costs	Costs faced by the organisation responsible for producing a good or service.
Privatisation	Transfer of ownership from the public to the private sector.
Production possibility curves	Different combinations of two goods or services which can be produced at a given time in a given economy.
Productive capacity	The maximum possible output that can be produced with existing resources and technology.
Productive efficiency	Producing goods and services at the lowest possible cost.
Productivity	Output per worker/hour.
Public goods	Goods for which the principles of non-exclusivity and non-rivalry apply.
Quota	A limit on imports.

Recession	A period of falling real GDP that lasts for at least six months.
Renewable resources	Natural resources which when used can be replaced.
Short run aggregate supply	Total supply over the time period when factor prices are unchanged.
Shoe leather costs	Time and effort involved in reducing holdings of cash and seeking the highest rate of interest.
Social benefits	Private benefits plus external benefits.
Social costs	Private costs plus external costs.
Social housing	Housing provided by the state or other agency as a merit good.
Specialisation	Concentrating on the production of a particular good or service, or on a particular stage of the productive process.
Subsistence	When societies produce only enough food and basic products to survive.
Substitutes	Goods which are similar. Goods which can be consumed instead of others.
Superior goods	Goods which have a positive income elasticity of demand greater than one.
Supply curve	Shows the likely relationship between the price of a good or service and the quantity supplied. These curves usually slope upwards from left to right showing that as price rises, supply is also likely to rise, whereas if price falls supply is likely to fall.
Supply-side policies	Policies designed to increase aggregate supply by raising the efficiency of markets.
Surpluses	When more is produced at a given price level than will be consumed.
Sustainable economic growth	Economic growth which does not lead to the depletion of non renewable resources.
Tariff	A tax on imports.

Tax relief	Allowances which can be given to firms and individuals which reduce the amount of direct taxes which have to be paid.
The Bank of England	The UK's central bank. Founded in 1694 it issues notes and coins and implements the government's monetary policy including changing interest rates when it is thought appropriate.
The invisible hand	Adam Smith's notion that markets will automatically ensure an optimum distribution of resources.
Trade unions	Organisations of workers designed to protect pay and conditions of employment.
Trend growth	Expected increase in productive capacity over time.
Weighted consumer price index	Changes in the prices of goods and services that people spend more on are given more importance than those on which they only spend a small amount.
World trade organisation	An international organisation that promotes free international trade and rules on international trade disputes.

Index